FUTURE

English for Work, Life, and Academic Success

Second Edition

Series Consultants
Sarah Lynn
Ronna Magy
Federico Salas-Isnardi

Authors
Marjorie Fuchs
Lisa Johnson
Sarah Lynn
Irene Schoenberg

Future 1
English for Work, Life, and Academic Success

Copyright © 2019 by Pearson Education, Inc.
All rights reserved. No part of this publication may be reproduced, stored in a retrieval system, or transmitted in any form or by any means, electronic, mechanical, photocopying, recording, or otherwise, without the prior permission of the publisher.

Pearson Education, 221 River Street, Hoboken, NJ 07030 USA

Staff credits: The people who made up the **Future** team, representing content development, design, manufacturing, marketing, multimedia, project management, publishing, rights management, and testing, are Pietro Alongi, Jennifer Castro, Dave Dickey, Gina DiLillo, Warren Fischbach, Pamela Fishman, Gosia Jaros-White, Joanna Konieczna, Michael Mone, Mary Rich, Katarzyna Starzyńska-Kościuszko, Claire Van Poperin, Joseph Vella, Gabby Wu

Text composition: ElectraGraphics, Inc.
Cover Design: EMC Design Ltd
Illustration credits: See Credits page 282.
Photo credits: See Credits page 282.
Audio: CityVox

Library of Congress Cataloging-in-Publication Data
A catalog record for the print edition is available from the Library of Congress.

ISBN-13: 9780135278314 (Student Book with App and MyEnglishLab)
ISBN-10: 0135278317 (Student Book with App and MyEnglishLab)

ISBN-13: 9780134857954 (Student Book with App)
ISBN-10: 013485795X (Student Book with App)

www.pearsoneltusa.com/future2e

CONTENTS

To the Teacher iv
Unit Tour vii
Scope and Sequence xiv
Correlations xx
About the Series Consultants and Authors xxii
Acknowledgments xxiii

PRE-UNIT	Getting Started	2
UNIT 1	Getting to Know You	5
UNIT 2	A Hard Day's Work	25
UNIT 3	Time for Class	45
UNIT 4	Family Ties	65
UNIT 5	Shop, Shop, Shop	85
UNIT 6	Home, Sweet Home	105
UNIT 7	Day After Day	125
UNIT 8	From Soup to Nuts	145
UNIT 9	Rain or Shine	165
UNIT 10	Around Town	185
UNIT 11	Health Matters	205
UNIT 12	Help Wanted	225

My Soft Skills Log 245
Grammar Review 247
Grammar Reference 259
ABCs and Numbers 261
Word List 262
Audio Script 265
Map of the United States and Canada 275
Map of the World 276
Index 278
Credits 282

TO THE TEACHER

Welcome to *Future: English for Work, Life, and Academic Success*

Future is a six-level, standards-based English language course for adult and young adult students. *Future* provides students with the contextualized academic language, strategies, and critical thinking skills needed for success in workplace, life, and academic settings. *Future* is aligned with the requirements of the Workforce Innovation and Opportunity Act (WIOA), the English Language Proficiency (ELP) and College and Career Readiness (CCR) standards, and the National Reporting System (NRS) level descriptors. The 21st century curriculum in *Future*'s second edition helps students acquire the basic literacy, language, and employability skills needed to meet the requirements set by the standards.

Future develops students' academic and critical thinking skills, digital literacy and numeracy, workplace and civic skills, and prepares students for taking standardized tests. Competency and skills incorporating standards are in the curriculum at every level, providing a foundation for academic rigor, research-based teaching strategies, corpus-informed language, and the best of digital tools.

In revising the course, we listened to hundreds of *Future* teachers and learners and studied the standards for guidance. *Future* continues to be the most comprehensive English communication course for adults, with its signature scaffolded lessons and multiple practice activities throughout. *Future*'s second edition provides enhanced content, rigorous academic language practice, and cooperative learning through individual and collaborative practice. Every lesson teaches the interpretive, interactive, and productive skills highlighted in the standards.

Future's Instructional Design

Learner Centered and Outcome Oriented

The student is at the center of *Future*. Lessons start by connecting to student experience and knowledge, and then present targeted skills in meaningful contexts. Varied and dynamic skill practice progresses from controlled to independent in a meticulously scaffolded sequence.

Headers highlighting Depth of Knowledge (DOK) terms are used throughout *Future* to illuminate the skills being practiced. Every lesson culminates in an activity in which students apply their learning, demonstrate their knowledge, and express themselves orally or in writing. A DOK glossary for teachers includes specific suggestions on how to help students activate these cognitive skills.

Varied Practice

Cognitive science has proven what *Future* always knew: Students learn new skills through varied practice over time. Content-rich units that contextualize academic and employability skills naturally recycle concepts, language, and targeted skills. Individual and collaborative practice activities engage learners and lead to lasting outcomes. Lessons support both student collaboration and individual self-mastery. Students develop the interpretative, productive, and interactive skills identified in the NRS guidelines, while using the four language skills of reading, writing, listening, and speaking.

Goal Setting and Learning Assessment

For optimal learning to take place, students need to be involved in setting goals and in monitoring their own progress. *Future* addresses goal setting in numerous ways. In the Student Book, Unit Goals are identified on the unit opener page. Checkboxes at the end of lessons invite students to evaluate their mastery of the material, and suggest additional online practice.

High-quality assessment aligned to the standards checks student progress and helps students prepare to take standardized tests. The course-based assessment program is available in print and digital formats and includes a bank of customizable test items. Digital tests are assigned by the teacher and reported back in the LMS online gradebook. All levels include a midterm and final test. Test items are aligned with unit learning objectives and standards. The course Placement Test is available in print and digital formats. Test-prep materials are also provided for specific standardized tests.

One Integrated Program

Future provides everything adult English language learners need in one integrated program using the latest digital tools and time-tested print resources.

Integrated Skills Contextualized with Rich Content

Future contextualizes grammar, listening, speaking, pronunciation, reading, writing, and vocabulary in meaningful activities that simulate real workplace, educational, and community settings. A special lesson at the end of each unit highlights soft skills at work. While providing relevant content, *Future* helps build learner knowledge and equips adults for their many roles.

Meeting Work, Life, and Education Goals

Future recognizes that every adult learner brings a unique set of work, life, and academic experiences, as well as a distinct skill set. With its diverse array

TO THE TEACHER

of print and digital resources, *Future* provides learners with multiple opportunities to practice with contextualized materials to build skill mastery. Specialized lessons for academic and workplace skill development are part of *Future*'s broad array of print and digital resources.

In addition to two units on employment in each level, every unit contains a Workplace, Life, and Community Skills lesson as well as a Soft Skills at Work lesson.

Workplace, Life, and Community Skills Lessons

In the second edition, the Life Skills lesson has been revised to focus on workplace, life, and community skills and to develop the real-life language and civic literacy skills required today. Lessons integrate and contextualize workplace content. In addition, every lesson includes practice with digital skills on a mobile device.

Soft Skills at Work Lessons

Future has further enhanced its development of workplace skills by adding a Soft Skills at Work lesson to each unit. Soft skills are the critical interpersonal communication skills needed to succeed in any workplace. Students begin each lesson by discussing a common challenge in the workplace. Then, while applying the lesson-focused soft skill, they work collaboratively to find socially appropriate solutions to the problem. The log at the back of the Student Book encourages students to track their own application of the soft skill, which they can use in job interviews.

Academic Rigor

Rigor and respect for the ability and experiences of the adult learner have always been central to *Future*. The standards provide the foundation for academic rigor. The reading, writing, listening, and speaking practice require learners to analyze, use context clues, interpret, cite evidence, build knowledge, support a claim, and summarize from a variety of text formats. Regular practice with complex and content-rich materials develop academic language and build knowledge. Interactive activities allow for collaboration and exchange of ideas in workplace and in academic contexts. *Future* emphasizes rigor by highlighting the critical thinking and problem solving skills required in each activity.

Writing Lessons

In addition to the increased focus on writing in Show What You Know activities, *Future* has added a cumulative writing lesson to every unit, a lesson that requires students to synthesize and apply their learning in a written outcome. Through a highly scaffolded approach, students begin by analyzing writing models before planning and finally producing written work of their own. Writing frameworks, Writing Skills, and a checklist help guide students through the writing process.

Reading lessons

All reading lessons have new, information-rich texts and a revised pedagogical approach in line with the CCR and ELP standards and the NRS descriptors. These informational texts are level appropriate, use high-frequency vocabulary, and focus on interpretation of graphic information. The readings build students' knowledge and develop their higher-order reading skills by teaching citation of evidence, summarizing, and interpretation of complex information from a variety of text formats.

Future Grows with Your Student

Future takes learners from absolute beginner level through low-advanced English proficiency, addressing students' abilities and learning priorities at each level. As the levels progress, the curricular content and unit structure change accordingly, with the upper levels incorporating more advanced academic language and skills in the text and in the readings.

Future Intro	Future Level 1	Future Level 2	Future Level 3	Future Level 4	Future Advanced
NRS Beginning ESL Literacy	NRS Low Beginning ESL	NRS High Beginning ESL	NRS Low Intermediate ESL	NRS High Intermediate ESL	NRS Advanced ESL
ELPS Level 1	ELPS Level 1	ELPS Level 2	ELPS Level 3	ELPS Level 4	ELPS Level 5
CCRS Level A	CCRS Level A	CCRS Level A	CCRS Level B	CCRS Level C	CCRS Level D
CASAS 180 and below	CASAS 181–190	CASAS 191–200	CASAS 201–210	CASAS 211–220	CASAS 221–235

TO THE TEACHER

Abundant Opportunities for Student Practice

The **Pearson Practice English App** provides easy mobile access to all of the audio files, plus Grammar Coach videos and activities. Listen and study on the go—anywhere, any time!

Student book is a complete student resource, including lessons in grammar, listening and speaking, pronunciation, reading, writing, vocabulary, and Soft Skills at Work, taught and practiced in contextual activities.

MyEnglishLab allows online independent self study and interactive practice in pronunciation, grammar, vocabulary, reading, writing, and listening. The MEL includes the popular Grammar Coach videos and new Pronunciation Coach videos and activities.

Workbook—with audio—provides additional practice for each lesson in the student book, with new readings and practice in writing, grammar, listening and speaking, plus activities for new Soft Skills at Work lessons.

Outstanding Teacher Resources

Teacher Edition and Lesson Planner includes culture notes, teaching tips, and numerous optional and extension activities, with lesson-by-lesson correlations to CCR and ELP standards. Rubrics are provided for evaluation of students written and oral communication.

ActiveTeach for front-of-classroom projection of the student book, includes audio at point of use and pop-up activities, including grammar examples, academic conversation stems, and reader's anticipation guide.

College and Career Readiness Plus Lessons supplement the student book with challenging reading and writing lessons for every level above Intro.

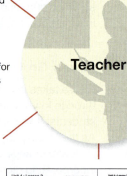

Assessment Program, accessed online with interactive and printable tests and rubrics, includes a Placement Test, multi-level unit, mid-term and final exams, and computer-based ExamView with additional ready-to-use and customizable tests. In addition, sample high-stakes test practice is included with CASAS test prep for listening and reading.

Multilevel Communicative Activities provide an array of reproducible communication activities and games that engage students through different modalities. Teachers' notes provide multilevel options for pre-level and above-level students, as well as extension activities for additional speaking and writing practice.

Go to the Teacher website for easy reference, correlations to federal and state standards, and course updates.
www.pearsoneltusa.com/future2e

UNIT TOUR

Preview questions activate student background knowledge and help the teacher assess how much students know about the unit theme.

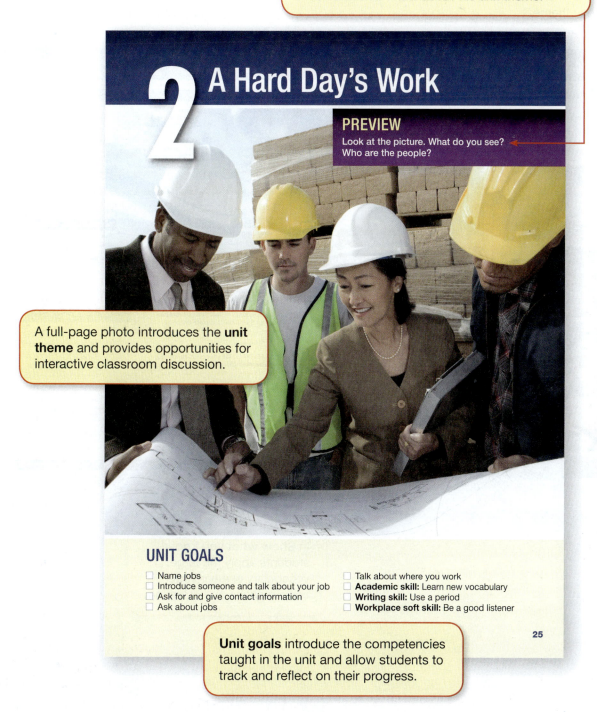

A full-page photo introduces the **unit theme** and provides opportunities for interactive classroom discussion.

Unit goals introduce the competencies taught in the unit and allow students to track and reflect on their progress.

Unit Tour   vii

UNIT TOUR

Key **vocabulary** is contextualized and practiced in connection to the unit theme.

Study tips introduce the learning skills and strategies students need to meet the rigor required by the CCRS.

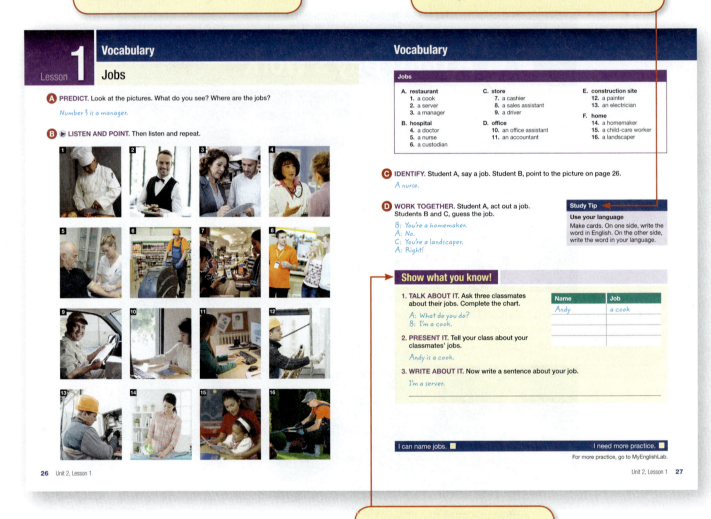

In **Show what you know!**, students apply the target vocabulary in meaningful conversations and in writing.

Unit Tour

UNIT TOUR

Three **Listening and Speaking** lessons provide students opportunities for realistic conversations in work, community, and educational settings.

Pronunciation activities help students learn, practice, and internalize the patterns of spoken English and relate them to their own lives.

Lesson 2 — Listening and Speaking
Introduce someone and talk about your job

1 BEFORE YOU LISTEN

TALK ABOUT IT. Look at the picture. Where are they?

Omar, this is Rosa. Rosa, this is Omar.
Hi, Omar. Nice to ____ you.
Hi, Rosa. ____ to meet you, ____.

2 LISTEN

A ▶ LISTEN. Complete the conversation in the picture.

B ▶ LISTEN. What is Rosa's question?
 a. What do you do? b. Where are you from?

C ▶ LISTEN FOR DETAILS. Complete the sentences.
 1. Omar is a landscaper and ____.
    a. a driver b. a student
 2. Rosa is a student and ____.
    a. a sales assistant b. a nurse

D ▶ EXPAND. Listen to the whole conversation. What is Emilio's job?

a.  b.

Listening and Speaking

3 PRONUNCIATION

Falling intonation in statements and Wh- questions

In *Wh-* questions and in statements, the voice goes down ↘ at the end.

A ▶ PRACTICE. Listen. Then listen and repeat.
 A: What do you do?   A: What's your name?
 B: I'm a student.   B: I'm Peter.

B ▶ APPLY. Practice saying the sentences. Then listen and repeat.
 Where are you from?
 I'm from China.
 What about you?

4 CONVERSATION

A ▶ LISTEN AND READ. Then listen and repeat.
 A: So, what do you do?
 B: I'm a landscaper. And I'm a student at Greenville Adult School.
 A: Really? I'm a student there, too. And I'm a sales assistant.
 B: Oh, that's interesting.

B ▶ WORK TOGETHER. Practice the conversation in Exercise A.

C ▶ CREATE. Make new conversations. Use the pictures.
 A: What do you do?
 B: I'm ____.
 A: Really? I'm ____, too. And I'm ____.
 B: Oh, that's interesting.

D ▶ MAKE CONNECTIONS. Make your own conversations.

I can introduce someone and talk about my job. ☐   I need more practice. ☐
For more practice, go to MyEnglishLab.

Multiple listening opportunities progress from listening for general understanding, to listening for details, to listening to an extended version of the conversation.

Predict activities focus students on the social context of the conversation.

Conversations carefully scaffold student learning and build language fluency.

Checkpoints at the end of lessons provide students an opportunity to reflect on their progress and identify further resources for more practice.

UNIT TOUR

Each unit presents three **Grammar** lessons in a systematic grammar progression. Every Grammar lesson focuses on language introduced in the preceding Listening and Speaking lesson. Additional grammar practice is available in the Grammar Review and online.

Images provide scaffolding for meaningful grammar practice.

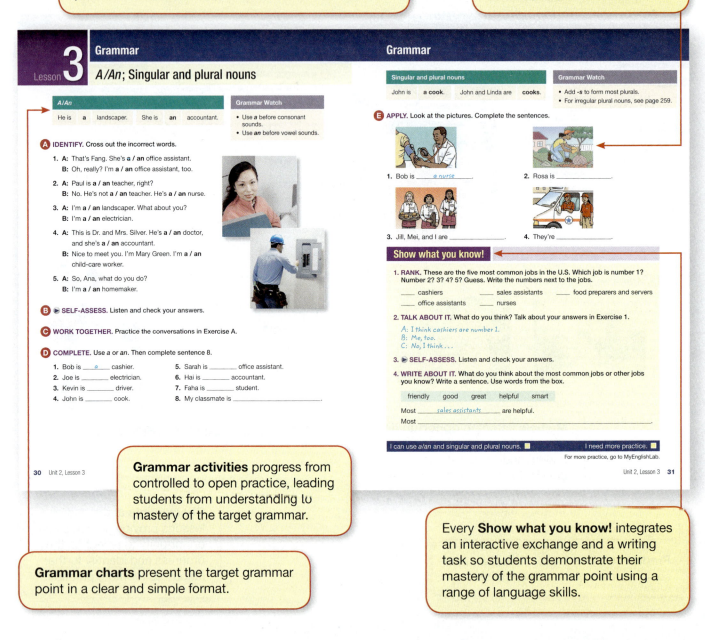

Grammar activities progress from controlled to open practice, leading students from understanding to mastery of the target grammar.

Grammar charts present the target grammar point in a clear and simple format.

Every **Show what you know!** integrates an interactive exchange and a writing task so students demonstrate their mastery of the grammar point using a range of language skills.

UNIT TOUR

Workplace, Life, and Community skills lessons develop real-life language and civic literacy while encouraging community participation.

Interactive activities develop real-life communication and collaboration skills.

Lesson 4 — Workplace, Life, and Community Skills
Ask for and give contact information

1 IDENTIFY PHONE NUMBERS

A MAKE CONNECTIONS. Think about numbers in your life. When do you use numbers? Do you use numbers at work?

B ▶ LISTEN AND POINT. Then listen and repeat.

0 zero	1 one	2 two	3 three	4 four
5 five	6 six	7 seven	8 eight	9 nine

C ▶ LISTEN. Circle the phone numbers you hear.

1. a. 212-960-5334   4. a. 323-865-4191
   b. 412-960-5334   b. 323-835-4191
2. a. 619-464-2083   5. a. 214-847-3726
   b. 619-464-2093   b. 214-847-3126
3. a. 305-576-1169   6. a. 773-395-2114
   b. 395-576-1169   b. 773-399-2114

Cumar Rahim
My number
(415) 555-7934

D ▶ COMPLETE. Listen to the voicemail messages. Write the missing numbers.

1. Mr. Fernandez
   Center Hospital
   Landscaper job
   (562) 555-____

2. Grace Simms
   Grace's Office Supplies
   Cashier Job
   (____) 555-____

3. Jin Wu
   Greenville Store
   Sales assistant job
   (____) 555-____

4. Ms. Rodriguez
   Carla's Restaurant
   Manager job
   (____) ____-____

Workplace, Life, and Community Skills

2 IDENTIFY EMAIL ADDRESSES

A MAKE CONNECTIONS. Think about email in your life. When do you use email? Do you use email at work?

B ▶ LISTEN AND POINT. Look at the email. Listen and point to the email addresses. Then listen and repeat.

From: amy.smith@mymail.com
To: rosa.medina@mymail.com
Subject: ESL class

C ▶ LISTEN. Circle the email addresses you hear.

1. a. dan.silver@ccmail.edu   3. a. tlopez719@gomail.com
   b. dans.ilver@ccmail.edu   b. tlopez715@gomail.com
2. a. gsimms@hmail.com   4. a. jin.wu@newmail.edu
   b. g.simms@hmail.com   b. jin.hu@newmail.edu

3 GET CONTACT INFORMATION

A ▶ LISTEN AND READ. Then listen and repeat.

A: What's your phone number?
B: 213-555-4963.
A: 213-555-4563?
B: No. It's 213-555-4963.
A: OK. And what's your email address?
B: asad.bilan@hmail.com.

B WORK TOGETHER. Ask two classmates for their phone number and email address. Complete the chart.

Name	Phone Number	Email address
Asad	(213) 555-4963	asad.bilan@hmail.com
1.		
2.		

C GO ONLINE. Add two new contacts in your phone.

I can ask for and give contact information. ☐   I need more practice. ☐
For more practice, go to MyEnglishLab.

In **Go Online** activities, students use their devices to practice concrete online tasks, such as researching information or inputting data.

UNIT TOUR

All new informational **Reading lessons** develop academic language and build content knowledge to meet the rigorous requirements of the CCRS.

Close-reading activities require that students return to the reading to find textual evidence of detail, to summarize for general understanding, and to make inferences.

Students develop **numeracy** skills by interpreting numeric information in charts and graphs.

Lesson 7 Reading
Read about healthcare jobs in the U.S.

1 BEFORE YOU READ

A CHOOSE. Complete the sentences with the vocabulary from the box.

| CNA | nursing home | orderly |

1. He's an _____.
2. She's a _____.
3. They live in a _____.

B TALK ABOUT IT. What kinds of jobs are there in a hospital?

2 READ

▶ Listen and read.

Academic Skill: Learn new vocabulary
The words in Exercise 1A will be important when you read *Healthcare Jobs in the U.S.* Write the words in your notebook. Underline the words when you see them in the article.

Healthcare Jobs in the U.S.

Many people in the U.S. work in healthcare. How many? More than 12 million.

The biggest number of jobs in healthcare is for nurses. They work in hospitals, doctors' offices, schools, and 5 nursing homes. You need a lot of training to be a nurse. Nurses go to school for many years.

That is not true for all jobs in healthcare. For some jobs, a high school diploma is enough. For example, you can be an orderly or a CNA. (CNA means "certified 10 nursing assistant.") Most orderlies get training on the job. CNAs take a training course and an exam.

The U.S. has more than 1.5 million CNAs and orderlies. They work in hospitals and nursing homes. They need to be strong because sometimes they lift 15 patients out of bed. They also help people eat, wash, or get dressed.

Hospitals and nursing homes need other kinds of workers, too. They need cooks, housekeepers, custodians, and electricians. They need clerks to do 20 office work.

Healthcare in the U.S. is growing. It will need more workers in the future.

Top Jobs in the U.S.

	What's the job?	How many people do it?	How much money do they make in a year?
1.	Sales assistant	4.5 million	about $25,000
2.	Cashier	3.3 million	about $20,000
3.	Food preparer and server	3.0 million	about $19,000
4.	Office assistant	2.8 million	about $30,000
5.	Registered nurse	2.7 million	about $69,000

Source: U.S. Bureau of Labor Statistics

38 Unit 2, Lesson 7

Reading
3 CLOSE READING

A CITE EVIDENCE. Complete the sentences. Where is the information? Write the line number.

Lines

1. More than _____ million people work in healthcare in the U.S.
   a. 12   b. 15   c. 21   _____
2. You need many years of school to be _____.
   a. a CNA   b. an orderly   c. a nurse   _____
3. _____ do office work in hospitals.
   a. Clerks   b. Housekeepers   c. Electricians   _____
4. There will be _____ jobs in healthcare in the future.
   a. more   b. the same number of   c. not so many   _____

B INTERPRET. Complete the sentences about the chart.

1. The chart shows _____ in the U.S.
   a. the jobs with the most workers   b. who makes the most money   c. the best jobs
2. There are _____ nurses in the U.S.
   a. 2.7 million   b. 7 million   c. 12 million
3. There are more nurses in the U.S. than _____.
   a. cashiers   b. office assistants   c. doctors
4. Most nurses make about _____ a year.
   a. $39,000   b. $69,000   c. $89,000

4 SUMMARIZE

Complete the summary with the words in the box.

| CNA | healthcare | nurses | training |

More than 12 million people in the U.S. work in (1) _____. The biggest number of jobs are for (2) _____. They need a lot of (3) _____, but you can be a (4) _____ or an orderly after you finish high school. There are many other jobs in healthcare, too.

Show what you know!

1. THINK ABOUT IT. Do you know people who work in healthcare? What are their jobs? Where do they work?
2. WRITE ABOUT IT. Now write about someone you know who works in healthcare.
   _____ works in healthcare. (He/She) is a _____. (He/She) works at _____.

I can learn new vocabulary. ☐   I need more practice. ☐

To read more, go to MyEnglishLab.

Unit 2, Lesson 7   39

Graphs and charts introduce students to information in a variety of formats, developing their visual literacy.

Academic tasks, such as summarizing, are introduced from the beginning and scaffolded to support low-level learners.

Informational readings containing level-appropriate complex text introduce academic language and build content knowledge.

xii   Unit Tour

UNIT TOUR

Writing lessons follow a robust and scaffolded writing-process approach, engaging students in analyzing writing models, planning, and producing a final product.

A **Writing Skill** explains and models appropriate writing. Later in the lesson, students apply the skill to their own writing.

New **Soft Skills at Work** lessons engage students in real-life situations that develop the personal, social, and cultural skills critical for career success, and help students meet the WIOA requirements.

A brief scenario introduces a common workplace problem that can be solved using **critical thinking** and **soft skills**.

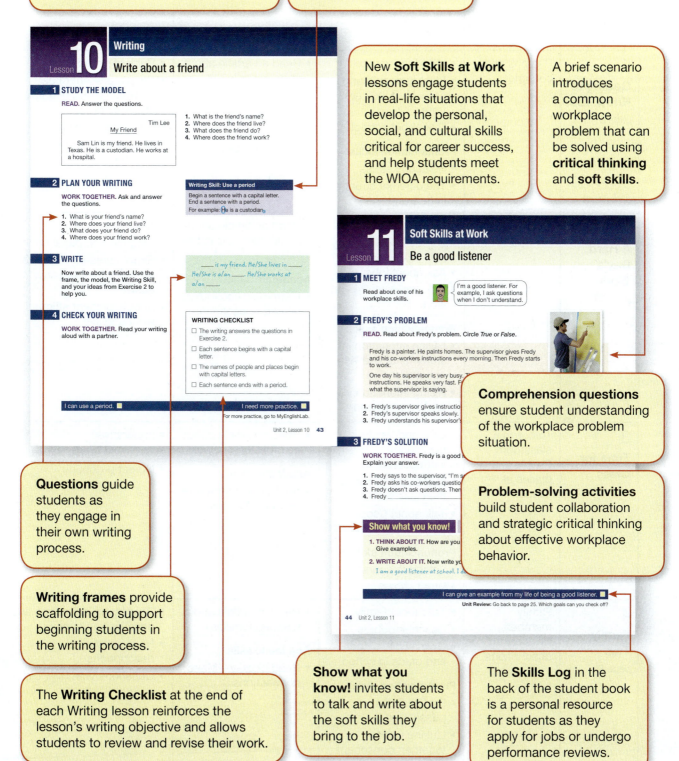

Comprehension questions ensure student understanding of the workplace problem situation.

Questions guide students as they engage in their own writing process.

Problem-solving activities build student collaboration and strategic critical thinking about effective workplace behavior.

Writing frames provide scaffolding to support beginning students in the writing process.

Show what you know! invites students to talk and write about the soft skills they bring to the job.

The **Writing Checklist** at the end of each Writing lesson reinforces the lesson's writing objective and allows students to review and revise their work.

The **Skills Log** in the back of the student book is a personal resource for students as they apply for jobs or undergo performance reviews.

Unit Tour **xiii**

SCOPE AND SEQUENCE

Unit	Vocabulary	Listening and Speaking	Reading	Grammar
Pre-Unit **Welcome to Class** page 2	Classroom instructions; Ask for help	• Follow classroom instructions • Ask for help	• Locate the U.S. map in your book	• Introduction to imperatives
1 **Getting to Know You** page 5	Regions and countries	• Introduce yourself • Identify people and ask where they are from • Talk about school **Pronunciation skills:** • Sentence stress • The different sounds in *he's* and *she's*	• Read an article about immigrants in the U.S. **Academic skill:** • Analyze text structure—Use the title	• Subject pronouns • Simple present of *be*: Affirmative and negative statements • Contractions with *be* • Negative contractions with *be*
2 **A Hard Day's Work** page 25	Jobs; Workplaces	• Introduce someone and talk about your job • Ask about jobs • Talk about where you work **Pronunciation skills:** • Falling intonation in statements and *Wh-* questions • Rising intonation in *yes/no* questions	• Read an article about healthcare jobs in the U.S. **Academic skill:** • Learn new vocabulary related to healthcare	• *A/an* • Singular and plural nouns • Simple present of *be*: *Yes/no* questions and short answers • Simple present affirmative: *work* and *live*
3 **Time for Class** page 45	Things in a classroom; People and places at school	• Give and follow classroom instructions • Talk about things in the classroom • Talk about people and places at school **Pronunciation skills:** • Voiced *th* sound • Word stress	• Read an article about helpful study habits **Academic skill:** • Analyze text structure—Use the headings	• Imperatives • *This, that, these, those* • Object pronouns
4 **Family Ties** page 65	Family members; Physical descriptions	• Talk about family • Describe people • Give a child's age and grade in school **Pronunciation skills:** • Pronunciation of possessive *'s* • Linking words together: consonant to vowel	• Read an article about blended families **Academic skill:** • Read closely—Make connections	• Possessive adjectives and possessive nouns • *Have* and *be* for descriptions • Questions with *How old*

Writing	Document Literacy Numeracy	Workplace, Life, and Community Skills	Soft Skills At Work
• Write about yourself **Writing skill:** • Use a capital letter for people and places	• Interpret a bar graph	• Say and spell first and last names • Use appropriate titles **Digital skill:** • Go online and find common American last names	• Be friendly
• Write about a friend **Writing skill:** • Begin a sentence with a capital letter • End a sentence with a period	• Learn cardinal numbers 0–9 • Interpret a chart	• Identify phone numbers • Identify email addresses • Ask for and give contact information **Digital skill:** • Go online and add new contacts in your phone	• Be a good listener
• Write about your study habits **Writing skill:** • Recognize and use a verb in a sentence	• Count classroom items	• Identify places at school • Give locations of places at school **Digital skill:** • Go online and find a school in your neighborhood	• Be flexible
• Write about a family member **Writing skill:** • Use a capital letter for months	• Interpret a calendar • Learn ordinal numbers 1st–31st • Interpret a pie chart • Understand percentages • Calculate age based on date of birth	• Talk about months • Talk about and write dates **Digital skill:** • Go online and find the date of the next holiday on your calendar	• Separate work and home life

SCOPE AND SEQUENCE

Unit	Vocabulary	Listening and Speaking	Reading	Grammar
5 **Shop, Shop, Shop** page 85	Colors and clothes	• Talk about things you need or want • Ask for sizes and colors • Return something to a store **Pronunciation skill:** • Sentence stress	• Read an article about credit cards and debit cards **Academic skill:** • Read closely—Make inferences	• Simple present affirmative • Simple present: *Yes/no* questions and short answers • Simple present negative
6 **Home, Sweet Home** page 105	Rooms of a house; Furniture and appliances	• Talk about a house for rent • Ask about an apartment for rent • Give directions **Pronunciation skill:** • Stress in compound nouns	• Read an article about smoke alarms and fire safety at home **Academic skill:** • Read closely—Read multiple times to get all the details	• *There is/There are* • *Is there/Are there* • Prepositions of direction and location
7 **Day After Day** page 125	Daily routines and leisure activities; Clock times	• Make plans with someone • Talk about weekend activities • Talk about ways to relax **Pronunciation skills:** • The weak pronunciation of *do you* in questions • Extra syllable in *-es* endings	• Read an article about how Americans spend their free time **Academic skill:** • Read closely—Make predictions	• Simple present: *When* and *What time* • Prepositions of time • Adverbs of frequency • Questions with *How often* • Expressions of frequency
8 **From Soup to Nuts** page 145	Common foods	• Talk about foods you like and don't like • Order a meal in a restaurant • Plan a healthy meal **Pronunciation skill:** • Intonation of choice questions with *or*	• Read an article about food safety **Academic skill:** • Analyze text structure—Read captions before reading an article	• Count and non-count nouns • Choice questions with *or* • Questions and short answers with *How many* and *How much*

Writing	Document Literacy Numeracy	Workplace, Life, and Community Skills	Soft Skills At Work
• Write about the clothes you wear **Writing skill:** • Use commas between words in a list	• Count U.S. money • Calculate the total on a receipt • Make a bar graph about where classmates shop • Interpret a pie chart	• Identify U.S. money • Talk about prices • Read receipts **Digital skill:** • Go online and find the tax rate in your city	• Be professional
• Write about your favorite room at home **Writing skill:** • Use details in your writing	• Talk about numbers of rooms in a home • Compare rents of two homes	• Say and write addresses • Read housing ads **Digital skill:** • Go online and find the address of a home for rent in or near your neighborhood	• Find information
• Write about your favorite day of the week **Writing skill:** • Use a capital letter for days of the week	• Tell time • Count hours worked in a day or week • Interpret a pie chart	• Talk about work schedules • Read and complete a time sheet **Digital skill:** • Go online and find the next event on your calendar	• Be a team player
• Write about the foods you usually eat **Writing skill:** • Choose the correct verb to use with food and drinks	• Understand U.S. measurements of weight • Read store flyers and compare prices • Understand nutritional information on food labels	• Compare food prices • Read food labels • Talk about healthy food **Digital skill:** • Go online and look up the number of calories in your favorite food	• Take action

Scope and Sequence xvii

SCOPE AND SEQUENCE

Unit	Vocabulary	Listening and Speaking	Reading	Grammar
9 **Rain or Shine** page 165	Weather, seasons, and temperature	• Talk about what you are doing now • Ask what someone is doing now • Understand a weather report	• Read an article about hurricanes **Academic skill:** • Read closely—Focus on details	• Present continuous: Statements • Present continuous: *Yes/no* questions and short answers • Adverbs of degree
10 **Around Town** page 185	Places in the community; Kinds of transportation	• Give locations of places in the community • Ask about bus routes and costs • Talk about weekend plans **Pronunciation skills:** • Stressed syllable in a two-syllable word • Unstressed words (*do, the, to, at*)	• Read an article about resources available at the public library **Academic skill:** • Read closely—Give your own examples	• Prepositions of place • Simple present questions with *How, How much,* and *Where* • Present continuous for future plans
11 **Health Matters** page 205	Parts of the body; Symptoms and illnesses	• Call to explain an absence • Talk about health problems • Give advice **Pronunciation skill:** • Pronunciation of *was/were* and *wasn't/weren't*	• Read an article about the health benefits of walking **Academic skill:** • Read closely—Apply what you read	• Review: Simple present • Past of *be*: Statements • Statements with *should*
12 **Help Wanted** page 225	Job duties	• Respond to a help-wanted sign • Talk about hours you can work • Talk about work experience **Pronunciation skills:** • Sentence stress: *Can* and *can't* in statements • Sentence stress: *Can* and *can't* in short answers	• Read an article about making a good first impression in a job interview **Academic skill:** • Read closely—Mark up a text when reading	• *Can*: Statements • *Can*: *Yes/no* questions and short answers • Past of *be*: Questions and answers

Writing	Document Literacy Numeracy	Workplace, Life, and Community Skills	Soft Skills At Work
• Write about the weather in your native country **Writing skill:** • Use *because* to give a reason	• Read a thermometer in degrees Fahrenheit	• Talk about bad weather and emergencies • Plan for an emergency **Digital skill:** • Go online and add emergency numbers to your phone	• Be ready to learn new skills
• Write about your street **Writing skill:** • Use the correct preposition in a sentence	• Understand traffic signs • Understand bus schedules	• Talk about kinds of transportation • Read traffic signs • Read bus signs and schedules **Digital skill:** • Go online and use a transportation website or app to find public transportation to a supermarket	• Be reliable
• Write about your healthy habits **Writing skill:** • Start each paragraph with a topic sentence	• Read medicine labels and understand correct dosages	• Make a doctor's appointment • Follow a doctor's instructions • Read medicine labels **Digital skill:** • Go online and find the phone number for a clinic in or near your neighborhood	• Make good decisions
• Write about a job you want and your job skills **Writing skill:** • Recognize and use a subject in a sentence	• Calculate weekly earnings based on hourly wages	• Read job postings • Identify different ways to find a job **Digital skill:** • Go online and find a job listing for a job you want	• Respond well to feedback

CORRELATIONS

Unit	CASAS Reading Standards (correlated to CASAS Reading Standards 2016)	CASAS Listening Standards (correlated to CASAS Listening Basic Skills Content Standards)
1	**L1:** RDG 1.1, 1.4, 1.5, 1.7, 2.1, 1.8, 3.2, 2.9, 3.4, 3.5; **L2:** RDG 1.1, 1.5, 1.7, 2.9; **L3:** RDG 1.1, 1.5, 1.7, 2.2, 2.9, 3.3, 3.10; **L4:** RDG 1.1, 1.5, 1.7, 2.2, 2.9; **L5:** RDG 1.1, 1.5, 1.7, 2.10, 2.9; **L6:** RDG 1.1, 1.5, 1.7, 1.8, 3.2, 3.4, 3.5, 3.8, 4.2; **L7:** RDG 1.1, 1.5, 1.7, 2.9; **L8:** RDG 1.1, 1.5, 1.7, 2.10, 2.9; **L10:** RDG 1.1, 1.5, 1.7, 1.8, 3.2, 3.14; **L11:** RDG 1.1, 1.5, 1.7, 1.8, 3.2	**L1:** 2.1, 2.3, 2.9; **L2:** 1.3, 1.4, 2.1, 2.3, 4.1, 4.2; **L3:** 1.3, 2.1, 2.2, 2.3, 4.1, 4.2; **L4:** 1.2, 2.1, 2.3, 4.1, 4.2; **L5:** 2.1, 2.3, 3.1, 3.3, 3.5, 4.1, 4.2; **L6:** 2.1, 2.3, 4.1, 4.2; **L7:** 2.1, 2.3, 4.1, 4.2, 4.3; **L8:** 2.1, 2.3, 3.1, 3.3, 3.5, 4.1, 4.2; **L9:** 2.1, 2.3, 3.1, 3.3, 3.5; **L10:** 2.1, 2.3; **L11:** 2.1, 2.3, 4.1, 4.2;
2	**L1:** RDG 2.3; **L2:** RDG 1.1, 1.5, 1.7, 2.9; **L3:** RDG 2.6, 1.8, 3.2, 2.9, 3.6, 1.4; **L4:** RDG 1.1, 1.5, 1.7, 2.9, 1.4; **L5:** RDG 1.1, 1.7, 2.9; **L6:** RDG 1.7, 3.6, 2.9; **L7:** RDG 1.1, 1.5, 1.7, 1.8, 3.2, 1.4, 3.4, 3.10, 4.2; **L8:** RDG 1.1, 1.7, 2.9; **L10:** RDG 1.1, 1.5, 1.7, 1.8, 3.2, 3.14; **L11:** RDG 1.1, 1.5, 1.7, 1.8, 3.2	**L1:** 2.1, 2.4, 2.9, 4.2; **L2:** 1.3, 1.4, 2.1, 2.3, 2.4, 3.6, 4.1, 4.2; **L3:** 1.2, 2.3, 2.4, 3.7, 4.2; **L4:** 1.3, 2.1, 2.3, 4.1, 4.2; **L5:** 1.3, 1.4, 2.1, 2.3, 2.4, 3.6, 4.1, 4.2; **L6:** 1.3, 1.4, 2.1, 2.3, 2.4, 3.3, 3.6, 4.1, 4.2; **L7:** 2.4, 2.9, 4.2; **L8:** 1.3, 2.1, 2.3, 2.4, 4.1, 4.2; **L9:** 2.1, 2.3, 3.1; **L10:** 2.1, 2.3, 3.6; **L11:** 2.1, 2.3
3	**L1:** RDG 2.3; **L2:** RDG 1.1, 1.5, 1.7, 2.9, 2.8, 3.6; **L3:** RDG 2.10, 3.6, 2.9; **L4:** RDG 1.1, 1.5, 1.7, 1.8, 3.2, 3.10, 4.2; **L5:** RDG 1.1, 1.5, 1.7, 2.9, 3.6; **L7:** RDG 1.1, 1.5, 1.7, 2.9, 3.6, 3.4, 3.5; **L8:** RDG 1.1, 1.5, 1.7, 2.9; **L10:** RDG 1.1, 1.5, 1.7, 1.8, 3.2, 3.14; **L11:** RDG 1.1, 1.5, 1.7, 1.8, 3.2	**L1:** 2.1, 2.4, 2.9, 4.2; **L2:** 1.3, 2.1, 2.3, 4.2, 5.4; **L3:** 1.3, 2.1, 2.3, 2.4, 3.3, 3.4, 4.1, 4.2; **L4:** 2.4, 2.9, 4.2; **L5:** 1.3, 2.1, 2.3, 2.9, 4.2; **L6:** 2.1, 2.3, 3.2, 3.6; **L7:** 1.3, 2.1, 2.3, 2.9, 4.2; **L8:** 1.3, 1.4, 2.1, 2.3, 2.9, 4.2; **L9:** 2.1, 2.3, 3.1, 3.2; **L10:** 2.1, 2.3, 3.6; **L11:** 2.1, 2.3
4	**L1:** RDG 2.3; **L2:** RDG 1.1, 1.5, 1.7, 2.9; **L3:** RDG 2.10, 2.6, 2.9; **L4:** RDG 1.1, 1.5, 1.7, 1.8, 3.2, 3.4, 3.5, 4.2; **L5:** RDG 1.1, 1.5, 1.7, 2.9; **L6:** RDG 1.1, 1.5, 1.7, 2.9; **L7:** RDG 1.1, 1.5, 1.7, 2.2, 1.4; **L8:** RDG 1.1, 1.5, 1.7, 2.9; **L10:** RDG 1.1, 1.5, 1.7, 1.8, 3.2, 3.14; **L11:** RDG 1.1, 1.5, 1.7, 1.8, 3.2	**L1:** 2.1, 2.9, 4.2; **L2:** 1.3, 2.1, 2.3, 4.2; **L3:** 1.2, 2.1, 2.3, 3.2, 3.3, 3.8; **L4:** 2.3, 2.9, 4.2; **L5:** 1.3, 2.1, 2.3, 4.2; **L6:** 2.1, 2.3, 3.1, 4.2; **L7:** 1.3, 2.1, 2.3, 4.2; **L8:** 1.1, 1.3, 1.4, 2.1, 2.3, 4.2; **L9:** 2.1, 2.3, 3.6; **L10:** 2.1, 2.3, 3.5; **L11:** 2.1, 2.3
5	**L1:** RDG 2.3, 2.11; **L2:** 1.1, 1.5, 1.7, 2.9; **L3:** 2.9; **L4:** 1.1, 1.5, 1.7, 2.9, 1.4; **L5:** 1.1, 1.5, 1.7, 2.9, 3.7, 3.10; **L6:** 2.9; **L7:** 1.1, 1.5, 1.7, 1.8, 3.2, 3.4, 3.5, 4.2, 4.3; **L8:** 1.1, 1.5, 1.7, 2.2, 2.9; **L10:** 1.1, 1.5, 1.7, 1.8, 3.2, 3.14; **L11:** 1.1, 1.5, 1.7, 1.8, 3.2	**L1:** 2.1, 2.9, 4.2; **L2:** 1.3, 2.1, 2.3, 2.4, 4.1, 4.2; **L3:** 1.2, 2.1, 2.3, 3.1, 4.2; **L4:** 1.3, 2.1, 2.3, 2.4, 4.2; **L5:** 1.3, 1.4, 2.1, 2.3, 2.4, 4.2; **L6:** 2.1, 2.3, 3.1, 3.3, 3.6, 4.2; **L7:** 2.3, 2.9, 4.2; **L8:** 1.3, 2.1, 2.3, 2.4, 4.2; **L9:** 2.1, 2.3, 3.1, 3.3, 3.5; **L10:** 2.1, 2.3, 3.6; **L11:** 2.1, 2.3
6	**L1:** RDG 2.3; **L2:** RDG 1.1, 1.5, 1.7, 2.9; **L3:** RDG 1.1, 1.5, 1.7, 2.10, 2.9, 1.4; **L4:** RDG 1.1, 1.5, 1.7, 1.8, 3.2, 3.4, 3.5, 3.7, 3.10, 4.2; **L5:** RDG 1.1, 1.5, 1.7, 2.9; **L6:** RDG 2.10; **L7:** RDG 1.1, 1.5, 1.3, 1.7, 2.2, 1.8, 3.2, 1.4; **L8:** RDG 1.1, 1.5, 1.7, 1.8, 3.2, 1.4, 3.4, 3.5; **L10:** RDG 1.1, 1.5, 1.7, 1.8, 3.2, 3.14; **L11:** RDG 1.1, 1.5, 1.7, 3.2	**L1:** 2.1, 2.4, 2.9, 4.2; **L2:** 1.3, 2.1, 2.3, 2.4, 4.2; **L3:** 2.1, 2.3, 3.1, 3.3, 4.2; **L4:** 2.3, 2.9, 4.2; **L5:** 1.3, 1.7, 2.1, 2.3, 2.4, 2.9, 4.2; **L6:** 2.1, 2.3, 3.1, 3.3, 4.2; **L7:** 2.3, 2.4, 2.9, 4.2; **L8:** 2.3, 2.3, 2.9, 4.2, 5.4; **L9:** 2.1, 2.3, 3.9;; **L10:** 2.1, 2.3, 3.6; **L11:** 2.1, 2.3, 2.4
7	**L1:** RDG 1.4, 2.3; **L2:** RDG 1.1, 1.5, 1.7, 1.8, 3.2, 1.4; **L3:** RDG 2.9, 3.4; **L4:** RDG 2.9, 3.4, 4.2; **L5:** RDG 1.1, 1.5, 1.7, 1.8, 3.2, 3.6; **L6:** RDG 2.9, 3.4, 4.2; **L7:** RDG 1.1, 1.5, 1.7, 1.8, 3.2, 3.4, 3.5, 3.7, 3.10, 3.8, 4.2; **L8:** RDG 1.1, 1.5, 1.7, 1.8, 3.2; **L10:** RDG 1.1, 1.5, 1.7, 1.8, 3.2, 3.14; **L11:** RDG 1.1, 1.5, 1.7, 1.8, 3.2	**L1:** 2.1, 2.4, 2.9, 4.2; **L2:** 1.4, 1.5, 2.3, 2.4, 4.2, 4.4; **L3:** 2.1, 2.3, 2.4, 3.1, 3.6, 4.2; **L4:** 2.3, 2.4, 4.2; **L5:** 1.4, 2.3, 2.4, 4.2; **L6:** 2.1, 2.3, 2.4, 3.9, 4.2; **L7:** 2.3, 2.9, 4.2; **L8:** 1.2, 2.3, 2.4, 2.9, 4.2; **L9:** 2.1, 2.3, 3.1, 3.9; **L10:** 2.1, 2.3, 3.6; **L11:** 2.1, 2.3, 2.4
8	**L1:** RDG 2.3, 3.4, 3.5; **L2:** RDG 1.1, 1.5, 1.7, 1.8, 3.2; **L3:** RDG 2.9; **L4:** RDG 1.1, 1.5, 1.7, 1.8, 3.2, 4.2, 3.10; **L5:** RDG 1.1, 1.5, 1.7, 1.8, 3.2, 3.6; **L7:** RDG 2.2, 1.4, 3.16; **L8:** RDG 1.1, 1.5, 1.7, 1.8, 3.2; **L9:** RDG 2.9; **L10:** RDG 1.1, 1.5, 1.7, 1.8, 3.2, 3.14; **L11:** RDG 1.1, 1.5, 1.7, 1.8, 3.2	**L1:** 2.1, 2.9, 4.2; **L2:** 2.3, 2.4, 2.9, 4.2; **L3:** 2.1, 2.3, 2.4, 3.7, 4.2; **L4:** 2.3, 2.4, 4.2; **L5:** 1.4, 2.3, 2.4, 4.2; **L6:** 2.1, 2.3, 2.4, 3.6, 4.2, 4.4; **L7:** 2.3, 2.4, 2.9, 4.2; **L8:** 2.3, 2.4, 2.9, 4.2; **L9:** 2.3, 3.6, 3.7; **L10:** 2.1, 2.3, 3.6; **L11:** 2.1, 2.3, 2.4
9	**L1:** RDG 1.3, 2.3; **L2:** RDG 1.1, 1.5, 1.7, 1.8, 3.2, 3.4, 3.5; **L3:** RDG 2.9; **L4:** RDG 1.1, 1.5, 1.7, 2.3, 1.8, 3.2, 1.4; **L5:** RDG 1.1, 1.5, 1.7, 1.8, 3.2, 2.3; **L6:** RDG 2.10, 2.9; **L7:** RDG 1.1, 1.5, 1.3, 1.7, 2.3, 1.8, 3.2, 3.4, 3.5, 3.7, 3.10, 4.2; **L8:** RDG 1.1, 1.5, 1.3, 1.7, 2.3, 1.8, 3.2, 3.4, 3.5; **L9:** RDG 1.1, 1.5, 1.7, 2.9; **L10:** RDG 1.1, 1.5, 1.7, 1.8, 3.2, 3.14; **L11:** RDG 1.1, 1.5, 1.7, 1.8, 3.2	**L1:** 2.1, 4.2; **L2:** 2.3, 2.4, 2.9, 4.2; **L3:** 2.1, 2.0, 0.0, 0.0, 1.2; **L4:** 2.3, 2.4, 4.2; **L5:** 2.3, 2.4, 4.2; **L6:** 2.1, 2.3, 2.4, 3.6, 4.2; **L7:** 2.1, 2.3, 2.4, 2.9, 4.2; **L8:** 2.3, 2.4, 2.9, 4.2; **L9:** 2.1, 2.3, 3.9; **L10:** 2.1, 2.3, 3.6; **L11:** 2.1, 2.3, 2.4
10	**L1:** RDG 2.3; **L2:** RDG 1.1, 1.5, 1.7, 1.8, 3.2, 3.4, 3.5; **L3:** RDG 2.9, 3.4, 3.5; **L4:** RDG 1.3, 2.2, 2.3, 1.4, 3.4; **L5:** RDG 1.1, 1.5, 1.7, 1.8, 3.2, 1.4, 2.3; **L6:** RDG 2.9; **L7:** RDG 1.1, 1.5, 1.7, 2.3, 1.8, 3.2, 3.7, 3.10, 4.2; **L8:** RDG 1.1, 1.5, 1.7, 2.3, 1.8, 3.2; **L9:** RDG 1.1, 1.5, 1.7, 2.9; **L10:** RDG 1.1, 1.5, 1.7, 1.8, 3.2, 3.14; **L11:** RDG 1.1, 1.5, 1.7, 1.8, 3.2	**L1:** 2.1, 2.3, 2.4, 4.2; **L2:** 1.4, 2.3, 2.4, 2.9, 4.2; **L3:** 2.3, 3.9, 4.2; **L4:** 2.3, 2.4, 4.2; **L5:** 1.4, 2.3, 2.4, 4.2; **L6:** 2.1, 2.3, 2.4, 3.6, 4.2; **L7:** 2.1, 2.3, 2.4, 2.9, 4.2; **L8:** 2.3, 2.4, 2.9, 4.2; **L9:** 2.1, 2.3, 3.9; **L10:** 2.1, 2.3, 3.6; **L11:** 2.3, 2.4
11	**L1:** RDG 2.3; **L2:** RDG 1.1, 1.5, 1.7, 1.8, 3.2; **L3:** RDG 2.9; **L4:** RDG 2.2, 2.3, 1.8, 3.2; **L5:** RDG 1.1, 1.5, 1.7, 1.8, 3.2, 1.4, 2.3; **L6:** RDG 2.10, 2.9, 3.4; **L7:** RDG 1.1, 1.5, 1.7, 2.3, 1.8, 3.2, 3.7, 3.10, 4.2; **L8:** RDG 1.1, 1.5, 1.7, 1.8, 3.2, 3.4; **L9:** RDG 1.1, 1.5, 1.7, 2.2, 2.10; **L10:** RDG 1.1, 1.5, 1.7, 1.8, 3.2, 3.14; **L11:** RDG 1.1, 1.5, 1.7, 1.8, 1.4	**L1:** 2.1, 2.2, 4.2; **L2:** 2.3, 2.4, 2.9, 4.2; **L3:** 3.1, 3.6, 4.2; **L4:** 2.3, 2.4, 4.2; **L5:** 1.4, 2.3, 2.4, 4.2; **L6:** 2.1, 2.3, 2.4, 3.9, 4.2; **L7:** 2.1, 2.3, 2.4, 2.9, 4.2; **L8:** 2.3, 2.4, 2.9, 4.2; **L9:** 2.1, 2.3, 3.3, 3.9; **L10:** 2.1, 2.3, 3.6; **L11:** 2.3, 2.4
12	**L1:** RDG 2.3; **L2:** RDG 1.1, 1.5, 1.7, 2.10, 1.8, 3.2; **L3:** RDG 2.10, 2.9, 3.4; **L4:** RDG 1.1, 1.5, 1.7, 2.2, 2.3, 1.8, 3.2, 1.4; **L5:** RDG 1.1, 1.5, 1.7, 2.10, 1.8, 3.2, 2.3, 1.4; **L6:** RDG ; **L7:** RDG 1.1, 1.5, 1.7, 2.3, 1.8, 3.2, 3.7, 3.10, 4.2; **L8:** RDG 1.1, 1.5, 1.7, 1.8, 3.2; **L9:** RDG 2.10; **L10:** RDG 1.1, 1.5, 1.7, 1.8, 3.2, 3.14; **L11:** RDG 1.1, 1.5, 1.7, 1.8, 3.2	**L1:** 2.1, 2.4, 4.2; **L2:** 1.4, 2.4, 2.9, 3.3, 4.2; **L3:** 2.1, 2.4, 3.1, 3.3, 3.5, 4.2; **L4:** 2.3, 2.4, 4.2; **L5:** 1.4, 2.3, 2.4, 4.2; **L6:** 2.1, 2.4, 3.6, 4.2; **L7:** 2.3, 2.4, 2.9, 4.2; **L8:** 2.3, 2.4, 2.9, 4.2; **L9:** 2.1, 2.4, 3.3, 3.9; **L10:** 2.1, 2.3, 2.4, 3.6; **L11:** 2.3, 2.4

CASAS: Comprehensive Adult Student Assessment System
CCRS: College and Career Readiness Standards (R=Reading; W=Writing; SL=Speaking/Listening; L=Language)
ELPS: English Language Proficiency Standards

CASAS Competencies (correlated to CASAS Competencies: Essential Life and Work skills for Youth and Adults)	CCRS Correlations, Level A	ELPS Correlations, Level 1
L1: 0.1.2, 0.1.5, 0.2.1, 7.4.1; L2: 0.1.2, 0.1.4, 0.1.5, 0.2.1; L3: 0.1.2, 0.1.4, 0.1.5, 0.1.6, 0.2.1, 0.2.2, 7.7.3; L4: 0.1.2, 0.1.4, 0.1.5, 0.1.6, 0.2.1; L5: 0.1.2, 0.1.4, 0.1.5, 0.1.6, 0.2.1, 7.4.1; L6: 0.1.2, 0.1.4, 0.1.5, 0.2.1, 6.7.2, 6.8.1; L7: 0.1.2, 0.1.4, 0.1.5, 0.1.6, 0.2.1; L8: 0.1.2, 0.1.4, 0.1.5, 0.1.6, 0.2.1; L9: 0.1.2; L10: 0.1.2, 0.1.5, 0.1.6, 0.2.1; L11: 0.1.2, 0.1.5;	L1: RI.1.4, SL.1.1, SL.K.6, L.1. 4, L1.5a, L1.5b, L1.5c, L1.6; L2: SL.K.3, SL.1.4; L3: W.1.7; W.1.8; L4: SL.K.3; SL.1.4; L5: L.1.1e, L.1.1f; L6: L.1.6, RI.1.2, RI.1.3, RI.1.4, RI.1.7, W.1.7, W.1.8, SL.K.2; L7: SL.K.3, SL.1.4; L8: L.1.1e, L.1.1f, L.1.1g; L9: L.1.1e, L.1.1g; L10: W.1.3, W.1.5, W.1.7, W.1.8, SL.1.1a, SL.1.1b, SL.1.1c, SL.K.6, L1.1l, L.1.2b; L11: RI.1.8	ELPS 1–3, 5–10
L1: 0.1.2, 0.1.5, 0.2.1, 7.4.1; L2: 0.1.2, 0.1.5, 0.2.1; L3: 0.1.2, 0.1.5, 0.1.6, 4.1.3, 4.1.8, 7.4.1, 7.4.2; L4: 0.1.2, 0.1.5, 0.2.1, 2.1.7, 7.7.3, 7.7.4; L5: 0.1.2, 0.1.5, 0.2.1, 4.1.8; L6: 0.1.2, 0.1.5, 0.1.6, 0.2.1, 4.1.8; L7: 0.1.2, 0.1.5, 0.2.1, 4.4.3, 7.4.1, 7.4.2; L8: 0.1.2, 0.1.5, 0.2.1, 4.1.8; L9: 0.1.2, 0.1.5, 0.2.1, 4.1.8; L10: 0.1.2, 0.1.5, 0.1.6, 0.2.1; L11: 0.1.2	L1: RI.1.4, L.1. 4, L.1.6, W.1.7, W.1.8, L.1.5a, L.1.5b, L.1.5c; L2: SL.K.3, SL.1.4; L3: L.1.1b, L.1.1c, L.1.1g, L.1.1i; L4: W.1.7, W.1.8, SL.1.1a, SL.1.1b, SL.1.1c, SL.K.6; L5: SL.K.3, SL.1.4, SL.1.1, SL.K.6; L6: L.1.1g, L.1.1k; L7: RI.1.4, RI.1.7, L.1.6; L8: SL.K.3, SL.1.4; L9: L.1.1c, L.1.1e, L.1.1g; L10: W.1.3, W.1.5, W.1.7, W.1.8, L.1.1i, L.1.2a, L.1.2b, L.1.2c, L.1.2d; L11: RI.1.8	ELPS 1–3, 5–10
L1: 0.1.2, 0.1.5, 7.4.1, 7.4.2, 7.4.3; L2: 0.1.2, 0.1.5, 0.1.7, 0.2.1; L3: 0.1.2, 0.1.5, 0.1.7; L4: 0.1.2, 0.1.5, 0.2.1, 7.4.1, 7.4.9; L5: 0.1.2, 0.1.5, 0.1.7, 0.2.1, 0.2.1; L7: 0.1.2, 0.1.5, 2.2.1; L8: 0.1.2, 0.1.4, 0.1.5, 4.1.8; L9: 0.1.2, 0.1.5, 0.1.7, 0.2.1, 2.2.1; L10: 0.1.2, 0.1.5, 0.2.1, 7.4.1; L11: 0.1.2, 0.1.5	L1: RI.1.4, L.1. 4a, L.1.6, L.1.5a, L.1.5b, L.1.5c; L2: SL.K.3, SL.1.4, SL.1.1a, SL.1.1b, SL.1.1c, SL.K.6; L3: L.1.1e, L.1.1g; L4: RI.1.4, RI.1.5, L.1.6, RI/RL.1.1, RI.1.2, RI.1.3, SL.K.2; L5: SL.K.3, SL.1.4, SL.1.1; L6: ; L7: W.1.7, W.1.8; L8: SL.K.3, SL.1.4; L9: L.1.1d; L10: W.1.2, W.1.5, W.1.7, W.1.8, L.1.1l, L.1.2a, L.1.2c, L.1.2d; L11: RI.1.8, SL.1.1a, SL.1.1b, SL.1.1c, SL.K.6	ELPS 1–3, 5–10
L1: 0.1.2, 0.1.5, 7.4.1, 7.4.2; L2: 0.1.2, 0.1.4, 0.1.5, 0.2.1; L3: 0.1.2, 0.1.5; L4: 0.1.2, 0.1.5, 0.2.1, 7.4.1; L5: 0.1.2, 0.1.5, 0.2.1; L6: 0.1.2, 0.1.5, 0.2.1; L7: 0.1.2, 0.1.5, 0.2.1; L8: 0.1.2, 0.1.4, 0.1.5, 0.2.1; L9: 0.1.2, 0.1.5 ; L10: 0.1.2, 0.1.5, 0.2.1; L11: 0.1.2, 0.1.5	L1: RI.1.4, L.1. 4a, L.1.6, L.1.5a, L.1.5b, L.1.5c, L.1.6; L2: SL.K.3, SL.1.4, SL.1.1a, SL.1.1b, SL.1.1c, SL.K.6; L3: L.1.1b, SL.1.1a, SL.1.1b, SL.1.1c, SL.K.6; L4: RI.1.4, RI.1.7, L.1.6, RI/RL.1.1, RI.1.2, RI.1.3, SL.K.2; L5: SL.K.3, SL.1.4; L6: L.1.1c, L.1.1e, L.1.1f, L.1.1g, W.1.7, W.1.8; L7: W.1.7, W.1.8; L8: SL.K.3, SL.1.4; L9: L.1.1k; L10: W.1.2, W.1.5, W.1.7, W.1.8, L.1.1l, L.1.2a, L.1.2c, L.1.2d; L11: RI.1.8	ELPS 1–3, 5–10
L1: 0.1.2, 0.1.5, 0.2.1, 7.4.1; L2: 0.1.2, 0.1.5, 0.2.1; L3: 0.1.2, 0.1.5, 0.2.1; L4: 0.1.2, 0.1.5, 0.2.1, 1.1.6, 1.6.4, 5.4.2, 7.7.3; L5: 0.1.2, 0.1.4, 0.1.5, 1.2.9; L6: 0.1.2, 0.1.5, 0.2.1; L7: 0.1.2, 0.1.5, 0.2.1, 1.3.1, 7.4.1; L8: 0.1.2, 0.1.4, 0.1.5, 1.3.3; L9: 0.1.2, 0.1.5; L10: 0.1.2, 0.1.5, 0.2.1; L11: 0.1.2, 0.1.5	L1: RI.1.4, L.1.4, L.1.6, W.1.7, W.1.8, L.1.5a, L.1.5b, L.1.5c; L2: SL.K.3, SL.1.4; L3: L.1.1c, L.1.1e, L.1.1g; L4: W.1.7, W.1.8; L5: SL.K.3, SL.1.4, SL.1.1a, SL.1.1b, SL.1.1c, SL.K.6; L6: L.1.1c, L.1.1e, L.1.1g, L.1.1k; L7: RI.1.4, RI.1.7, L.1.6, RI/RL.1.1, RI.1.2, RI.1.3, SL.K.2; L8: SL.K.3, SL.1.4; L9: L.1.1e, L.1.1g; L10: W.1.2, W.1.5, W.1.2, SL.1.1, SL.K.6, L.1.1l, L.1.2a, L.1.2c, L.1.2d, L.1.2e, L.1.2g, L.1.2h, L.1.2i; L11: RI.1.8	ELPS 1–10
L1: 0.1.2, 0.1.5, 7.4.1, 7.4.2; L2: 0.1.2, 0.1.5, 1.4.1; L3: 0.1.2, 0.1.5, 1.4.1, 1.4.2; L4: 0.1.2, 0.1.5, 0.2.1, 1.4.1, 7.4.1; L5: 0.1.2, 0.1.5, 1.4.1; L6: 0.1.2, 0.1.5, 1.4.1; L7: 0.1.2, 0.1.5, 0.2.1, 1.4.1, 1.4.2; L8: 0.1.2, 0.1.5, 0.2.1, 2.2.1; L9: 0.1.2, 0.1.5, 2.2.1; L10: 0.1.2, 0.1.5, 0.2.1, 1.4.1; L11: 0.1.2, 0.1.4, 0.1.5	L1: RI.1.4, L.1. 4a, L.1.6, L.1.5a, L.1.5b, L.1.5c; L2: SL.K.3, SL.1.4; L3: L.1.1g; L4: RI.1.4, RI.1.7, L.1.6, RI/RL.1.1, RI.1.2, RI.1.3, SL.K.2; L5: SL.K.3, SL.1.4; L6: L.1.1g; L7: W.1.7, W.1.8, SL.1.1a, SL.1.1b, SL.1.1c, SL.K.6; L8: SL.K.3, SL.1.4, SL.1.1a, SL.1.1b, SL.1.1c, SL.K.6; L9: L.1.1j; L10: W.1.2, W.1.5, W.1.7, W.1.8, L.1.1l; L11: RI.1.8	ELPS 1–3, 5–10
L1: 0.1.2, 0.1.5, 0.2.1, 0.2.4, 7.4.1, 7.4.3; L2: 0.1.2, 0.1.4, 0.1.5, 0.2.1, 0.2.4; L3: 0.1.2, 0.1.5, 0.2.1, 0.2.4, 7.1.2; L4: 0.1.2, 0.1.5, 0.2.1, 2.8.3, 4.2.1, 7.4.4, 7.7.3; L5: 0.1.2, 0.1.4, 0.1.5, 0.2.1, 0.2.4; L6: 0.1.2, 0.1.5, 0.2.1, 0.2.4; L7: 0.1.2, 0.1.5, 0.2.1, 7.4.1; L8: 0.1.2, 0.1.5, 0.2.1, 0.2.4, 2.2.1; L9: 0.1.2, 0.1.5, 2.8.3; L10: 0.1.2, 0.1.5, 0.2.1, 0.2.4; L11: 0.1.2, 0.1.4, 0.1.5	L1: RI.1.4, L.1. 4, L.1.6, L.1.5a, L.1.5b, L.1.5c; L2: SL.K.3, SL.1.4; L3: L.1.1e, L.1.1g, L.1.1j, RI.1.7, W.1.7, W.1.8; L4: SL.1.1a, SL.1.1b, SL.1.1c, SL.K.6, W.1.7, W.1.8; L5: SL.1.1a, SL.1.1b, SL.1.1c, SL.K.3, SL.1.4, SL.K.6; L6: RI.1.4, L.1.6; L7: RI/RL.1.1, RI.1.2, RI.1.3, RI.1.7, SL.K.2; L8: SL.K.3, SL.1.4; L9: L.1.1k; L10: W.1.2, W.1.5, W.1.7, W.1.8, L.1.1l, L.1.2; L11: RI.1.8	ELPS 1–3, 5–10
L1: 0.1.2, 0.1.5, 0.2.4, 1.2.8, 7.4.1, 7.4.3; L2: 0.1.2, 0.1.5, 0.2.1, 0.2.4, 1.2.8; L3: 0.1.2, 0.1.5, 1.2.8; L4: 0.1.2, 0.1.5, 0.2.1, 1.6.1, 1.2.8, 3.5.3; L5: 0.1.2, 0.1.4, 0.1.5, 0.2.1, 0.2.4, 1.2.8, 2.6.4; L6: 0.1.2, 0.1.5, 0.2.1, 0.2.4, 1.2.8; L7: 0.1.2, 0.1.5, 0.2.1, 1.2.1, 1.2.2, 1.2.8, 3.5.1, 3.5.2; L8: 0.1.2, 0.1.5, 0.2.1, 0.2.4, 1.2.8, 3.5.2, 3.5.3; L9: 0.1.2, 0.1.5, 1.2.8; L10: 0.1.2, 0.1.5, 0.2.1, 0.2.4, 1.2.8; L11: 0.1.2, 0.1.4, 0.1.5, 1.2.8, 4.6.4, 7.3.1, 7.3.2	L1: RI.1.4, L.1. 4a, L.1.6; L2: SL.K.3, SL.1.4; L3: L.1.1b, L.1.1c, L.1.1g; L4: RI.1.4, RI.1.5, L.1.6, RI/RL.1.1, RI.1.2, RI.1.3, SL.K.2; L5: SL.K.3, SL.1.4; L6: L.1.1h, L.1.1k; L7: L.1.5a, L.1.5b, L.1.5c, W.1.7, W.1.8; L8: SL.1.1a, SL.1.1b, SL.1.1c, SL.K.3, SL.1.4, SL.K.6; L9: SL.1.1a, SL.1.1b, SL.1.1c, SL.K.6, L.1.1k; L10: W.1.2, W.1.5, W.1.7, L.1.1l; L11: RI.1.8	ELPS 1–3, 5–10
L1: 0.1.2, 0.1.5, 2.3.3, 7.4.1; L2: 0.1.2, 0.1.4, 0.1.5, 0.2.1, 0.2.4, 2.3.3; L3: 0.1.2, 0.1.5, 2.3.3; L4: 0.1.2, 0.1.5, 0.2.1, 2.3.1, 2.3.3, 7.7.3; L5: 0.1.2, 0.1.5, 0.2.1; L6: 0.1.2, 0.1.5, 0.2.1; L7: 0.1.2, 0.1.5, 0.2.1, 2.3.3; L8: 0.1.2, 0.1.5, 0.2.1, 2.3.3; L9: 0.1.2, 0.1.5, 0.2.1, 2.3.3; L10: 0.1.2, 0.1.5, 0.2.1, 2.3.3; L11: 0.1.2, 0.1.4, 0.1.5, 7.3.2, 7.5.7	L1: RI.1.4, L.1. 4a, L.1.6, W.1.7, W.1.8; L2: SL.K.3, SL.1.4, L.1.5a, L.1.5b, L.1.5c, SL.1.1a, SL.1.1b, SL.1.1c, SL.K.6; L3: L.1.1e, L.1.1g, L.1.2g, L.1.2h, L.1.2i; L4: W.1.7, W.1.8; L5: SL.K.3, SL.1.4; L6: L.1.1e, L.1.1g, L.1.1k; L7: RI/RL.1.1, RI.1.2, RI.1.3, RI.1.4, RI.1.7, SL.K.2, L.1.6; L8: SL.K.3, SL.1.4; L9: L.1.1f, L.1.1j; L10: W.1.2, W.1.5, W.1.7, W.1.8, SL.1.1a, SL.1.1b, SL.1.1c, SL.K.6, L.1.1l; L11: RI.1.8	ELPS 1–10
L1: 0.1.2, 0.1.5, 2.2.1, 7.4.1; L2: 0.1.2, 0.1.4, 0.1.5, 0.2.1, 2.2.1; L3: 0.1.2, 0.1.5, 2.2.1; L4: 0.1.2, 0.1.5, 0.2.1, 2.2.4, 2.3.1, 7.4.4, 7.7.3; L5: 0.1.2, 0.1.3, 0.1.4, 0.1.5; L6: 0.1.2, 0.1.5, 0.2.1; L7: 0.1.2, 0.1.5, 2.5.6, 7.4.1; L8: 0.1.2, 0.1.5, 0.2.1, 0.2.4; L9: 0.1.2, 0.1.5, 0.2.1; L10: 0.1.2, 0.1.5, 0.2.1; L11: 0.1.2, 0.1.4, 0.1.5, 7.3.2, 7.5.7	L1: L.1.4a, L.1.5a, L.1.5b, L.1.5c, L.1.6; L2: SL.K.3, SL.1.4; L3: L.1.1j; L4: W.1.7, W.1.8; L5: SL.1.1a, SL.1.1b, SL.1.1c, SL.K.3, SL.1.4, SL.K.6; L6: SL.1.1a, SL.1.1b, SL.1.1c, SL.K.6, L.1.1e, L.1.1g, L.1.1k; L7: RI/RL.1.1, RI.1.2, RI.1.3, RI.1.4, RI.1.7, SL.K.2, L.1.6; L8: SL.K.3, SL.1.4; L9: L.1.1e; L10: W.1.2, W.1.5, W.1.7, W.1.8, L.1.1j, L.1.1l; L11: RI.1.8	ELPS 1–3, 5–10
L1: 0.1.2, 0.1.5, 3.6.1, 7.4.1, 7.4.3; L2: 0.1.2, 0.1.4, 0.1.5, 2.8.6, 3.6.1; L3: 0.1.2, 0.1.5, 0.1.8; L4: 0.1.2, 0.1.5, 3.3.1, 3.3.2, 3.3.4, 7.7.3; L5: 0.1.2, 0.1.3, 0.1.4, 0.1.5; L6: 0.1.2, 0.1.5; L7: 0.1.2, 0.1.5, 3.5.9, 7.4.1; L8: 0.1.2, 0.1.3, 0.1.5, 3.6.3, 3.6.4; L9: 0.1.2, 0.1.3, 0.1.5, 3.4.1; L10: 0.1.2, 0.1.3, 0.1.5, 0.2.1, 3.5.9; L11: 0.1.2, 0.1.5, 3.5.9, 7.3.2, 7.5.7	L1: RI.1.4, L.1.4a, L.1.5a, L.1.5b, L.1.5c, L.1.6; L2: SL.K.3, SL.1.4; L3: L.1.1e, L.1.1g; L4: W.1.7, W.1.8, SL.1.1a, SL.1.1b, SL.1.1c, SL.K.6; L5: SL.K.3, SL.1.4; L6: L.1.1e, L.1.1g; L7: RI/RL.1.1, RI.1.2, RI.1.3, RI.1.4, RI.1.7, SL.K.2, L.1.6; L8: SL.K.3, SL.1.4; L9: L.1.1g; L10: W.1.2, W.1.5, W.1.7, W.1.8, L.1.1l; L11: RI.1.8, SL.1.1a, SL.1.1b, SL.1.1c, SL.K.6	ELPS 1–3, 5–10
L1: 0.1.2, 0.1.5, 4.1.8, 7.4.1, 7.4.2, 7.4.3; L2: 0.1.2, 0.1.4, 0.1.5, 4.1.3, 4.1.8; L3: 0.1.2, 0.1.5, 4.1.8; L4: 0.1.2, 0.1.5, 4.1.3, 4.1.8, 7.4.4, 7.7.3; L5: 0.1.2, 0.1.4, 0.1.5; L6: 0.1.2, 0.1.5, 4.1.8; L7: 0.1.1, 0.1.2, 0.1.5, 4.1.5, 4.1.7, 7.4.1; L8: 0.1.2, 0.1.5, 0.2.1; L9: 0.1.2, 0.1.5, 4.1.5; L10: 0.1.2, 0.1.5, 0.2.1, 4.1.8; L11: 0.1.2, 0.1.3, 0.1.5, 4.6.1, 7.3.2, 7.5.3, 7.5.7	L1: RI.1.4, W.1.7, L.1.4a, L.1.5a, L.1.5b, L.1.5c, L.1.6; L2: SL.K.3, SL.1.4; L3: ; L4: W.1.7, W.1.8; L5: SL.K.3, SL.1.4; L6: L.1.1k; L7: RI/RL.1.1, RI.1.2, RI.1.3, RI.1.4, RI.1.7, SL.1.1a, SL.1.1b, SL.1.1c, SL.K.2, L.1.6; L8: SL.1.1a, SL.1.1b, SL.1.1c, SL.K.3, SL.1.4, SL.K.6; L9: L.1.1e, L.1.1g, L.1.1k; L10: W.1.2, W.1.5, W.1.7, W.1.8, L.1.1l; L11: RI.1.8	ELPS 1–3, 5–10

All units of *Future* meet most of the **EFF Content Standards**. For details, as well as for correlations to other state standards, go to www.pearseneltusa.com/future 2e.

ABOUT THE SERIES CONSULTANTS AND AUTHORS

AUTHOR, SERIES CONSULTANT, AND LEARNING EXPERT

Sarah Lynn is an ESOL teacher trainer, author, and curriculum design specialist. She has taught adult learners in the U.S. and abroad for decades, most recently at Harvard University's Center for Workforce Development. As a teacher-trainer and frequent conference presenter throughout the United States and Latin America, Ms. Lynn has led sessions and workshops on topics such as: fostering student agency and resilience, brain-based teaching techniques, literacy and learning, and teaching in a multilevel classroom. Collaborating with program leaders, teachers, and students, she has developed numerous curricula for college and career readiness, reading and writing skill development, and contextualized content for adult English language learners. Ms. Lynn has co-authored several Pearson ELT publications, including *Business Across Cultures, Future, Future U.S. Citizens,* and *Project Success.* She holds a master's degree in TESOL from Teachers College, Columbia University.

SERIES CONSULTANTS

Ronna Magy has worked as an ESOL classroom teacher, author, teacher-trainer, and curriculum development specialist. She served as the ESL Teacher Adviser in charge of professional development for the Division of Adult and Career Education of the Los Angeles Unified School District. She is a frequent conference presenter on the College and Career Readiness Standards (CCRS), the English Language Proficiency Standards (ELPS), and on the language, literacy, and soft skills needed for academic and workplace success. Ms. Magy has authored/co-authored and trained teachers on modules for CALPRO, the California Adult Literacy Professional Development Project, including modules on integrating and contextualizing workforce skills in the ESOL classroom and evidence-based writing instruction. She is the author of adult ESL publications on English for the workplace, reading and writing, citizenship, and life skills and test preparation. Ms. Magy holds a master's degree in social welfare from the University of California at Berkeley.

Federico Salas-Isnardi has worked in adult education as a teacher, administrator, professional developer, materials writer, and consultant. He contributed to a number of state projects in Texas including the adoption of adult education content standards and the design of statewide professional development and accountability systems.

Over nearly 30 years he has conducted professional development seminars for thousands of teachers, law enforcement officers, social workers, and business people in the United States and abroad. His areas of concentration have been educational leadership, communicative competence, literacy, intercultural communication, citizenship, and diversity education. He has taught customized workplace ESOL and Spanish programs as well as high-school equivalence classes, citizenship and civics, labor market information seminars, and middle-school mathematics. Mr. Salas-Isnardi has been a contributing writer or series consultant for a number of ESL publications, and he has co-authored curriculum for site-based workforce ESL and Spanish classes.

Mr. Salas-Isnardi is a certified diversity trainer. He has a Masters Degree in Applied Linguistics and doctoral level coursework in adult education.

AUTHORS

Marjorie Fuchs has taught ESL at New York City Technical College and LaGuardia Community College of the City University of New York and EFL at Sprach Studio Lingua Nova in Munich, Germany. She has a master's degree in applied English linguistics and a certificate in TESOL from the University of Wisconsin–Madison. She has authored or co-authored many widely used books and multimedia materials, notably *Focus on Grammar: An Integrated Skills Approach* (levels 3 and 4), *Longman English Interactive 3 and 4, Grammar Express* (*Basic and Intermediate*), *OPD Workplace Skills Builder,* and workbooks for the *Oxford Picture Dictionary* (*High Beginning and Low Intermediate*), *Grammar Express Basic,* and *Focus on Grammar* (levels 3 and 4).

Lisa Johnson has taught ESL in the United States and abroad and is currently an instructor and curriculum specialist at City College of San Francisco, where she has taught for the past two decades. Ms. Johnson holds a master's degree in TESOL from the University of Northern Iowa. She co-authored *Apply Yourself: English for Job Search Success,* co-authored or edited the Communication Companions for the Pearson English Interactive course, and contributed to *Talking Business Intermediate: Mastering the Language of Business.* She has also developed curricula for numerous ESL and VESL projects.

Irene Schoenberg has taught ESL for more than two decades at Hunter College's International English Language Institute and at Columbia University's American Language Program. Ms. Schoenberg holds a master's degree in TESOL from Teachers College, Columbia University. She has trained teachers at Hunter College, Columbia University, and the New School University, and she has given workshops and academic presentations at ESL programs and conferences throughout the world. Ms. Schoenberg is the author or co-author of numerous publications, including *True Colors; Speaking of Values 1; Topics from A to Z,* Books 1 and 2; and *Focus on Grammar: An Integrated Skills Approach* (levels 1 and 2).

ACKNOWLEDGMENTS

The Publisher would like to acknowledge the teachers, students, and survey and focus-group participants for their valuable input. Thank you to the following reviewers and consultants who made suggestions, contributed to this *Future* revision, and helped make *Future: English for Work, Life, and Academic Success* even better in this second edition. There are many more who also shared their comments and experiences using *Future*—a big thank you to all.

Fuad Al-Daraweesh The University of Toledo, Toledo, OH

Denise Alexander Bucks County Community College, Newtown, PA

Isabel Alonso Bergen Community College, Hackensack, NJ

Veronica Avitia LeBarron Park, El Paso, TX

Maria Bazan-Myrick Houston Community College, Houston, TX

Sara M. Bulnes Miami Dade College, Miami, FL

Alexander Chakshiri Santa Maria High School, Santa Maria, CA

Scott C. Cohen, M.A.Ed. Bergen Community College, Paramus, NJ

Judit Criado Fiuza Mercy Center, Bronx, NY

Megan Ernst Glendale Community College, Glendale, OH

Rebecca Feit-Klein Essex County College Adult Learning Center, West Caldwell, NJ

Caitlin Floyd Nationalities Service Center, Philadelphia, PA

Becky Gould International Community High School, Bronx, NY

Ingrid Greenberg San Diego Continuing Education, San Diego Community College District, San Diego, CA

Steve Gwynne San Diego Continuing Education, San Diego, CA

Robin Hatfield, M.Ed. Learning Institute of Texas, Houston,TX

Coral Horton Miami Dade College, Kendall Campus, Miami, FL

Roxana Hurtado Miami-Dade County Public Schools, Miami, FL

Lisa Johnson City College of San Francisco, San Francisco, CA

Kristine R. Kelly ATLAS @ Hamline University, St. Paul, MN

Jennifer King Austin Community College, Austin, TX

Lia Lerner, Ed.D. Burbank Adult School, Burbank, CA

Ting Li The University of Toledo, Ottawa Hills, OH

Nichole M. Lucas University of Dayton, Dayton, OH

Ruth Luman Modesto Junior College, Modesto, CA

Josephine Majul El Monte-Rosemead adult School, El Monte, CA

Dr. June Ohrnberger Suffolk County Community College, Selden, NY

Sue Park The Learning Institute of Texas, Houston, TX

Dr. Sergei Paromchik Adult Education Department, Hillsborough County Public Schools, Tampa, FL

Patricia Patton Uniontown ESL, Uniontown, PA

Matthew Piech Amarillo College, Amarillo, TX

Guillermo Rocha Essex County College, NJ

Audrene Rowe Essex County School, Newark, NJ

Naomi Sato Glendale Community College, Glendale, CA

Alejandra Solis Lone Star College, Houston, TX

Geneva Tesh Houston Community College, Houston, TX

Karyna Tytar Lake Washington Institute of Technology, Kirkland, WA

Miguel Veloso Miami Springs Adult, Miami, FL

Minah Woo Howard Community College, Columbia, MD

Pre-Unit

Welcome to Class

1 MEET YOUR TEACHER

▶ Look at the picture. Listen. Then listen and repeat.

2 FOLLOW CLASSROOM INSTRUCTIONS

Look at the pictures. Listen to your teacher. Repeat the sentences.

Take out your book.

Point to the picture.

Read the information.

Put away your book.

Look at the board.

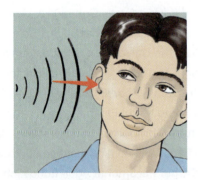

Listen to your teacher.

Open your notebook.

Write sentences.

Use a pencil./Use a pen.

Welcome to Class

3 ASK FOR HELP

A Look at the pictures. Complete the conversations.

> ~~Can you speak more slowly?~~   Can you repeat that?
> How do you pronounce this?   How do you spell that?
> What does this word mean?   What's this called in English?

1.

2.

3.

4.

5.

6.

B **WORK TOGETHER.** Practice the conversations in Exercise A.

Pre-Unit 3

Welcome to Class

4 LEARN ABOUT *FUTURE*

A Turn to page iii. Answer the questions.

1. How many units are in this book? _____
2. Which unit is about families? _____
3. Which unit is about health? _____
4. Which units are about work? _____
5. Which unit is about shopping? _____
6. Which unit is about education/school? _____

B Look in the back of your book. Find each section. Write the page numbers.

Map of the World _____
Grammar Reference _____
Map of the U.S. and Canada _____
Grammar Review _____
Alphabet _____
Numbers _____
Word List _____
Audio Script _____

C Look at Unit 1. Write the page numbers.

Lesson 1: Vocabulary _____
Lesson 2: Listening and Speaking _____
Lesson 3: Grammar _____
Lesson 4: Workplace, Life, and Community Skills _____
Lesson 6: Reading _____
Lesson 10: Writing _____
Lesson 11: Soft Skills at Work _____

D Look inside the front cover. How will you get the audio?
_____

5 THINK ABOUT YOUR ENGLISH

A **THINK ABOUT IT.** What is most important for you? Put number 1 next to it. Then number 2-6.

_____ Listening
_____ Speaking
_____ Writing
_____ Grammar
_____ Vocabulary
_____ Reading

B **TALK ABOUT IT.** Tell the class what is most important for you.

Pre-Unit

1 Getting to Know You

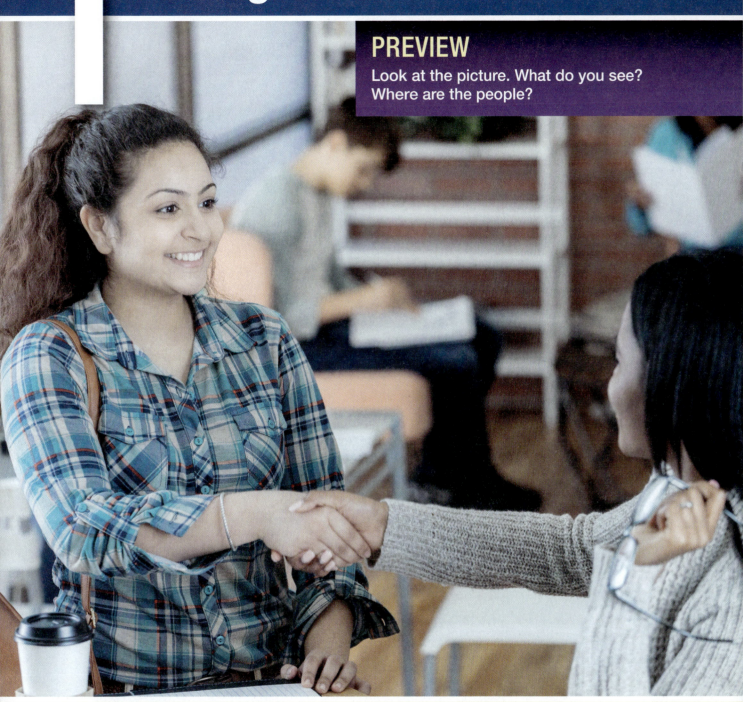

PREVIEW
Look at the picture. What do you see? Where are the people?

UNIT GOALS

- Identify regions and countries
- Introduce yourself
- Say and spell names
- Use titles
- Identify people and ask where they are from
- Talk about school
- **Academic skill:** Use the title to help understand a reading
- **Writing skill:** Use a capital letter for names and places
- **Workplace soft skill:** Be friendly

Lesson 1

Vocabulary

Regions and countries

A **PREDICT.** Look at the map. What are the regions and countries?

Letter A is North America. Number 2 is the United States.

B ▶ **LISTEN AND POINT.** Then listen and repeat.

6   Unit 1, Lesson 1

Vocabulary

Regions and countries

A. North America
1. Canada
2. the United States

B. Central America
3. Mexico
4. Cuba
5. El Salvador

C. South America
6. Peru
7. Brazil

D. Europe
8. Poland
9. Russia

E. The Middle East
10. Syria
11. Iraq

F. Africa
12. Ethiopia
13. Somalia

G. Asia
14. China
15. South Korea
16. Vietnam

C IDENTIFY. Student A, look at the map. Say a country. Student B, point to the country.

Vietnam.

D NAME. Student A, look at the word box. Say the region and the first letter of a country. Student B, say the country.

A: It is in Europe. The first letter is P.
B: Poland?
A: Yes!

Study Tip

Test yourself

Cover the word box. Say the words you remember.

Show what you know!

1. **TALK ABOUT IT.** What country are you from? Point to the map. Tell your group.

   A: I'm from China. What about you?
   B: I'm from Mexico. What about you?
   C: I'm from Somalia.

2. **PRESENT IT.** Tell your class about one classmate from your group.

   Ana is from Mexico.

3. **WRITE ABOUT IT.** Now write a sentence about where you are from.

   I'm from the United States.

   _____

I can identify regions and countries. ◻   I need more practice. ◻

For more practice, go to MyEnglishLab.

Lesson 2: Listening and Speaking — Introduce yourself

1 BEFORE YOU LISTEN

A LABEL. Write the words under the pictures.

> bow   hug   shake hands

1. _____   2. _____   3. _____

B MAKE CONNECTIONS. In the United States and Canada, people shake hands when they meet for the first time. What about in your native country?

2 LISTEN

A PREDICT. Look at the picture of Carla and Boris. Where are they?

B LISTEN. Choose the correct picture for the conversation.

a.    b.

C LISTEN FOR DETAILS. What does Carla say?

a. Nice to meet you, too.   b. Nice to meet you.

D EXPAND. Listen to the whole conversation. Complete the sentences.

1. Boris is from ____.   a. Russia   b. Poland
2. Carla is from ____.   a. Mexico   b. Peru

Listening and Speaking

3 PRONUNCIATION

A ▶ **PRACTICE.** Listen. Then listen and repeat.

•Nice to •meet you.   •Nice to meet •you, •too.

Sentence stress
In English, important words in a sentence are stressed. Stressed words sound long and strong.

B ▶ **APPLY.** Listen. Then listen again and put a dot (•) on the stressed words.

Where are you from?   I'm from China.   What about you?

4 CONVERSATION

A ▶ **LISTEN AND READ.** Then listen and repeat.

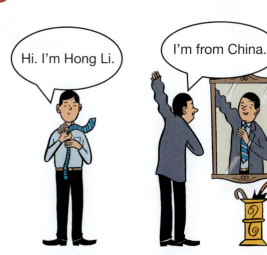

B **WORK TOGETHER.** Practice the conversation. Use your own names and countries.

A: Hi, I'm _____.
B: Hi, I'm _____.
A: Nice to meet you.
B: Nice to meet you, too.
A: Where are you from?
B: I'm from _____. What about you?
A: I'm from _____.

C **MAKE CONNECTIONS.** Walk around the room. Meet other classmates.

I can introduce myself. ▪   I need more practice. ▪

For more practice, go to MyEnglishLab.

Lesson 3: Workplace, Life, and Community Skills

Spell names and use titles

1 SAY AND SPELL YOUR NAME

A ▶ **LISTEN AND READ.** Then listen and repeat.

A: What's your first name?
B: My first name is Andre.
A: How do you spell that?
B: A-N-D-R-E.
A: A-N-D-R-E?
B: Right.
A: And what's your last name?
B: Mirov.
A: OK. Thanks.

B **MAKE CONNECTIONS.** Practice the conversation. Talk to five classmates. Write their names.

First Name	Last Name
Andre	Mirov

C **GO ONLINE.** Find common American last names.

_____   _____
_____   _____
_____   _____
_____   _____
_____   _____
_____   _____

I can say and spell my first and last name. ■   I need more practice. ■

For more practice, go to MyEnglishLab.

10 Unit 1, Lesson 3

Workplace, Life, and Community Skills

2 USE TITLES

A ▶ **LISTEN AND POINT.** Then listen and repeat.

Mr. Johnson   Miss Chan / Ms. Chan   Mrs. Brown / Ms. Brown

B **MAKE CONNECTIONS.** Read the information. Which title do you use?

> **Using Titles**
>
> Use *Mr.* for both single and married men.
> Use *Ms.* for both single and married women.
> Use *Miss* for single women.
> Use *Mrs.* for married women.
> Use titles with last names, not first names.
>   *John Smith = Mr. Smith, not ~~Mr. John~~*

C **IDENTIFY.** Look at the pictures. Check (✓) the correct title.

1.
☐ Mr. Rivas
☐ Mrs. Rivas

2.
☐ Miss Parker
☐ Mrs. Parker

3.
☐ Ms. Lee
☐ Mr. Lee

D ▶ **APPLY.** Listen. Complete the form.

1.
Student Registration
Title
● Mr. ○ Miss ○ Mrs. ○ Ms.
Name
[   ] [Chen]
First   Last

2.
Student Registration
Title
○ Mr. ○ Miss ○ Mrs. ○ Ms.
Name
[Vera] [   ]
First   Last

3.
Student Registration
Title
○ Mr. ○ Miss ○ Mrs. ○ Ms.
Name
[Ana]   [   ]
First   Last

I can use titles. ▪   I need more practice. ▪

For more practice, go to MyEnglishLab.

Unit 1, Lesson 3

Lesson 4 Listening and Speaking
Identify people and ask where they are from

1 BEFORE YOU LISTEN

A READ. Look at the pictures and read.

B IDENTIFY. Look at your classmates. Answer the question.

Who is absent?

_____

2 LISTEN

A PREDICT. Look at the picture. Carla and Sen are classmates. Where are they?

a. in their classroom
b. outside their classroom

B ▶ LISTEN. Circle the questions Carla asks.

a. Who's that?
b. Where is he?
c. Where's he from?

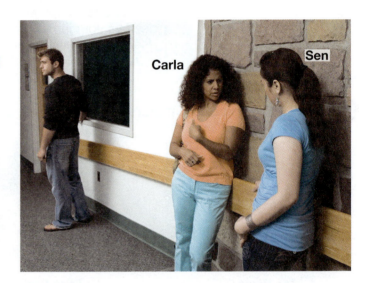

C ▶ LISTEN FOR DETAILS. Complete the sentences.

1. The man in the picture is _____.
   a. Max   b. Boris

2. Max is from _____.
   a. Mexico   b. Russia

D ▶ EXPAND. Listen to the whole conversation. Choose the correct picture of Boris.

a.

b.

12   Unit 1, Lesson 4

Listening and Speaking

3 PRONUNCIATION

A ▶ **PRACTICE.** Listen. Notice the different sounds in *he's* and *she's*. Then listen and repeat.

He's from Mexico.   She's absent.

> he = 👨   she = 👩
> he's = he is   she's = she is

B ▶ **CHOOSE.** Listen. Circle the words you hear.

1. a. He's   (b.) She's   4. a. He's   b. She's
2. a. He's   b. She's   5. a. He's   b. She's
3. a. He's   b. She's   6. a. He's   b. She's

4 CONVERSATION

A ▶ **LISTEN AND READ.** Then listen and repeat.

A: Who's that?
B: That's Boris.
A: No, that's not Boris.
B: Oh, you're right. That's Max.
A: Max? Where's he from?
B: He's from Mexico.

B **WORK TOGETHER.** Practice the conversation in Exercise A.

C **CREATE.** Make new conversations. Use the information in the boxes.

A: Who's that?
B: That's the teacher.
A: No, that's not the teacher.
B: Oh, you're right. That's _____.
A: _____? Where's _____ from?
B: _____'s from _____.

 Jin Su — he — South Korea

 Laura — she — Mexico

 Sagal — she — Somalia

D **MAKE CONNECTIONS.** Make your own conversations. Ask about your classmates.

I can identify people and ask where they are from. ■   I need more practice. ■

For more practice, go to MyEnglishLab.

Lesson 5 Grammar

Be with I, he, she

Affirmative of be with I, he, and she		
I	am	
He		from Russia.
She	is	
Boris		

Grammar Watch

We usually use contractions in conversation.

Contractions
I am = **I'm**
he is = **he's**
she is = **she's**

A REWRITE. Write contractions for the underlined words.

1. My name is Carla Cruz. <u>I am</u> (I'm) in level 1. I am from Peru.
2. That's Victor. <u>He is</u> in my class.
3. Ms. Reed is the teacher. <u>She is</u> from Canada.
4. Pedro is a new student. <u>He is</u> from Mexico.
5. Frida is from Mexico, too. <u>She is</u> in Level 3.

B ▶ SELF-ASSESS. Listen and check your answers.

C COMPLETE. Look at the pictures. Complete the sentences. Use contractions.

1. __I'm__ from Mexico. 2. __She's__ from Vietnam. 3. _____ from El Salvador.

4. _____ from Peru. 5. _____ from South Korea. 6. _____ from China.

Grammar

Negative of *be* with *I*, *he*, and *she*

I	am		
He			
She	is	not	in Level 3.
Carla			

Grammar Watch

Contractions
I am not = **I'm not**
he is not = **he's not**
she is not = **she's not**

D IDENTIFY. Look at the identification cards. Cross out the incorrect words.

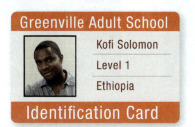

1. **She's / ~~She's not~~** from Peru.
2. **She's / She's not** from Ethiopia.
3. **He's / He's not** in Level 3.
4. **He's / He's not** in Level 1.

E WORK TOGETHER. Look at the chart. Student A, make sentences about a person. Student B, guess the person.

A: *She's from Peru. She's absent.*
B: *Carla?*
A: *No! Dora.*

Level 1 Attendance		Monday		
Name	Country	Here	Absent	Late
Mr. Carlos Delgado	Mexico			✓
Ms. Carla Cruz	Peru	✓		
Ms. Ting Wong	China	✓		
Ms. Mi Young Lim	South Korea		✓	
Ms. Dora Moreno	Peru		✓	
Mr. Kofi Solomon	Ethiopia	✓		

Show what you know!

1. TALK ABOUT IT. Say a sentence about yourself.

A: *I'm Carmen Garcia.*
B: *I'm not from Peru.*
C: *I'm a student.*

2. WRITE ABOUT IT. Now write two sentences about a classmate.

Mi Young is not from Peru.

_____

_____

I can use affirmative and negative *be* with *I*, *he*, and *she*. ▪   I need more practice. ▪

For more practice, go to MyEnglishLab.

Lesson 6 Reading

Read about immigrants to the U.S.

1 BEFORE YOU READ

A CHOOSE. Complete the sentences with the vocabulary in the box.

easy   hard   safe

1. They are _____.

2. This is _____.

3. This is not easy. It is _____.

B TALK ABOUT IT. Talk about living in the U.S. What's hard? What's easy?

2 READ

▶ Listen and read.

Academic Skill: Use the title

Before you read an article, look at the title. It can help you understand the article.

IMMIGRANTS IN THE U.S.

Every year, many immigrants come to the U.S. They come from different places and for different reasons.

Why do immigrants come to the U.S.?
Some people come for work. They get jobs in the U.S. Some people come to be safe. There are problems in their countries. Some people come to be with their family.
5 For example, the parents come first. The children come later to be with their parents.

Where are immigrants from?
Many immigrants come from Central or South America. They come from countries
10 like Mexico and Brazil. Many immigrants come from countries in Asia. For example, they come from China or India. Some immigrants are from Europe or Africa. Some are from other places.

15 *Are immigrants happy to be here in the U.S.?*
It is not easy to leave your home. It is hard to start a new life in a new country. But more than 70% of immigrants in the U.S. say they are happy to be here.

Source: www.publicagenda.org

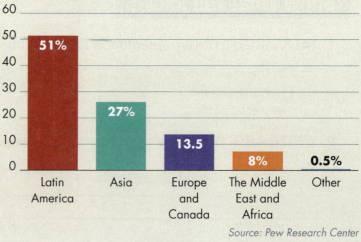

Immigrants Living in the U.S. by Region of Birth

- Latin America: 51%
- Asia: 27%
- Europe and Canada: 13.5
- The Middle East and Africa: 8%
- Other: 0.5%

Source: Pew Research Center

Reading

3 CLOSE READING

A CITE EVIDENCE. Complete the sentences. Where is the information? Write the line number.

Lines

1. People come to live in the U.S. for different _____.
   a. families
   b. reasons
   c. immigrants   _____

2. Some immigrants come to _____ in the U.S.
   a. get jobs
   b. live an easy life
   c. make new friends   _____

3. More than _____ percent (%) of immigrants in the U.S. say they are happy here.
   a. 50
   b. 70
   c. 90   _____

B INTERPRET. Complete the sentences about the bar graph.

1. More than 50% of immigrants living in the U.S. are from _____.
   a. Europe
   b. Latin America
   c. Africa

2. About _____ of immigrants living in the U.S. are from Asia.
   a. 17%
   b. 24%
   c. 27%

3. About 8% of immigrants living in the U.S. are from _____.
   a. Africa and the Middle East
   b. Europe and Canada
   c. North America

4 SUMMARIZE

Complete the summary with the words in the box.

| family | happy | immigrants | safe |

Many (1) _____ come to the U.S. They come for different reasons. Some come to work, some come to be (2) _____, and some come to be with their (3) _____. Most immigrants say they are (4) _____ living in the U.S.

Show what you know!

1. **TALK ABOUT IT.** Complete the chart with information about the other people in your group. Ask, "What's your name? Where are you from?"

Name	Country	Region

2. **WRITE ABOUT IT.** Now write about 3 people from your group. Tell where they are from.

_____ *is from* _____. *It's in* _____.

I can use the title to help understand a reading. ■   I need more practice. ■

To read more, go to MyEnglishLab.

Unit 1, Lesson 6   17

Lesson 7 Listening and Speaking

Talk about school

1 BEFORE YOU LISTEN

A **LABEL.** Write the words under the pictures.

| boring | easy | ~~good~~ |
| great | hard | interesting |

B **COMPARE.** Look at your answers. Compare with a partner.

1. _good_   2. _____   3. _____

 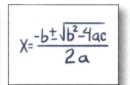 

4. _____   5. _____   6. _____

2 LISTEN

A ▶ **LISTEN.** Look at the picture. Listen to the conversation. What are they talking about?

   a. a test   b. a class   c. a book

B ▶ **LISTEN FOR DETAILS.** Complete the sentences.

1. Boris and Mimi are in _____.
   a. Level 1   b. Level 2

2. The students are _____.
   a. interesting   b. great

C ▶ **EXPAND.** Listen to the whole conversation. Complete the sentence.

Boris says, "English! It's _____."

18   Unit 1, Lesson 7

Listening and Speaking

3 CONVERSATION

A ▶ **LISTEN AND READ.** Then listen and repeat.

A: Hi. So, what class are you in?
B: We're in Level 1.
A: Oh. How is it?
C: It's good. The teacher is great.
A: How are the students?
B: They're great, too.

B **WORK TOGETHER.** Practice the conversation in Exercise A.

C **CREATE.** Make new conversations. Use the words in the boxes.

A: Hi. What class are you in?
B: We're in Level 1.
A: Oh. How is it?
C: It's _____. The teacher is _____.
A: How are the students?
B: They're _____, too.

easy	great	interesting
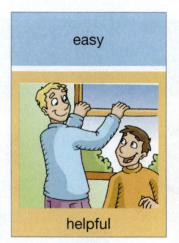	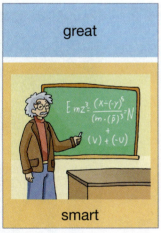	
helpful	smart	friendly

D **MAKE CONNECTIONS.** Make your own conversations. Talk about your English class.

I can talk about school. ▪   I need more practice. ▪

For more practice, go to MyEnglishLab.

Lesson 8 Grammar

Be with *we*, *you*, *they*, and *it*

Affirmative of *be* with *we*, *you*, *they*, and *it*					
We Carla and I					
You	are	in Level 1.	It The book	is	interesting.
They Sen and Boris					

Grammar Watch

Contractions
we are = **we're**
you are = **you're**
they are = **they're**
it is = **it's**

you
(singular)

you
(plural)

A APPLY. Complete the sentences. Use contractions.

1. **Mr. Salas:** You_'re_____ in Level 1.

   Student A: Thanks.

2. **Mr. Salas:** Here. You_____ in Level 2.

   Student B: Thank you.

3. **Student A:** So, you and Tom are in Level 2.

   Student B: Yes. We_____ in Level 2.

   Student A: How is your class?

   Student B: It_____ interesting.

   Student A: And how are the students?

   Student B: They_____ great.

B WORK TOGETHER. Practice the conversations in Exercise A.

Grammar

Negative of *be* with *we*, *you*, *they*, and *it*							
We Carla and I							
You	are	not	late.	It The book	is	not	easy.
They Sen and Boris							

Grammar Watch

Contractions
we are not = **we're not**
you are not = **you're not**
they are not = **they're not**
it is not = **it's not**

C IDENTIFY. Read the conversations. Cross out the incorrect words.

1. **Students:** Oh, no. **We're / We're not** late.
   Teacher: It's OK. You're on time. **You're / You're not** late.

2. **Teacher:** Where are the students? **They're / They're not** here.
   Students: Oh. **We're / We're not** here. Sorry we're late.

3. **Student A:** My class is good. **It's / It's not** interesting. How is your class?
   Student B: My class **is / is not** interesting, too.

4. **Student A:** How are the students?
   Student B: They're great. **They're / They're not** friendly.

D WORK TOGETHER. Practice the conversations.

Show what you know!

1. **TALK ABOUT IT.** Talk about your class. Use words from the box.

   boring   easy   friendly   good   great   hard   helpful   interesting   smart

   A: How is your class?
   B: It's not good ...

2. **WRITE ABOUT IT.** Now write an affirmative and a negative sentence about your class.

   My class is good. It's not boring.
   _____
   _____

I can use affirmative and negative of *be* with *we*, *you*, *they*, and *it*. ▪   I need more practice. ▪

For more practice, go to MyEnglishLab.

Unit 1, Lesson 8   **21**

Lesson 9

Grammar

Other negative contractions with *be*

Other negative contractions with *be*		
He	isn't	
She		
Carla		late.
You	aren't	
We		
They		

Grammar Watch

Contractions
isn't = is not
aren't = are not

A COMPLETE. Write *isn't* or *aren't*.

1. My teacher ____isn't____ from Canada.
2. My classmates _____ from the United States.
3. Ana _____ absent.
4. Our books _____ boring.
5. It _____ easy.
6. Her last name _____ Brown. It's Wilson.

B COMPLETE. Write *is*, *isn't*, *are*, or *aren't*.

1. Carlos ____isn't____ in Peru. He's in the United States.
2. Ana _____ absent. She's here.
3. My book _____ hard. It isn't easy.
4. My classmates _____ here. They're absent.
5. Lila and Rob _____ in Level 2. They aren't in Level 1.
6. They _____ from Canada. They're from the United States.

C ▶ LISTEN. Complete the sentences.

1. _____ in Level 3.
   a. He's   (b.) He's not
2. Level 3 _____ easy.
   a. is   b. isn't
3. _____ late.
   a. We're   b. We're not
4. _____ in my class.
   a. They're   b. They're not
5. _____ absent.
   a. They're   b. They aren't
6. The teachers _____ helpful.
   a. are   b. aren't

I can use other negative contractions with *be*. ◻   I need more practice. ◻

For more practice, go to MyEnglishLab.

Lesson 10 Writing

Write about yourself

1 STUDY THE MODEL

READ. Answer the questions.

> Marta Banas
> My Class
>
> I'm Marta Banas. My first name is Marta. My last name is Banas. I'm from Warsaw, Poland. Now I'm in Chicago, Illinois. I'm an English student. My class is helpful. The students are friendly.

1. What are the writer's first and last names?
2. Where is she from?
3. Where is she now?
4. How is her class?

2 PLAN YOUR WRITING

WORK TOGETHER. Ask and answer the questions.

1. What are your first and last names?
2. Where are you from?
3. Where are you now?
4. How is your class?

Writing Skill: Use capital letters

Names of people and places begin with a capital letter. For example:
Marta Banas, Warsaw

3 WRITE

Now write about yourself. Use the frame, the model, the Writing Skill, and your ideas from Exercise 2 to help you.

> I'm _____. My first name is _____. My last name is _____. I'm from _____, _____. Now I'm in _____, _____. I'm a/an _____ student. My class is _____. The students are _____.

4 CHECK YOUR WRITING

WORK TOGETHER. Read your writing aloud with a partner.

WRITING CHECKLIST

☐ The writing answers the questions in Exercise 2.

☐ The names of people and places begin with a capital letter.

I can use a capital letter for names and places. ■   I need more practice.

For more practice, go to MyEnglishLab.

Lesson 11: Soft Skills at Work

Be friendly

1 MEET AKI

Read about one of her workplace skills.

I'm friendly. For example, I smile and say hi to my co-workers. I call my co-workers by their first name.

2 AKI'S PROBLEM

READ. Circle *True* or *False*.

Aki works at a store. She is a sales assistant. She works with people from different countries. She learns their names. She asks her co-workers questions to get to know them.

One day, Aki sees a new co-worker. The co-worker says, "Hi, Aki." Aki wants to talk to her, but she doesn't know her name.

1. Aki works with people from her native country.   True   False
2. Aki asks her co-workers questions.   True   False
3. Aki knows the new co-worker's name.   True   False

3 AKI'S SOLUTION

A WORK TOGETHER. Aki is friendly. What is the friendly thing to do? Explain your answer.

1. Aki says "Hi" and leaves.
2. Aki says, "Hi. I'm sorry. I don't know your name."
3. Aki says nothing.
4. Aki says, "_____."

B ROLE-PLAY. Look at your answers to 3A. Role-play Aki's conversation.

Show what you know!

1. **THINK ABOUT IT.** How are you friendly at school? At work? Give examples.

2. **WRITE ABOUT IT.** Now write your example in your Skills Log.

   I smile and say "hi" to my classmates.

I can give an example of how I am friendly. ▪

Unit Review: Go back to page 5. Which goals can you check off?

2 A Hard Day's Work

PREVIEW
Look at the picture. What do you see? Who are the people?

UNIT GOALS

☐ Name jobs
☐ Introduce someone and talk about your job
☐ Ask for and give contact information
☐ Ask about jobs
☐ Talk about where you work
☐ **Academic skill:** Learn new vocabulary
☐ **Writing skill:** Use a period
☐ **Workplace soft skill:** Be a good listener

Lesson 1

Vocabulary

Jobs

A PREDICT. Look at the pictures. What do you see? Where are the jobs?

Number 3 is a manager.

B ▶ LISTEN AND POINT. Then listen and repeat.

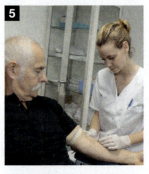

Vocabulary

Jobs

A. restaurant
1. a cook
2. a server
3. a manager

B. hospital
4. a doctor
5. a nurse
6. a custodian

C. store
7. a cashier
8. a sales assistant
9. a driver

D. office
10. an office assistant
11. an accountant

E. construction site
12. a painter
13. an electrician

F. home
14. a homemaker
15. a child-care worker
16. a landscaper

C IDENTIFY. Student A, say a job. Student B, point to the picture on page 26.

A nurse.

D WORK TOGETHER. Student A, act out a job. Students B and C, guess the job.

B: You're a homemaker.
A: No.
C: You're a landscaper.
A: Right!

Study Tip

Use your language
Make cards. On one side, write the word in English. On the other side, write the word in your language.

Show what you know!

1. **TALK ABOUT IT.** Ask three classmates about their jobs. Complete the chart.

    A: What do you do?
    B: I'm a cook.

Name	Job
Andy	a cook

2. **PRESENT IT.** Tell your class about your classmates' jobs.

    Andy is a cook.

3. **WRITE ABOUT IT.** Now write a sentence about your job.

    I'm a server.

    _____

I can name jobs. ☐   I need more practice. ☐

For more practice, go to MyEnglishLab.

Lesson 2 Listening and Speaking
Introduce someone and talk about your job

1 BEFORE YOU LISTEN

TALK ABOUT IT. Look at the picture. Where are they?

2 LISTEN

A ▶ **LISTEN.** Complete the conversation in the picture.

B ▶ **LISTEN.** What is Rosa's question?

a. What do you do?   b. Where are you from?

C ▶ **LISTEN FOR DETAILS.** Complete the sentences.

1. Omar is a landscaper and _____.
   a. a driver   b. a student

2. Rosa is a student and _____.
   a. a sales assistant   b. a nurse

Omar, this is Rosa. Rosa, this is Omar.

Hi, Omar. Nice to _____ you.

Hi, Rosa. _____ to meet you, _____.

D ▶ **EXPAND.** Listen to the whole conversation. What is Emilio's job?

a.

b.

Listening and Speaking

3 PRONUNCIATION

A ▶ **PRACTICE.** Listen. Then listen and repeat.

A: What do you do?   A: What's your name?
B: I'm a student.   B: I'm Peter.

> **Falling intonation in statements and *Wh-* questions**
>
> In *Wh-* questions and in statements, the voice goes down ↘ at the end.

B ▶ **APPLY.** Practice saying the sentences. Then listen and repeat.

Where are you from?
I'm from China.
What about you?

4 CONVERSATION

A ▶ **LISTEN AND READ.** Then listen and repeat.

A: So, what do you do?
B: I'm a landscaper. And I'm a student at Greenville Adult School.
A: Really? I'm a student there, too. And I'm a sales assistant.
B: Oh, that's interesting.

B **WORK TOGETHER.** Practice the conversation in Exercise A.

C **CREATE.** Make new conversations. Use the pictures.

A: What do you do?
B: I'm  .
A: Really? I'm _____, too. And I'm _____ .
B: Oh, that's interesting.

D **MAKE CONNECTIONS.** Make your own conversations.

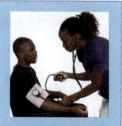

I can introduce someone and talk about my job. ▪   I need more practice. ▪

For more practice, go to MyEnglishLab.

Lesson 3 Grammar
A/An; Singular and plural nouns

A/An						
He is	a	landscaper.	She is	an	accountant.	

Grammar Watch
- Use *a* before consonant sounds.
- Use *an* before vowel sounds.

A IDENTIFY. Cross out the incorrect words.

1. **A:** That's Fang. She's **a / an** office assistant.
   B: Oh, really? I'm **a / an** office assistant, too.

2. **A:** Paul is **a / an** teacher, right?
   B: No. He's not **a / an** teacher. He's **a / an** nurse.

3. **A:** I'm **a / an** landscaper. What about you?
   B: I'm **a / an** electrician.

4. **A:** This is Dr. and Mrs. Silver. He's **a / an** doctor, and she's **a / an** accountant.
   B: Nice to meet you. I'm Mary Green. I'm **a / an** child-care worker.

5. **A:** So, Ana, what do you do?
   B: I'm **a / an** homemaker.

B ▶ SELF-ASSESS. Listen and check your answers.

C WORK TOGETHER. Practice the conversations in Exercise A.

D COMPLETE. Use *a* or *an*. Then complete sentence 8.

1. Bob is ___a___ cashier.
2. Joe is _____ electrician.
3. Kevin is _____ driver.
4. John is _____ cook.
5. Sarah is _____ office assistant.
6. Hai is _____ accountant.
7. Faha is _____ student.
8. My classmate is _____.

Grammar

Singular and plural nouns			
John is	**a cook**.	John and Linda are	**cooks**.

Grammar Watch
- Add **-s** to form most plurals.
- For irregular plural nouns, see page 259.

E APPLY. Look at the pictures. Complete the sentences.

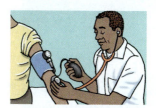

1. Bob is ___a nurse___.

2. Rosa is _____.

3. Jill, Mei, and I are _____.

4. They're _____.

Show what you know!

1. **RANK.** These are the five most common jobs in the U.S. Which job is number 1? Number 2? 3? 4? 5? Guess. Write the numbers next to the jobs.

   ___ cashiers   ___ sales assistants   ___ food preparers and servers
   ___ office assistants   ___ nurses

2. **TALK ABOUT IT.** What do you think? Talk about your answers in Exercise 1.

   A: I think cashiers are number 1.
   B: Me, too.
   C: No, I think . . .

3. ▶ **SELF-ASSESS.** Listen and check your answers.

4. **WRITE ABOUT IT.** What do you think about the most common jobs or other jobs you know? Write a sentence. Use words from the box.

   | friendly | good | great | helpful | smart |

   Most ___sales assistants___ are helpful.
   Most _____.

I can use *a/an* and singular and plural nouns. ☐   I need more practice. ☐

For more practice, go to MyEnglishLab.

Lesson 4: Workplace, Life, and Community Skills

Ask for and give contact information

1 IDENTIFY PHONE NUMBERS

A **MAKE CONNECTIONS.** Think about numbers in your life. When do you use numbers? Do you use numbers at work?

B ▶ **LISTEN AND POINT.** Then listen and repeat.

| 0 zero | 1 one | 2 two | 3 three | 4 four |
| 5 five | 6 six | 7 seven | 8 eight | 9 nine |

C ▶ **LISTEN.** Circle the phone numbers you hear.

1. a. 212-960-5334
   b. 412-960-5334

2. a. 619-464-2083
   b. 619-464-2093

3. a. 305-576-1169
   b. 395-576-1169

4. a. 323-865-4191
   b. 323-835-4191

5. a. 214-847-3726
   b. 214-847-3126

6. a. 773-395-2114
   b. 773-399-2114

D ▶ **COMPLETE.** Listen to the voicemail messages. Write the missing numbers.

1. Mr. Fernandez
   Center Hospital
   Landscaper job
   (562) 555-_____

2. Grace Simms
   Grace's Office Supplies
   Cashier Job
   (_____) 555-_____

3. Jin Wu
   Greenville Store
   Sales assistant job
   (_____) 555-_____

4. Ms. Rodriguez
   Carla's Restaurant
   Manager job
   (_____) _____-_____

32 Unit 2, Lesson 4

Workplace, Life, and Community Skills

2 IDENTIFY EMAIL ADDRESSES

A **MAKE CONNECTIONS.** Think about email in your life. When do you use email? Do you use email at work?

B ▶ **LISTEN AND POINT.** Look at the email. Listen and point to the email addresses. Then listen and repeat.

From: amy.smith@mymail.com
To: rosa.medina@mymail.com
Subject: ESL class

C ▶ **LISTEN.** Circle the email addresses you hear.

1. a. dan.silver@ccmail.edu
   b. dans.ilver@ccmail.edu

2. a. gsimms@hmail.com
   b. g.simms@hmail.com

3. a. tlopez719@gomail.com
   b. tlopez715@gomail.com

4. a. jin.wu@newmail.edu
   b. jin.hu@newmail.edu

3 GET CONTACT INFORMATION

A ▶ **LISTEN AND READ.** Then listen and repeat.

A: What's your phone number?
B: 213-555-4963.
A: 213-555-4563?
B: No. It's 213-555-4963.
A: OK. And what's your email address?
B: asad.bilan@hmail.com.

B **WORK TOGETHER.** Ask two classmates for their phone number and email address. Complete the chart.

Name	Phone Number	Email address
Asad	(213) 555-4963	asad.bilan@hmail.com
1.		
2.		

C **GO ONLINE.** Add two new contacts in your phone.

I can ask for and give contact information. ☐   I need more practice. ☐

For more practice, go to MyEnglishLab.

Lesson 5: Listening and Speaking

Ask about jobs

1 BEFORE YOU LISTEN

LABEL. Write the jobs under the pictures.

cashier   cook   homemaker   ~~server~~

1. _server_   2. _____   3. _____   4. _____

2 LISTEN

A PREDICT. Look at the picture. Where are they?

B ▶ LISTEN. Complete the sentence.

Sara is a _____.
a. student   b. teacher

C ▶ LISTEN FOR DETAILS. Complete the sentences.

1. Sara is a _____, too.
   a. cashier   b. nurse

2. Boris is a _____.
   a. server   b. cook

D ▶ EXPAND. Listen to the whole conversation. Complete the sentences.

1. Marta says, "I'm _____." (Choose all the correct answers.)
   a. an electrician   c. a cook   e. a server
   b. a child-care worker   d. a cashier   f. a doctor

2. Marta is _____. (Choose one answer.)
   a. a homemaker   b. a landscaper   c. a painter

34 Unit 2, Lesson 5

Listening and Speaking

3 PRONUNCIATION

A ▶ **PRACTICE.** Listen. Then listen and repeat.

Are you a student?   Is he a cook?

> **Rising intonation in *yes/no* questions**
>
> In *yes/no* questions, the voice goes up (↗) at the end.

B ▶ **CHOOSE.** Listen to the sentences. Does the voice go up (↗) or down (↘) at the end?

	1.	2.	3.	4.	5.	6.	7.	8.
Up	✓	☐	☐	☐	☐	☐	☐	☐
Down	☐	☐	☐	☐	☐	☐	☐	☐

4 CONVERSATION

A ▶ **LISTEN AND READ.** Then listen and repeat.

A: Who's that? Is she a teacher?
B: No, she's not. She's a student. And she's a cashier at Al's Restaurant.
A: Oh, that's interesting. And what do you do?
B: I'm a cook.

B **WORK TOGETHER.** Practice the conversation in Exercise A.

C **CREATE.** Make new conversations. Use the words in the boxes.

A: Who's that? Is _____ a teacher?
B: No, _____ 's not. _____ 's a student. And _____ 's _____ .
A: Oh, that's interesting. And what do you do?
B: I'm _____ .

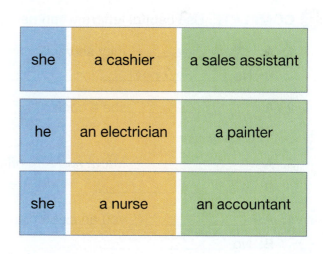

she	a cashier	a sales assistant
he	an electrician	a painter
she	a nurse	an accountant

D **MAKE CONNECTIONS.** Make your own conversations. Ask about people and their jobs.

I can ask about jobs. ▢   I need more practice. ▢

For more practice, go to MyEnglishLab.

Lesson 6 Grammar
Be: Yes/no questions and short answers

Yes/no questions			Short answers			
Are	you	a teacher?	Yes,	I am.	No,	I'm not.
Is	he / she			he is. / she is.		he's not / he isn't. / she's not / she isn't.
Are	you / they	teachers?		we are. / they are.		we're not / we aren't. / they're not / they aren't.

A APPLY. Now write yes/no questions.

1. John / a / landscaper / Is — <u>Is John a landscaper?</u>
2. cook / she / a / Is — _____
3. they / Are / sales assistants — _____
4. a / Are / server / you — _____
5. Is / painter / he / a — _____
6. managers / you / Are — _____

Is she a cook?

B COMPLETE. Use capital letters when necessary.

1. A: <u>Are</u> they servers?
   B: No, <u>they're not</u>. (OR <u>they aren't</u>.)

2. A: _____ she a cook?
   B: Yes, _____.

3. A: _____ Marta and Kim office assistants?
   B: Yes, _____.

4. A: _____ you an electrician?
   B: No, _____.

5. A: _____ he an accountant?
   B: No, _____.

6. A: _____ Mr. Garcia a painter?
   B: Yes, _____.

Grammar

C **APPLY.** Look at the pictures. Complete the conversations. Add *a* or *an* when necessary.

1. A: <u>Is she an</u> accountant?
   B: <u>Yes, she is.</u>

2. A: _____ drivers?
   B: _____

3. A: _____ electrician?
   B: _____

4. A: _____ nurse?
   B: _____

5. A: _____ landscapers?
   B: _____

6. A: _____ server?
   B: _____

Show what you know!

1. **ACT IT OUT.** Student A, choose a job. Act it out. Students B and C, guess the job.

   B: Are you a painter?
   A: No, I'm not.
   C: Are you a cook?
   A: Yes, I am.

2. **WRITE ABOUT IT.** Now write two *yes/no* questions and short answers about your classmates' jobs.

   Is Tom a driver? Yes, he is.

   _____
   _____

I can ask *yes/no* questions and give short answers with *be*. ■   I need more practice. ■

For more practice, go to MyEnglishLab.

Unit 2, Lesson 6

Lesson 7 Reading

Read about healthcare jobs in the U.S.

1 BEFORE YOU READ

A CHOOSE. Complete the sentences with the vocabulary from the box.

| CNA | nursing home | orderly |

1. He's an _____.
2. She's a _____.
3. They live in a _____.

B TALK ABOUT IT. What kinds of jobs are there in a hospital?

2 READ

▶ Listen and read.

Academic Skill: Learn new vocabulary

The words in Exercise 1A will be important when you read *Healthcare Jobs in the U.S.* Write the words in your notebook. Underline the words when you see them in the article.

Healthcare Jobs in the U.S.

Many people in the U.S. work in healthcare. How many? More than 12 million.

The biggest number of jobs in healthcare is for nurses. They work in hospitals, doctors' offices, schools, and
5 nursing homes. You need a lot of training to be a nurse. Nurses go to school for many years.

That is not true for all jobs in healthcare. For some jobs, a high school diploma is enough. For example, you can be an orderly or a CNA. (CNA means "certified
10 nursing assistant.") Most orderlies get training on the job. CNAs take a training course and an exam.

The U.S. has more than 1.5 million CNAs and orderlies. They work in hospitals and nursing homes. They need to be strong because sometimes they lift
15 patients out of bed. They also help people eat, wash, or get dressed.

Hospitals and nursing homes need other kinds of workers, too. They need cooks, housekeepers, custodians, and electricians. They need clerks to do
20 office work.

Healthcare in the U.S. is growing. It will need more workers in the future.

Top Jobs in the U.S.

	What's the job?	How many people do it?	How much money do they make in a year?
1.	Sales assistant	4.5 million	about $25,000
2.	Cashier	3.3 million	about $20,000
3.	Food preparer and server	3.0 million	about $19,000
4.	Office assistant	2.8 million	about $30,000
5.	Registered nurse	2.7 million	about $69,000

Source: U.S. Bureau of Labor Statistics

Reading

3 CLOSE READING

A **CITE EVIDENCE.** Complete the sentences. Where is the information? Write the line number.

Lines

1. More than _____ million people work in healthcare in the U.S.
   a. 12   b. 15   c. 21   _____
2. You need many years of school to be _____.
   a. a CNA   b. an orderly c. a nurse   _____
3. _____ do office work in hospitals.
   a. Clerks   b. Housekeepers c. Electricians _____
4. There will be _____ jobs in healthcare in the future.
   a. more   b. the same number of c. not so many _____

B **INTERPRET.** Complete the sentences about the chart.

1. The chart shows _____ in the U.S.
   a. the jobs with the most workers   b. who makes the most money   c. the best jobs
2. There are _____ nurses in the U.S.
   a. 2.7 million   b. 7 million   c. 12 million
3. There are more nurses in the U.S. than _____.
   a. cashiers   b. office assistants   c. doctors
4. Most nurses make about _____ a year.
   a. $39,000   b. $69,000   c. $89,000

4 SUMMARIZE

Complete the summary with the words in the box.

| CNA | healthcare | nurses | training |

More than 12 million people in the U.S. work in (1) _____. The biggest number of jobs are for (2) _____. They need a lot of (3) _____, but you can be a (4) _____ or an orderly after you finish high school. There are many other jobs in healthcare, too.

Show what you know!

1. **THINK ABOUT IT.** Do you know people who work in healthcare? What are their jobs? Where do they work?

2. **WRITE ABOUT IT.** Now write about someone you know who works in healthcare.

   _____ works in healthcare. (He/She) is a _____. (He/She) works at _____.

I can learn new vocabulary. ■   I need more practice. ■

To read more, go to MyEnglishLab.

Lesson 8 Listening and Speaking

Talk about where you work

1 BEFORE YOU LISTEN

TALK ABOUT IT. Look at the picture. What do they do? Where do they work?

2 LISTEN

A ▶ **LISTEN.** Dora, Omar, and Sali are at a party. What is Sali talking about?

a. her school b. her job

B ▶ **LISTEN FOR DETAILS.** Where does Sali work?

a.

b.

C ▶ **EXPAND.** Listen to the whole conversation. Complete the sentences.

1. Omar is a _____.
   a. nurse b. teacher c. student

2. Omar says, "It's _____."
   a. an interesting job b. a hard job c. a great job

D **DISCUSS.**

Sali says, "That's not a job." Omar says, "Yes, it is." Who is right, Sali or Omar?

Listening and Speaking

3 CONVERSATION

A ▶ **LISTEN AND READ.** Then listen and repeat.

A: So, what do you do?
B: I'm a nurse.
A: Really? Where do you work?
B: I work at a school on Main Street. I'm a school nurse.
A: Oh. That's nice.

B **WORK TOGETHER.** Practice the conversation in Exercise A.

C **CREATE.** Make new conversations. Use the information in the boxes.

A: What do you do?
B: I'm _____.
A: Really? Where do you work?
B: I work at _____ on Main Street.
A: Oh. That's nice.

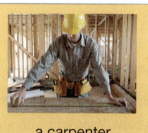
a carpenter
a construction site

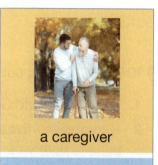
a caregiver
a nursing home

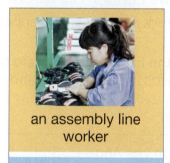
an assembly line worker
a factory

a stock clerk
a supermarket

D **MAKE CONNECTIONS.** Make your own conversations. Ask where your partner works.

A: Where do you work?
B: Oh, I'm a server at Alice's Restaurant. What about you?
A: I'm a server, too. I work at . . .

E **NETWORK.** Find classmates with the same job as you. Form a group. Ask the people in your group, *Where do you work?*

I can talk about where I work. ▪   I need more practice. ▪

For more practice, go to MyEnglishLab.

Lesson 9 Grammar
Simple present affirmative: *work* and *live*

Simple present affirmative: *work* and *live*		
I		
You	**live**	
We	**work**	
They		in Miami.
He		
She	**lives**	
Kate	**works**	

Grammar Watch

For spelling rules for the simple present, see page 259.

A IDENTIFY. Cross out the incorrect words.

1. That's my friend George. He ~~work~~ / **works** at a store.
2. George **live** / **lives** in New York. My wife and I **live** / **lives** in New York, too.
3. I **work** / **works** at a store, too! I'm a cashier.
4. This is Gloria. She **live** / **lives** in Florida. She **work** / **works** at a hospital.
5. Olga and Marcos **work** / **works** at a hospital, too. They're clerks.

B COMPLETE. Look at the ID cards. Complete the sentences. Use the verbs in parentheses and write the jobs.

1. Helen Lam (be) ___is___ a _____. She (live) _____ in Los Angeles. She (work) _____ at General Hospital.

2. Luis Mendoza and Nadif Fall (be) _____ _____. They (live) _____ in Tampa. They (work) _____ for Andrews Accounting.

C WORK TOGETHER. Talk about what you do and where you work.

A: I'm a cook. I work at a restaurant.
B: Paul is a cook. He works at a restaurant. I'm a sales assistant. I work at a store.
C: Paul is a cook. He works at a restaurant. Sara is a sales assistant. She . . .

I can use the simple present affirmative with *work* and *live*. ■   I need more practice. ■

For more practice, go to MyEnglishLab.

Lesson 10 Writing

Write about a friend

1 STUDY THE MODEL

READ. Answer the questions.

> Tim Lee
>
> My Friend
>
> Sam Lin is my friend. He lives in Texas. He is a custodian. He works at a hospital.

1. What is the friend's name?
2. Where does the friend live?
3. What does the friend do?
4. Where does the friend work?

2 PLAN YOUR WRITING

WORK TOGETHER. Ask and answer the questions.

1. What is your friend's name?
2. Where does your friend live?
3. What does your friend do?
4. Where does your friend work?

Writing Skill: Use a period

Begin a sentence with a capital letter.
End a sentence with a period.
For example: He is a custodian.

3 WRITE

Now write about a friend. Use the frame, the model, the Writing Skill, and your ideas from Exercise 2 to help you.

> _____ is my friend. He/She lives in _____. He/She is a/an _____. He/She works at a/an _____.

4 CHECK YOUR WRITING

WORK TOGETHER. Read your writing aloud with a partner.

WRITING CHECKLIST

☐ The writing answers the questions in Exercise 2.

☐ Each sentence begins with a capital letter.

☐ The names of people and places begin with capital letters.

☐ Each sentence ends with a period.

I can use a period. ■ I need more practice.

For more practice, go to MyEnglishLab.

Lesson 11 — Soft Skills at Work

Be a good listener

1 MEET FREDY

Read about one of his workplace skills.

"I'm a good listener. For example, I ask questions when I don't understand."

2 FREDY'S PROBLEM

READ. Read about Fredy's problem. Circle *True* or *False*.

> Fredy is a painter. He paints homes. The supervisor gives Fredy and his co-workers instructions every morning. Then Fredy starts to work.
>
> One day his supervisor is very busy. The supervisor gives many instructions. He speaks very fast. Fredy doesn't understand what the supervisor is saying.

1. Fredy's supervisor gives instructions every morning.   True   False
2. Fredy's supervisor speaks slowly.   True   False
3. Fredy understands his supervisor's instructions.   True   False

3 FREDY'S SOLUTION

WORK TOGETHER. Fredy is a good listener. What is the right thing to do? Explain your answer.

1. Fredy says to the supervisor, "I'm sorry. Could you please repeat that?"
2. Fredy asks his co-workers questions when the supervisor leaves.
3. Fredy doesn't ask questions. Then he starts to work.
4. Fredy _____.

Show what you know!

1. **THINK ABOUT IT.** How are you a good listener at school? At work? At home? Give examples.

2. **WRITE ABOUT IT.** Now write your example in your Skills Log.

   I am a good listener at school. I don't talk when another student talks.

I can give an example from my life of being a good listener. ☐

Unit Review: Go back to page 25. Which goals can you check off?

3 Time for Class

PREVIEW
Look at the picture. What do you see? Where are the people?

UNIT GOALS

- ☐ Identify things in the classroom
- ☐ Give and follow classroom instructions
- ☐ Talk about things in the classroom
- ☐ Talk about places at school
- ☐ Talk about people and places at school
- ☐ **Academic skill:** Use headings to help understand a reading
- ☐ **Writing skill:** Recognize and use a verb in a sentence
- ☐ **Workplace soft skill:** Be flexible

Lesson 1 Vocabulary

Things in the classroom

A **PREDICT.** Look at the pictures. What do you see? What are the things?

Number 3 is a tablet.

B ▶ **LISTEN AND POINT.** Then listen and repeat.

46   Unit 3, Lesson 1

Vocabulary

Things in the classroom

1. a desk
2. a laptop
3. a tablet
4. a phone
5. a projector
6. a board
7. a marker
8. a book
9. a dictionary
10. a piece of paper
11. a sticky note
12. a notebook
13. an eraser
14. a three-ring binder
15. a folder
16. a backpack

C IDENTIFY. Student A, say a thing. Student B, point to the picture on page 46.

A dictionary.

D CATEGORIZE. Write the things in the chart. Then compare answers.

Digital devices	Things you can read	Things you can write on
a laptop		

Study Tip

Draw pictures

Make cards. On one side, write the word in English. On the other side, draw a picture.

Show what you know!

1. **TALK ABOUT IT.** Talk about the things you have in your classroom. How many do you see?

   A: *We have one projector.*
   B: *We have twenty-five desks.*

2. **MAKE CONNECTIONS.** Talk about the things you have.

   I have a phone, a folder, and a book.

3. **WRITE ABOUT IT.** Now write a sentence about the things you have.

   I have _____.

I can identify things in the classroom. ◼   I need more practice. ◼

For more practice, go to MyEnglishLab.

Lesson 2: Listening and Speaking

Give and follow classroom instructions

1 BEFORE YOU LISTEN

MATCH. Look at the pictures. Complete the sentences with the words in the box.

| borrow | put away | take out | ~~turn off~~ |

1. Please _turn off_ your phone.
2. Please _____ your books.
3. Please _____ your notebook.
4. Can I _____ your pen?

2 LISTEN

A ▶ **LISTEN.** Look at the picture. Listen to the conversation. Complete the sentence.

The teacher is giving _____ to the students.
a. books
b. instructions
c. pencils

B ▶ **LISTEN FOR DETAILS.** Check (✓) the teacher's instructions.

☐ Take out your books.
☐ Put away your books.
☐ Borrow a pencil.
☐ Take out a piece of paper.

C ▶ **EXPAND.** Listen to the whole conversation. A phone is ringing. Complete the sentence.

It's _____ phone.
a. a student's
b. the teacher's

Listening and Speaking

3 CONVERSATION

A ▶ **LISTEN AND READ.** Then listen and repeat.

Teacher: OK, everyone. Please put away your books.
Take out a piece of paper.
Student A: Can I borrow a pencil?
Student B: Sure. Here you go.

B **WORK TOGETHER.** Practice the conversation in Exercise A.

C **CREATE.** Make new conversations. Use the pictures.

Teacher: Please put away your _____.
Take out _____.
Student A: Can I borrow _____?
Student B: Sure. Here you go.

D **ROLE-PLAY.** Make your own conversations. Student A, you're a teacher. Give instructions. Student B, you're a student. Follow the instructions.

A: Please take out your notebook.
B: OK.

I can give and follow classroom instructions. ▪   I need more practice. ▪

For more practice, go to MyEnglishLab.

Lesson 3 Grammar
Imperatives

Imperatives				Grammar Watch
Affirmative		**Negative**		Use *please* to be polite:
Use	a pencil.	Don't use	a pen.	***Please** turn off your phones.*

A MATCH. Write the letters to match the pictures and the sentences.

__d__ 1. Turn off your laptop. ____ 5. Don't turn off your laptop.
____ 2. Don't use your dictionary. ____ 6. Use your dictionary.
____ 3. Write in your book. ____ 7. Take out your notebook.
____ 4. Don't take out your notebook. ____ 8. Don't write in your book.

a.
b.
c.

d.
e.
f.

g.
h.

Grammar

B IDENTIFY. Look at the pictures. Cross out the incorrect words.

1.
Use / **Don't use** a Number 2 pencil.

2.
Use / **Don't use** a pen.

3.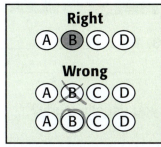
Fill in / Don't fill in the circles.

4.
Look / **Don't look** at your classmate's test.

C APPLY. Complete the sentences about classroom rules. Use the words in the box. Add *Don't* when necessary.

| answer | ~~bring~~ | come | ~~eat~~ | follow | listen |

1. ___Bring___ a notebook and pencil.
2. ___Don't eat___ in class.
3. _____ to class on time.
4. _____ to your classmates.
5. _____ your teacher's instructions.
6. _____ your phone in class.

Show what you know!

1. **TALK ABOUT IT.** What are some *Dos* and *Don'ts* in your classroom?

   A: Speak English in class.
   B: Don't come late.

2. **WRITE ABOUT IT.** Now write one *Do* and one *Don't* for your class.

   _____   _____

I can use imperatives. ☐   I need more practice. ☐

For more practice, go to MyEnglishLab.

Lesson 4 Reading

Read about good study habits

1 BEFORE YOU READ

A CHOOSE. Complete the sentences with the vocabulary in the box.

| looking at study goals | studying for a short period | throwing out papers |

1. He's _____.
2. He's _____.
3. He's _____.

B MAKE CONNECTIONS. What are your study habits? Where do you usually study? When do you usually study?

2 READ

▶ Listen and read.

Academic Skill: Use headings

Headings are titles for each part of a reading. They are often in **bold**, so they are easy to see.

HELPFUL STUDY HABITS

Sam and Tim are in the same class. Sam plans to study vocabulary every Sunday night for 60 minutes. Tim plans to study vocabulary for 10 minutes 5 nights a week. Whose plan is better?

5 Scientists study how people learn. They study how the brain remembers new information. What can scientists tell students?

Set study goals. Keep your goals small and write them in your notebook. For example, write "Listening: Watch TV 10 in English for ten minutes. Do it five days a week." Look at your goals every day. When you reach a goal, make a check mark ✓ next to it.

Be organized. Keep all your things for school in a bag or backpack. Keep important papers in a binder. Throw 15 out papers you don't need.

Do one thing at a time. You cannot learn when you are thinking about other things. Don't watch TV. Don't

Scientists study how we learn.

listen to music. Don't text friends when you study. Turn off your phone.

20 **Get enough sleep.** Most adults need about 7.5 hours of sleep. Sleep helps your brain work better.

Study for a short period every day. That's better than studying for a long time on one day. You will remember more. (Tim has the right idea!)

Reading

3 CLOSE READING

CITE EVIDENCE. Complete the sentences. Where is the information? Write the line number.

Lines

1. The information about study habits comes from _____.
   a. students   b. parents   c. scientists   _____

2. It is a good idea to write your _____ in your notebook.
   a. study goals   b. sleep habits   c. phone number   _____

3. Keep all your school things in a bag or backpack. It will help you _____.
   a. remember new words   b. be organized   c. read faster   _____

4. _____ papers you don't need.
   a. Throw out   b. Put away   c. Organize   _____

5. You cannot learn when you are _____.
   a. using your brain   b. studying for short periods   c. doing two things at the same time   _____

6. Most adults need about _____ hours of sleep.
   a. 6.5   b. 7.5   c. 8   _____

4 SUMMARIZE

Complete the summary with the words in the box.

| goals | learn | organized | period |

Good study habits help you (1) _____ better. For example, set study (2) _____. Be (3) _____ and keep all your school things in a bag or backpack. Do one thing at a time. Get the sleep your brain needs. Study for a short (4) _____ every day.

Show what you know!

1. **THINK ABOUT IT.** Think about your study habits and the ideas in the article. What can you do better? Make a plan.

2. **TALK ABOUT IT.** Talk about your study habits. Ask, *What can you do better? What is your plan?*

3. **WRITE ABOUT IT.** Now write about ways to have good study habits.
   Don't _____. Try to _____.

I can use headings to help understand a reading. ■   I need more practice. ■

To read more, go to MyEnglishLab.

Lesson 5 — Listening and Speaking
Talk about things in the classroom

1 BEFORE YOU LISTEN

LABEL. Look at the pictures. Write the words from the box on the lines.

keyboard
mouse
printer
screen

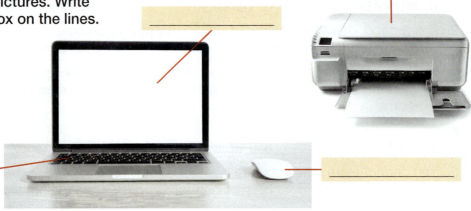

2 LISTEN

A **PREDICT.** Look at the picture. Where are Carlos and Mimi? What are they looking at?

a. their books
b. their notebooks
c. their phones

B ▶ **LISTEN.** Carlos asks, "What's this called in _____?"

a. English
b. Spanish

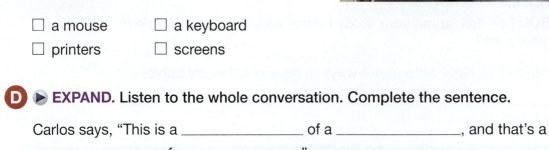

C ▶ **LISTEN FOR DETAILS.** What is Carlos asking about? Check (✓) all the correct answers.

☐ a mouse   ☐ a keyboard
☐ printers   ☐ screens

D ▶ **EXPAND.** Listen to the whole conversation. Complete the sentence.

Carlos says, "This is a _____ of a _____, and that's a _____ of _____."

54   Unit 3, Lesson 5

Listening and Speaking

3 PRONUNCIATION

Voiced *th* sound

To say the *th* sound in *this*, *these*, and *that's*, put your tongue between your teeth.

A ▶ **PRACTICE.** Listen. Then listen and repeat.

This   **Th**is is a laptop.
These **Th**ese are printers.
That's **Th**at's a keyboard.

B ▶ **CHOOSE.** Listen. Then listen again and check (✓) the correct words.

1. ☐ ten   ☐ then
2. ☐ day   ☐ they
3. ☐ Ds   ☐ these

4 CONVERSATION

A ▶ **LISTEN AND READ.** Then listen and repeat.

A: What's this called in English?
B: It's a mouse.
A: And these? What are these called?
B: They're printers.

B **WORK TOGETHER.** Practice the conversation in Exercise A.

C **CREATE.** Make new conversations. Use the pictures.

A: What's this called in English?
B: It's _____.
A: And these? What are these called?
B: They're _____.

D **MAKE CONNECTIONS.** Make your own conversations. Ask about things in your classroom.

I can talk about things in the classroom. ▪   I need more practice. ▪

For more practice, go to MyEnglishLab.

Lesson 6 Grammar

This, that, these, those

This, that, these, those: Statements

Singular		Plural	
This is	a good dictionary.	These are	good dictionaries.
That's	a great picture.	Those are	great pictures.

A IDENTIFY. Cross out the incorrect words.

1. **This is** / ~~These are~~ a good book.
2. **That's / Those are** my classmates.
3. **This is / These are** my markers.
4. **That's / Those are** my folders.
5. **That's / Those are** called a screen.

Grammar Watch

- Use *this* and *these* for people or things near you.
- Use *that* or *those* for people or things <u>not</u> near you.

Contraction
that is = **that's**

B COMPLETE. Look at the pictures. Complete the sentences with *This is*, *That's*, *These are*, and *Those are*.

1. *These are* our books.
2. _____ our teacher.
3. _____ nice binders.
4. _____ my backpack.

C WRITE. Write two sentences about things in your classroom. Use *this*, *that*, *these*, or *those*.

This is my book.

_____

_____

Grammar

This, that, these, those: Questions and answers

| Is | this / that | your book? | Yes, **it** is. | What is | this? / that? | It's a pen. |
| Are | these / those | your books? | Yes, **they** are. | What are | these? / those? | They're pens. |

D WORK TOGETHER. Look at the picture. Complete the conversations.

Show what you know!

1. **TALK ABOUT IT.** Student A, you have ten seconds. Draw a picture of one or two things in your classroom. Student B, guess the object or objects.

   A: What are these?
   B: Are they folders?
   A: No. They're notebooks.

2. **WRITE ABOUT IT.** Now write a question and an answer about something in your classroom.

   A: _____
   B: _____

I can use *this, that, these, those*.   I need more practice.

For more practice, go to MyEnglishLab.

Unit 3, Lesson 6   **57**

Lesson 7: Workplace, Life, and Community Skills

Talk about places at school

1 IDENTIFY PLACES AT SCHOOL

A LABEL. Look at the floor plan. How many places around school do you know? Write the words from the box on the lines.

| cafeteria | computer lab | elevator | hall |
| library | office | ~~restroom~~ | stairs |

1. _restroom_
2. _____
3. _____
4. _____
5. _____
6. _____
7. _____
8. _____

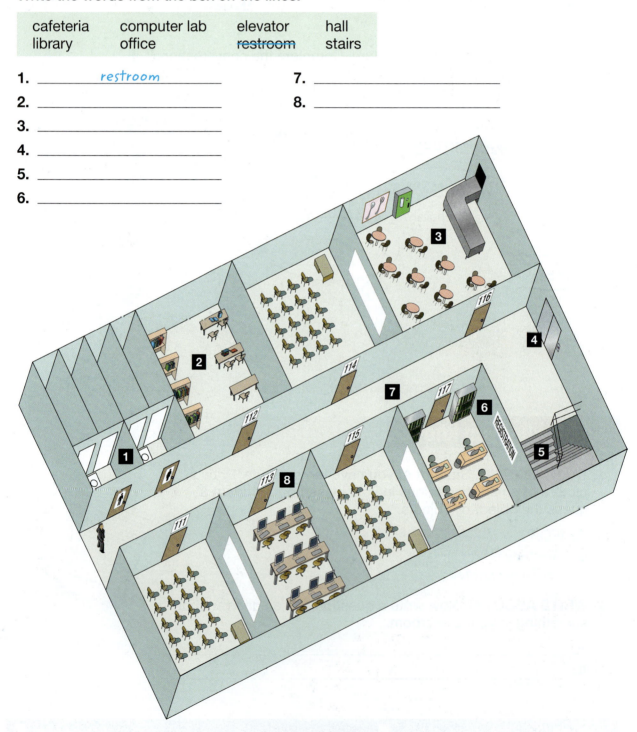

B ▶ SELF-ASSESS. Listen and check your answers. Then listen and repeat.

Workplace, Life, and Community Skills

2 GIVE LOCATIONS OF PLACES AT SCHOOL

A INTERPRET. Look at the diagram. Then look at the floor plan on page 58. Circle *True* or *False*.

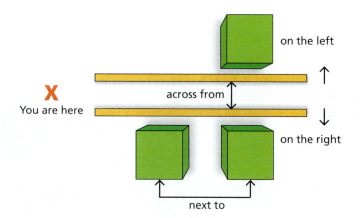

1. The library is on the right.   True   False
2. Room 115 is next to the computer lab.   True   False
3. Room 111 is across from the office.   True   False
4. The stairs are on the left.   True   False
5. The cafeteria is next to the restrooms. True   False

B REWRITE. Correct the sentences in Exercise 2A.

C ▶ LISTEN AND READ. Then listen and repeat.

A: Where is Room 114?
B: It's on the left, next to the library.
A: Where is the computer lab?
B: It's on the right, across from the library.

D ROLE-PLAY. Make new conversations about other rooms on the floor plan on page 58.

E GO ONLINE. Find a school in your neighborhood.

I can talk about places at school. ▪   I need more practice. ▪

For more practice, go to MyEnglishLab.

Unit 3, Lesson 7

Lesson 8
Listening and Speaking
Talk about people and places at school

1 BEFORE YOU LISTEN

IDENTIFY. Look at the pictures. Which people work at your school? Check (✓) the people. What other people work at your school?

☐ custodian

☐ director

☐ librarian

☐ computer lab assistant

2 LISTEN

A PREDICT. Look at the picture. What do you see?

B ▶ LISTEN. Ken is asking a question. Complete the sentence.

Ken's first words are _____.
a. Help me.
b. Excuse me.
c. Look at me.

C ▶ LISTEN FOR DETAILS. Answer the questions.

1. What is Ken's question?
   a. Where is the computer lab?
   b. Is the computer lab open?
   c. Is the computer lab upstairs?

2. Who is the man in the room with Ken and Berta?
   a. a teacher
   b. an office assistant
   c. the computer lab assistant

Listening and Speaking

3 PRONUNCIATION

A ▶ **PRACTICE.** Listen. Then listen and repeat.

of fice   ex **cuse**   **li** brar y   li **brar** i an   caf e **te** ri a

> **Word stress**
>
> A syllable is part of a word. One syllable in each word has the most stress.

B ▶ **APPLY.** Listen to the words. Mark (•) the syllable with the most stress.

1. o pen   2. com pu ter   3. as sist ant   4. di rec tor   5. cus to di an

4 CONVERSATION

A ▶ **LISTEN AND READ.** Then listen and repeat.

A: Excuse me. Is the computer lab open?
B: Sorry. I don't know. Ask him.
A: Oh, OK. But . . . Who is he?
B: He's the computer lab assistant.

B **WORK TOGETHER.** Practice the conversation in Exercise A.

C **CREATE.** Make new conversations. Use the words in the boxes.

A: Excuse me. Is the _____ open?
B: Sorry. I don't know. Ask _____ .
A: Oh, OK. But . . . Who is _____ ?
B: _____ 's the _____ .

Ask him.   Ask her.

cafeteria	him	he	custodian
office	her	she	office assistant
library	him	he	librarian
director's office	her	she	director

D **ROLE-PLAY.** Make your own conversations. Talk about places at your school.

I can talk about people and places at school. ▪   I need more practice. ▪

For more practice, go to MyEnglishLab.

Unit 3, Lesson 8   **61**

Lesson 9 Grammar

Object pronouns

Subject pronouns		Object pronouns	
I	am		me.
He			him.
She	is	Please help	her.
We			us.
They	are		them.

Grammar Watch

Subject Pronoun	Object Pronoun	
you	you	Are you the librarian? Can I ask **you** a question?
it	it	It's interesting. Read **it**.

A IDENTIFY. Cross out the incorrect words.

1. **A:** Where's the cafeteria?
   B: Sorry. I don't know. Ask ~~he~~ / **him**.

2. **A:** Are these the answers?
   B: Yes, but don't look at **they / them**.

3. **A:** Please show **us / we** your new pictures.
   B: Sure. Here they are.

4. **A:** What's the word for this in English?
   B: Sorry. I don't know. Ask **her / she**.

B APPLY. Change the underlined words. Use *him*, *her*, *it*, *us*, or *them*.

1. Take out your book. Open ~~the book~~ *it* to page 10.

2. Please close <u>your notebooks</u>. Thanks.

3. Please don't use your phone in class. Use <u>your phone</u> in the cafeteria.

4. Ask <u>Ms. Adams</u> about the computer lab hours. She's the computer lab assistant.

5. Mr. and Mrs. Lin are new here. Please show <u>Mr. and Mrs. Lin</u> the library.

6. Mr. Tran doesn't understand. Please help <u>Mr. Tran</u>.

7. Ask <u>Mr. Benson and me</u>. We're both Level 1 teachers.

I can use object pronouns. ■   I need more practice. ■

For more practice, go to MyEnglishLab.

Lesson 10 Writing

Write about study habits

1 STUDY THE MODEL

READ. Answer the questions.

> Marc Booker
> My Study Habits
>
> I study English four nights a week. I sit at my kitchen table. I read my class notes. I do my homework. I write new words in my notebook.

1. How many nights a week does Marc study?
2. Where does he study?
3. What does he read?
4. What does he write?

2 PLAN YOUR WRITING

WORK TOGETHER. Ask and answer the questions.

1. How many times a week do you study?
2. Where do you study?
3. What do you read?
4. What do you write?

Writing Skill: Recognize and use verbs

Every sentence has a verb. For example:
I (study) English four nights a week.

3 WRITE

Now write about your study habits. Use the frame, the model, the Writing Skill, and your ideas from Exercise 2 to help you.

> I study _____ times a week. I sit _____. I read _____. I write _____.

4 CHECK YOUR WRITING

WORK TOGETHER. Read your writing aloud with a partner.

WRITING CHECKLIST

- ☐ The writing answers the questions in Exercise 2.
- ☐ Each sentence begins with a capital letter.
- ☐ Each sentence has a verb.
- ☐ Each sentence ends with a period.

I can recognize and use a verb in a sentence. ■   I need more practice. ■

For more practice, go to MyEnglishLab.

Lesson 11 Soft Skills at Work

Be flexible

1 MEET YING

Read about one of her workplace skills.

 I'm flexible. For example, sometimes the work I do changes. I can make changes in my life.

2 YING'S PROBLEM

READ. Circle *True* or *False*.

Ying works in a restaurant. She is a server. She works every day from 9:00 to 5:00. She takes an English class in the evening. She really likes the class. The teacher is great, and the students are friendly.

One day the manager says to Ying, "You need to work in the evening." Ying wants to continue learning English, but she needs the job. She finds an online class. This is her first online class. It's not so friendly.

1. Ying works in a restaurant every day.   True   False
2. Ying doesn't like her English class.   True   False
3. Ying likes online classes.   True   False

3 YING'S SOLUTION

WORK TOGETHER. Ying is flexible. What is the flexible thing to do? Explain your answer.

1. Ying doesn't take the online class. She wants to wait until she works during the day again.
2. Ying takes the online class. Learning English is very important to her.
3. Ying quits her job so she can go to her class in the evening.
4. Ying _____.

Show what you know!

1. **THINK ABOUT IT.** How are you flexible at school? At work? At home? Give examples.

2. **WRITE ABOUT IT.** Now write your example in your Skills Log.

   Sometimes my schedule changes at school. That's OK for me.

3. **PRESENT IT.** Give a short presentation to show how you are flexible.

I can give an example from my life of being flexible. ■

Unit Review: Go back to page 45. Which goals can you check off?

4 Family Ties

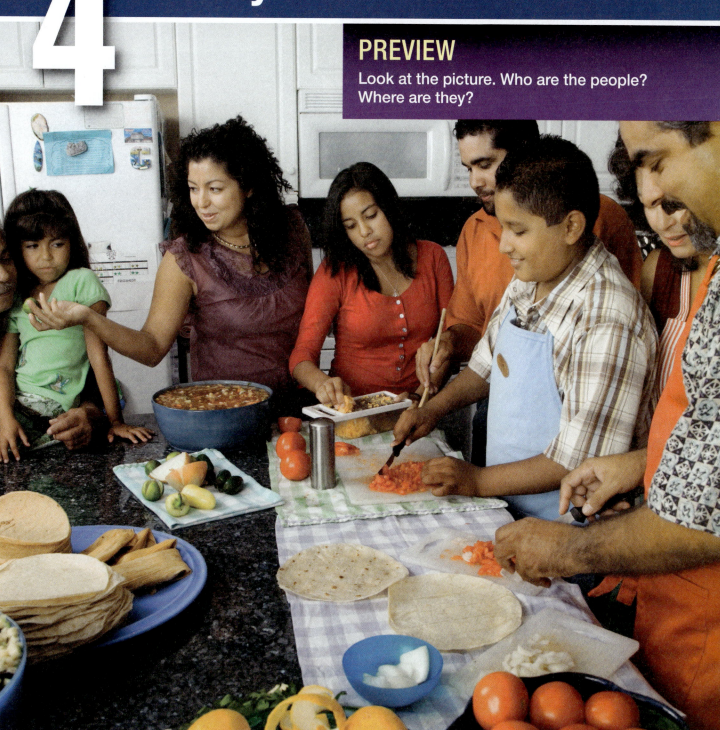

PREVIEW
Look at the picture. Who are the people? Where are they?

UNIT GOALS

- Identify family members
- Talk about family
- Describe people
- Say and write dates
- Give a child's age and grade in school
- **Academic skill:** Make connections
- **Writing skill:** Use a capital letter for months
- **Workplace soft skill:** Separate work and home life

Lesson 1

Vocabulary

Family members

A **PREDICT.** Look at the pictures of Sue's family. What are the family words?

Number 3 is Sue's mother.

Sue

B ▶ **LISTEN AND POINT.** Then listen and repeat.

Vocabulary

Family members

1. sister
2. brother
3. mother
4. father
5. parents
6. husband
7. wife
8. daughter
9. son
10. children
11. grandmother
12. grandfather

C IDENTIFY. Student A, point to a person in a picture on page 66. Talk about the person.

A: Who's this?
B: Sue's mother.

Study Tip

Test yourself

Cover the word box. Look at the pictures. Write the words you remember. Look at the word box and check your work.

D MATCH. Student A, say a family member. Student B, say the matching male or female word.

A: Brother.
B: Sister.

E LABEL. Look at Sue's family tree. Write family words in the correct places.

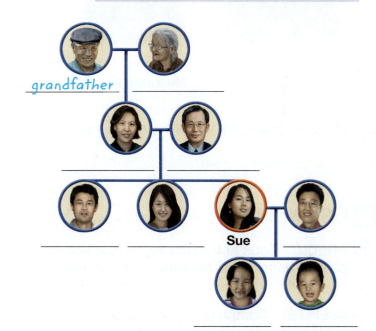

grandfather

Sue

Show what you know!

1. **DRAW A PICTURE.** Draw your family tree. Use names.

2. **TALK ABOUT IT.** Talk about your family.

   Ben is my brother.

3. **WRITE ABOUT IT.** Now write a sentence about your family.

   _____ is my _____.

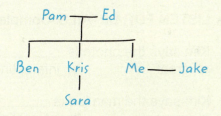

I can identify family members. ☐   I need more practice. ☐

For more practice, go to MyEnglishLab.

Lesson 2 Listening and Speaking

Talk about family

1 BEFORE YOU LISTEN

A READ.

This is Dev Patel.
He is an actor.

This is my brother.
He **looks like** Dev Patel.

B MAKE CONNECTIONS. Who do people in your family look like?

My sister looks like me.

2 LISTEN

A PREDICT. Look at the picture. Gina is showing a photo to Kim. What are they talking about?

B ▶ LISTEN. Complete the sentence.

The man in the photo is _____.
a. Gina's father   b. Gina's grandfather

C ▶ LISTEN FOR DETAILS. Complete the sentences.

1. Kim says the photo is _____.
   a. great   b. interesting   c. nice

2. Kim says the man looks _____.
   a. great   b. interesting   c. nice

D ▶ EXPAND. Listen to the whole conversation. Read the sentences. Circle *True* or *False*.

1. Kim thinks Gina looks like the woman in the photo.   True   False
2. The woman is Gina's sister.   True   False

Listening and Speaking

3 CONVERSATION

A ▶ **LISTEN AND READ.** Then listen and repeat.

A: That's a great photo. Who's that?
B: My father.
A: Oh, he looks nice.
B: Thanks.

B **WORK TOGETHER.** Practice the conversation in Exercise A.

C **CREATE.** Make new conversations. Use the family tree.

A: That's a great photo. Who's that?
B: My _____.
　　　　(family member)
A: Oh, _____ looks nice.
　　　　(he / she)
B: Thanks.

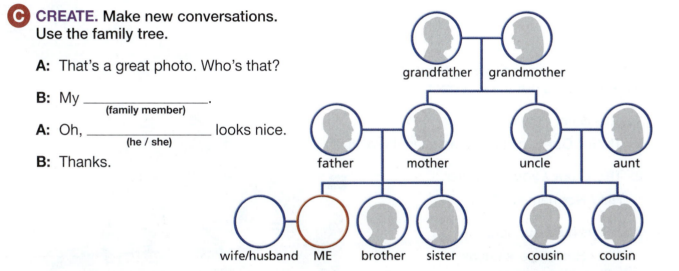

D **MAKE CONNECTIONS.** Make your own conversations. Use a photo of a person in your family. Talk about that person.

I can talk about family. ■　　　　I need more practice. ■

For more practice, go to MyEnglishLab.

Unit 4, Lesson 2　**69**

Lesson 3 Grammar

Possessive adjectives and possessive nouns

Possessive adjectives

Subject pronouns			Possessive adjectives	
I	am		My	
You	are		Your	
He	is	in the U.S.	His	family is in Peru.
She			Her	
We	are		Our	
They			Their	

A IDENTIFY. Maria is showing family photos to a friend. Cross out the incorrect words.

1. This is ~~his~~ / **my** husband and me.
   Their / **Our** two children aren't in the picture.

2. This is **our** / **your** daughter.
   His / **Her** name is Sara.

3. This is **his** / **our** son.
   His / **Her** name is Lucas.

4. These are **my** / **our** parents.
   Her / **Their** names are Frida and Luis.

B COMPLETE. Maria is showing more photos to her friend. Complete their conversation with *my, your, his, her,* and *their*.

Maria: This is ____my____ daughter with _____ friend from school.
This is _____ son with _____ cousin. And here are
the children with _____ classmates.
Friend: Nice. _____ son looks like you.
Maria: I know. And _____ daughter looks like my husband.

C ▶ SELF-ASSESS. Listen and check your answers.

Grammar

Possessive nouns		
Dora **Luis**	is in the U.S.	**Dora's** **Luis's** family is in Peru. **Dora and Luis's**

Grammar Watch

Add **'s** to names to show possession.

Pronunciation of possessive 's

The **'s** adds an extra syllable after the sounds *s*, *z*, *sh*, and *ch* (*Luis's, Alex's, Liz's, Josh's,* and *Mitch's*).

D INTERPRET. Look at the family tree. Complete the sentences.

1. Ryan is ____Eva's____ husband.
2. Meg is _____ wife.
3. Eva is Ross and _____ daughter.
4. Tess is _____ grandmother.
5. Ed is _____ husband.
6. Pat is Mary and _____ granddaughter.

E SELF-ASSESS. Listen and check your answers. Then listen and repeat.

Show what you know!

1. **TALK ABOUT IT.** Say the names of two people in the family tree. Your partner says their relationship.

   A: Ross and Alex.
   B: Ross is Alex's grandfather.

2. **WRITE ABOUT IT.** Now write about a person in your family. Describe your relationship in two ways.

   Rosa is my sister. I'm Rosa's brother.

I can use possessive adjectives and possessive nouns. ☐   I need more practice. ☐

For more practice, go to MyEnglishLab.

Lesson 4 Reading

Read about blended families

1 BEFORE YOU READ

A CHOOSE. Complete the sentences with the vocabulary in the box.

| divorced | married | step-sister |

1. In 2008, Jimmy's parents got _____.

2. In 2016, Jimmy's parents got _____.

3. Jimmy now lives with his mother, step-father, and _____.

B MAKE CONNECTIONS. Do you have a big family? Who's in your family?

2 READ

▶ Listen and read.

Academic Skill: Make connections

When you read, try to make connections between the article and your own life. Does the article make you think about people you know?

The Blended Family

In 2015, Jimmy Peterson had a small family. He had a mother and a father. He had no brothers or sisters. In 2016, his parents got divorced.

In 2017, Jimmy's mother got married again. In 2018, his
5 father remarried. Now Jimmy lives in two homes. Each home has a blended family. From Monday to Friday, Jimmy lives with his mother, step-father, and step-sister. On weekends, he lives with his father, step-mother, and two step-brothers. Jimmy says, "My life is different now,
10 but I love my big family."

Jimmy's family life isn't simple, but it is common. Today in the U.S., many people marry, divorce, and remarry. Many children live in blended families. Just 46% of

Jimmy with his father, step-mother, and step-brothers

children live with two parents who are married
15 for the first time.

Source: www.pewsocialtrends.org

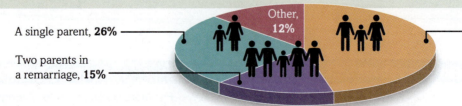

A single parent, **26%**

Two parents in a remarriage, **15%**

Other, **12%**

Two parents in their first marriage, **46%**

72 Unit 4, Lesson 4

Reading

3 CLOSE READING

CITE EVIDENCE. Answer the questions. Complete the sentences. Where is the information? Write the line number.

Lines

1. What happened in 2016?
   Jimmy's parents _____. _____

2. What happened in 2017?
   Jimmy's mother _____. _____

3. What happened in 2018?
   Jimmy's father _____. _____

4. Who does Jimmy live with during the week?
   His _____. _____

5. Who does Jimmy live with on weekends?
   His _____. _____

6. What does Jimmy say about his family?
   " _____." _____

4 SUMMARIZE

Complete the summary with the words in the box.

| common | divorced | families | remarried | step-father |

In 2016, Jimmy Peterson's parents got (1) _____. Later, his mother got married again, and his father (2) _____, too. Now Jimmy has two blended (3) _____. During the week, he lives with his mother, (4) _____, and step-sister. On weekends, he lives with his father, step-mother, and step-brothers. Blended families are (5) _____ in the U.S.

Show what you know!

1. **TALK ABOUT IT.** Do you know someone who is part of a blended family? Who? Talk about the people in his or her family.

2. **WRITE ABOUT IT.** Now write about the person you know and his or her blended family.

   _____ *is part of a blended family. (He/She) has* _____.

I can make connections. ■   I need more practice. ■

To read more, go to MyEnglishLab.

Unit 4, Lesson 4

Lesson 5: Listening and Speaking — Describe people

1 BEFORE YOU LISTEN

A ▶ **READ.** Look at the picture of Pam's parents and brother. Then listen and read.

Pam's father is *average height* and *heavy*. He has a *mustache*. Her mother is *short* and *average weight*. She has *long hair*. Her brother is *tall* and *thin*. He has a *beard*.

B **IDENTIFY.** Answer the questions.

1. Who has a mustache? _____
2. Who has a beard? _____
3. Who is average weight? _____

2 LISTEN

A ▶ **LISTEN.** Look at the picture of Pam and Leo. Listen to the conversation. Check (✓) the correct answer.

Who is Leo talking about?
- ☐ his father
- ☐ his grandfather
- ☐ his brother

B ▶ **LISTEN FOR DETAILS.** Check (✓) all the correct answers.

Leo's brother is _____.

- ☐ a painter
- ☐ a carpenter
- ☐ great
- ☐ interesting
- ☐ fun
- ☐ smart
- ☐ short
- ☐ tall
- ☐ heavy
- ☐ thin

C ▶ **EXPAND.** Listen to the whole conversation. Check (✓) the correct answers.

1. Which picture shows Leo's brother?

   a.   b.   c.

2. Is Leo's brother married?
   ☐ yes   ☐ no

Listening and Speaking

3 CONVERSATION

A ▶ **LISTEN AND READ.** Then listen and repeat.

A: Is your family here in this country?
B: My brother is here. He's a carpenter.
A: Oh. What's he like?
B: He's great. He's a lot of fun.
A: Does he look like you?
B: No. He's tall and thin, and he has long hair.

B **WORK TOGETHER.** Practice the conversation in Exercise A.

C **CREATE.** Make new conversations. Talk about a family member in this country.

A: Is your family here in this country?
B: My _____ is here.
A: Oh. What's _____ like?
              (he / she)
B: _____'s great.
   (He / She)
    _____'s a lot of fun.
   (He / She)
A: Does _____ look like you?
         (he / she)
B: Yes/No. _____'s
           (He / She)
   _____ and
   _____ and
   has _____.

uncle	aunt	cousin
tall	short	average height
thin	heavy	average weight
short hair	long hair	short hair

D **MAKE CONNECTIONS.** Make your own conversations. Student A, ask about your partner's family. Student B, talk about one person.

A: What's your brother like?
B: He's great. He's a lot of fun.
A: Does he look like you?
B: No. He's tall and thin and has short hair.

I can describe people. ▪   I need more practice. ▪

For more practice, go to MyEnglishLab.

Lesson 6 Grammar

Have and *be* for descriptions

Descriptions with *have*

| I / You / We / They | **have** | long hair. |
| He / She / Marco | **has** | short hair. |

A IDENTIFY. Cross out the incorrect words.

1. My name is Paul. I **have / ~~has~~** short hair.
2. My parents both **have / has** short hair, too.
3. My brother and I both **have / has** mustaches. But I also **have / has** a beard.
4. Our sister looks like our mother. But she **have / has** long hair.

B DECIDE. Look at the picture in Exercise A. Circle Paul.

C APPLY. Look at the pictures. Describe the people. Use *have* or *has*.

1. Ali *has a mustache.*

2. Aya _____

3. Kim and Rita _____

4. Feng _____

5. Karl and Nick _____

6. Max _____

Grammar

Descriptions with *be* and *have*

Be			Have		
I	am		I	have	
She	is	tall.	She	has	long hair.
We			We		
They	are		They	have	

D IDENTIFY. Read about Donna's family. Cross out the incorrect words.

Donna's mother **is / has** average height and weight, but her sister **is / are** short and heavy. Her sister and her mother both **has / have** short hair. Donna's father **is / has** a beard, and her brother **is / has** a mustache. Her father and her brother both **are / have** short hair. Her father **is / has** thin, but her brother **is / has** heavy.

E WORK TOGETHER. Look at the pictures of Donna and her husband. Talk about the differences.

A: In Picture A, Donna is average weight. In Picture B, she's heavy.
B: In Picture A, she has ...

A May 2011

B April 2017

Show what you know!

1. **TALK ABOUT IT.** Look at your classmates. Complete the chart. Write the number of students. Talk about your classmates.

Beard	Mustache	Long hair	Short hair	Tall	Short

A: Who has a beard?
B: Carlos and Chen have beards. What about mustaches?

2. **WRITE ABOUT IT.** Now write two sentences about two classmates.

_____ _____

I can use *have* and *be* for descriptions. ■   I need more practice. ■

For more practice, go to MyEnglishLab.

Unit 4, Lesson 6 **77**

Lesson 7

Workplace, Life, and Community Skills

Say and write dates

1 TALK ABOUT MONTHS

A ▶ **LISTEN AND POINT.** Then listen and repeat.

January	_____	February	_____	March	_____
April	_____	May	_____	June	_____
July	_____	August	_____	September	_____
October	_____	November	_____	December	_____

B **USE ABBREVIATIONS.** Look at the calendar. Write the abbreviations for the months in Exercise 1A.

C **WORK TOGETHER.** Student A, say a month. Student B, repeat the month and say the next month. Student C, continue. Then Student B, say a new month.

A: March.
B: March, April.
C: March, April, May.
B: August.

2 TALK ABOUT AND WRITE DATES

A ▶ **LISTEN AND POINT.** Then listen and repeat.

1st	2nd	3rd	4th	5th	6th
7th	8th	9th	10th	11th	12th
13th	14th	15th	16th	17th	18th
19th	20th	21st	22nd	23rd	24th
25th	26th	27th	28th	29th	30th
31st					

B ▶ **LISTEN AND POINT.** Look at the calendar for January. Listen and point to the dates.

Workplace, Life, and Community Skills

C APPLY. Look at the calendars. Write the dates. Use this year.

February 24, _____   _____   _____   _____

D REWRITE. Look at the calendars in Exercise 2C. Write the dates in numbers.

1. 2/24/_____   2. _____   3. _____   4. _____

E ▶ CHOOSE. Circle the dates you hear.

1. a. 3/4/87   (b.) 3/14/87   4. a. 8/30/05   b. 8/31/05
2. a. 10/2/11   b. 2/10/11   5. a. 12/17/69   b. 12/7/69
3. a. 6/28/98   b. 5/28/98   6. a. 9/2/72   b. 9/22/62

F ▶ LISTEN AND READ. Then listen and repeat.

A: When is your birthday?
B: My birthday is July 29. When is your birthday?

G MAKE CONNECTIONS. Ask three classmates for their birthdays. Write the names and dates.

Name	Birthday
Han	7/29

H PRESENT. Tell your class about your classmates' birthdays.

I GO ONLINE. Find the date of the next holiday on your calendar.

I can say and write dates. ▢   I need more practice. ▢

For more practice, go to MyEnglishLab.

Unit 4, Lesson 7   79

Lesson 8 Listening and Speaking

Give a child's age and grade in school

1 BEFORE YOU LISTEN

INTERPRET. Look at the picture. Answer the questions.

1. How old is the little girl?
2. What grade is she in?

2 LISTEN

A PREDICT. Look at the pictures. Ellen is babysitting for her friend's kids. What do you see?

B ▶ LISTEN. Where is Ellen?

a. at school   b. at home   c. at a friend's house

C ▶ LISTEN FOR DETAILS. Complete the sentences.

1. The boy is in the _____ grade.
   a. fourth   b. fifth   c. sixth

2. The girl is in the _____ grade.
   a. first   b. third   c. fourth

D ▶ EXPAND. Listen to the whole conversation. Answer the questions.

1. Who says Terry is friendly?
   a. Ellen   b. Ellen's friend   c. Ken

2. Who calls Terry "Terry the Terrible"?
   a. Ellen   b. Ellen's friend   c. Ken

Listening and Speaking

3 PRONUNCIATION

A ▶ **PRACTICE.** Listen. Then listen and repeat.

Her son is eleven.

He's in the fifth grade.

Where are you?

> **Linking words together: consonant to vowel**
>
> We connect a consonant sound at the end of a word to a vowel sound at the beginning of the next word.

B ▶ **APPLY.** Practice saying the sentences. Then listen and repeat.

1. How old are they?
2. She's in the first grade.

4 CONVERSATION

A ▶ **LISTEN AND READ.** Then listen and repeat.

A: Hi, Ellen. Where are you?
B: I'm at my friend's house. I'm babysitting for her kids.
A: Oh. How old are they?
B: Well, her son is in the fifth grade. I think he's eleven. And her daughter is six. She's in the first grade.

B **WORK TOGETHER.** Practice the conversation in Exercise A.

C **CREATE.** Make new conversations. Use the information in the boxes.

A: Hi! Where are you?
B: I'm at my friend's house. I'm babysitting for her kids.
A: Oh. How old are they?
B: Well, her son is _____. He's in the _____. And her daughter is _____. She's in the _____.

12 (years old) 6th grade

8 (years old) 3rd grade

14 (years old) 8th grade

13 (years old) 7th grade

D **MAKE CONNECTIONS.** Make your own conversations. Talk about children you know.

A: My sister has two children.
B: Oh, really? How old are they?

7 (years old) 2nd grade

10 (years old) 4th grade

I can give a child's age and grade in school. ▪   I need more practice. ▪

For more practice, go to MyEnglishLab.

Unit 4, Lesson 8   **81**

Lesson 9 Grammar

Questions with *How old*

Questions with *How old*					
How old	are	you? they? your friend's children?	**How old**	is	he? she? Terry?

A COMPLETE. Ask about age.

Date of birth: Jan. 4, 1985

Date of birth: May 6, 2014

Date of birth: Oct. 4, 1997

1. **A:** How old __is__ Dean's son?
   B: He's _____.

2. **A:** How old _____ Eric's cousins?
   B: They're _____.

3. **A:** _____ Marco's sisters?
   B: _____.

Date of birth: Aug. 11, 1936

Date of birth: June 2, 2010
Date of birth: Sept. 30, 2013

Date of birth: You

4. **A:** _____ Barry's grandmother?
   B: _____.

5. **A:** _____ Eva's kids?
   B: Her son _____ and her daughter _____.

6. **A:** How old _____ you?
   B: I'd rather not say!

B WORK TOGETHER. Look at these photos of famous people. Guess. How old are they?

Zhang Ziyi

George Clooney

Cristiano Ronaldo

Rihanna

A: How old is Zhang Ziyi?
B: I don't know. I think she's (around) thirty.
A: Oh, no. I think she's (around) forty.

I can ask questions with *How old*.   I need more practice.

For more practice, go to MyEnglishLab.

Lesson 10 Writing

Write about a family member

1 STUDY THE MODEL

READ. Answer the questions.

> Ana Montes
> My Sister
>
> My sister's name is Betta. She's 40 years old. Her birthday is in March. She's tall and thin. She has long hair. She's fun and smart.

1. Who is Betta?
2. How old is she?
3. When is her birthday?
4. What does she look like?
5. What is she like?

2 PLAN YOUR WRITING

WORK TOGETHER. Ask and answer the questions.

1. Who is one of your family members?
2. How old is he/she?
3. When is his/her birthday?
4. What does he/she look like?
5. What is he/she like?

Writing Skill: Use a capital letter for months

Months always begin with a capital letter.
For example:
(M)arch

3 WRITE

Now write about a family member. Use the frame, the model, the Writing Skill, and your ideas from Exercise 2 to help you.

> My ____'s name is ____. He's/She's ____ years old. His/Her birthday is in ____. He's/She's ____ and ____. He/She has ____ hair. He/She is ____ and ____.

4 CHECK YOUR WRITING

WORK TOGETHER. Read your writing aloud with a partner.

WRITING CHECKLIST
- ☐ The writing answers the questions in Exercise 2.
- ☐ Each sentence begins with a capital letter.
- ☐ The month begins with a capital letter.
- ☐ Each sentence ends with a period.

I can use a capital letter for months. ☐   I need more practice. ☐

For more practice, go to MyEnglishLab.

Lesson 11 Soft Skills at Work

Separate work and home life

1 MEET HANI

Read about one of her workplace skills.

I can separate work and home life. When I am at work, I think about my work. I don't make personal phone calls at work.

2 HANI'S PROBLEM

READ. Circle *True* or *False*.

Hani is an accountant. She works in a busy office. The office has many rules. One rule is "Work calls only."

Her father lives alone in another city. He calls Hani at work every day, but Hani can't talk on the phone at work.

1. Hani is busy at work.   True   False
2. Hani lives with her father.   True   False
3. Hani's father likes to talk to Hani on the phone.   True   False

3 HANI'S SOLUTION

WORK TOGETHER. Hani separates work and home life. What is the right thing to do? Explain your answer.

1. Hani answers the phone and talks quietly.
2. Hani doesn't answer the phone. She texts her father at work.
3. Hani calls her father during the break and says, "I can't talk on the phone at work. Please call me at home."
4. Hani says, "_____."

Show what you know!

1. **THINK ABOUT IT.** How do you separate work and home life? Give examples.

2. **WRITE ABOUT IT.** Now write your example in your Skills Log.

    I don't text friends or family members at work.

I can give an example from my life of separating work and home life. ■

Unit Review: Go back to page 65. Which goals can you check off?

5 Shop, Shop, Shop

PREVIEW

Look at the picture. What do you see? Where are the people?

UNIT GOALS

- ☐ Name colors and clothes
- ☐ Talk about things you need or want
- ☐ Identify U.S. money
- ☐ Talk about money and prices and read receipts
- ☐ Ask for sizes and colors
- ☐ Return something to a store
- ☐ **Academic skill:** Make inferences
- ☐ **Writing skill:** Use commas between words in a list
- ☐ **Workplace soft skill:** Be professional

Lesson 1 Vocabulary

Colors and clothes

A PREDICT. Look at the pictures. What do you see? What are the clothes and colors?

Number 1 is a dress. Number 4 is orange.

B ▶ LISTEN AND POINT. Then listen and repeat.

Vocabulary

Colors and clothes

1. a blue dress
2. a green shirt
3. a purple skirt
4. an orange blouse
5. a pink sweater
6. black jeans
7. a red jacket
8. a yellow T-shirt
9. khaki pants
10. gray socks
11. white sneakers
12. brown shoes

C   IDENTIFY. Look at the pictures and the list of clothes. Which clothes come in pairs? Write the words.

pants   _____   _____

_____   _____

D   WORK TOGETHER. Ask and answer questions about the pictures.

A: What's number 12?
B: Shoes.
A: What color are they?
B: Brown. What's number 3?
A: A skirt.
B: What color is it?
A: Purple.

Study Tip

Use an online dictionary
Look up three words about clothes on the Longman Online Dictionary. Listen to and repeat the pronunciation of the words.

Show what you know!

1. **IDENTIFY.** Student A, look around the room. Say what a classmate is wearing. Student B, guess the classmate.

   A: Who's wearing gray pants and a red sweater?
   B: Paul.
   A: Right!
   B: Who's wearing . . . ?

2. **TALK ABOUT IT.** Talk about your clothes.

   A: I'm wearing a green T-shirt, blue jeans, and black sneakers.
   B: And I'm wearing . . .

3. **WRITE ABOUT IT.** Now write a sentence about your clothes.

   I'm wearing _____.

I can name colors and clothes. ■   I need more practice. ■

For more practice, go to MyEnglishLab.

Lesson 2 — Listening and Speaking
Talk about things you need or want

1 BEFORE YOU LISTEN

CHOOSE. Complete the sentences with the words in the box.

wants	needs

She _____ a sweater.   She _____ those shoes.

2 LISTEN

A ▶ LISTEN. Look at the picture. Listen to the conversation. What's the conversation about?

a. a birthday gift   b. a shirt

B ▶ LISTEN FOR DETAILS. Read the sentences. Circle *True* or *False*.

1. Meg's birthday is next week.   True   False
2. Meg's brother needs clothes.   True   False
3. Meg's brother wants clothes.   True   False

C ▶ EXPAND. Listen to the whole conversation. Complete the sentence.

Carlos wants a _____.

a.    b.    c.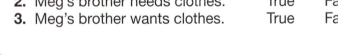

Listening and Speaking

3 CONVERSATION

A ▶ **LISTEN AND READ.** Then listen and repeat.

A: I need a gift for my brother. It's his birthday next week.
B: How about clothes?
A: Well, he needs clothes, but he wants a backpack!

B **WORK TOGETHER.** Practice the conversation in Exercise A.

C **CREATE.** Make new conversations. Use the information in the boxes.

A: I need a gift for my _____.

It's _____ birthday next
(his / her)
week.

B: How about clothes?

A: Well, _____ needs
(he / she)
clothes, but _____
(he / she)
wants _____!

friend

mother

father

a wallet

a handbag

a watch

D **MAKE CONNECTIONS.** Make your own conversations. Use different people and gifts.

A: I need a gift for my friend. It's her birthday tomorrow.
B: How about a handbag?
A: That's a good idea.

I can talk about things I need or want. ▪   I need more practice. ▪

For more practice, go to MyEnglishLab.

Unit 5, Lesson 2   **89**

Lesson 3 Grammar

Simple present affirmative

Simple present affirmative					
I	need		He	needs	
You	want	new clothes.	She	wants	new clothes.
They	have		Bob	has	

Grammar Watch

- With **he**, **she**, or **it**, the simple present verb ends in **-s**.
- Remember: The verb **have** is irregular. Use **has** with *he*, *she*, or *it*.

A IDENTIFY. Cross out the incorrect words.

1. Mr. Garcia ~~have~~ / **has** an orange shirt.
   He **want / wants** a green shirt.

2. Amy and Jeff **have / has** black sneakers.
   I **want / wants** black sneakers, too.

3. Our teacher **need / needs** a new jacket.
   He **need / needs** new pants, too.

B COMPLETE. Use the verbs in parentheses.

1. My sister ___needs___ a skirt.
   (need)
   She _____ a pink skirt.
   (want)

2. My brothers _____ new shoes.
   (have)
   Now they _____ new socks.
   (need)

3. Allen _____ brown jeans.
   (have)
   We _____ brown jeans, too.
   (want)

4. You _____ a nice new wallet.
   (have)
   I _____ a new wallet, too.
   (want)

Grammar

C **WORK TOGETHER.** Look at the picture. What do they need? What do they want? There is more than one correct answer.

A: What does he need?
B: He needs new shoes. He also needs...
A: Yes. But he really wants...

D **WRITE.** Complete the sentences.

He needs _____
_____
_____.

He wants _____
_____
_____.

She needs _____
_____
_____.

She wants _____
_____
_____.

Show what you know!

1. **THINK ABOUT IT.** Complete the chart.

2. **TALK ABOUT IT.** Talk about your clothes.

    A: I have a blue T-shirt. I need a white T-shirt, and I want a blue jacket.
    B: I have a blue T-shirt, too, and I want blue pants.

Clothes I have	Clothes I need	Clothes I want

3. **WRITE ABOUT IT.** Now write three sentences about your partner. What does he or she have, need, and want?

    My partner has blue pants. She needs _____. She _____.

I can use the simple present affirmative. ☐   I need more practice. ☐

For more practice, go to MyEnglishLab.

Unit 5, Lesson 3   **91**

Workplace, Life, and Community Skills

Lesson 4

Talk about money and prices and read receipts

1 IDENTIFY U.S. MONEY

A **MAKE CONNECTIONS.** Where do you shop for clothes? Do you pay with cash?

B ▶ **LISTEN AND POINT.** Then listen and repeat.

1. one dollar ($1.00)

2. five dollars ($5.00)

3. ten dollars ($10.00)

4. twenty dollars ($20.00)

C ▶ **LISTEN AND POINT.** Then listen and repeat.

1. a penny (1¢)   2. a nickel (5¢)   3. a dime (10¢)   4. a quarter (25¢)

D **CALCULATE.** Count the money. Write the amount.

1. ___65¢___

2. _____

3. _____

4. _____

E ▶ **SELF-ASSESS.** Listen and check your answers. Then listen and repeat.

I can identify U.S. money. ■   I need more practice. ■

For more practice, go to MyEnglishLab.

Workplace, Life, and Community Skills

2 TALK ABOUT PRICES

A ▶ **LISTEN AND READ.** Then listen and repeat.

Customer: Excuse me. How much is this **skirt**?
Assistant: It's **$15.99**.
Customer: And how much are these **jeans**?
Assistant: They're **$17.99**.

B ▶ **LISTEN.** Write the prices.

1.  2.  3.  4.

C **ROLE-PLAY.** Ask about prices. Use the pictures in Exercise 2B.

D **INTERPRET.** Look at the receipt. Answer the questions.

1. What is the date on the receipt?

   Write it in words. _____

2. How much are the jeans? _____

3. How much is the tax? _____

4. How much are the clothes before tax? _____

5. How much are the clothes after tax? _____

6. How much is the change? _____

E **GO ONLINE.** Find the tax rate in your city and calculate the total on the receipt in Exercise 2D.

_____

```
             IMAGINE
       Los Angeles, CA 90027
        (213) 555-6111

08-06-18
                            2:25 P.M.

WOMEN'S JEANS              18.99
WOMEN'S SWEATERS           13.99
WOMEN'S T-SHIRTS            7.99
SUBTOTAL                   40.97
TAX 8% ON 40.97             3.28
TOTAL
                           44.25
CASH AMOUNT PAID           45.00
CHANGE DUE                   .75

Please keep receipt for
returns.
Thank you for shopping
at IMAGINE.
```

I can talk about money and prices and read receipts. ■   I need more practice. ■

For more practice, go to MyEnglishLab.

Unit 5, Lesson 4   **93**

Lesson 5 Listening and Speaking
Ask for sizes and colors

1 BEFORE YOU LISTEN

A LABEL. Look at the pictures. Write the sizes under the shirts.

| extra large | extra small | medium | large | small |

_____ _____ _____ _____ _____

B IDENTIFY. Some clothes come in sizes with letters, and some clothes come in sizes with numbers. Check (✓) the clothes that come in sizes with numbers.

☐ shoes   ☐ socks   ☐ sweaters   ☐ jeans   ☐ T-shirts

2 LISTEN

Kofi

A PREDICT. Look at the picture. Where are they? What do you see?

B ▶ LISTEN. Complete the sentence.

Kofi wants clothes for his _____.
a. mother   b. sister   c. wife

C ▶ LISTEN FOR DETAILS. Complete the sentences.

1. Kofi wants a _____.
   a. sweater   b. blouse   c. jacket

2. His sister needs a _____.
   a. small   b. medium   c. large

D ▶ EXPAND. Listen to the whole conversation. What does Kofi get?

a.   b.   c.

Listening and Speaking

3 PRONUNCIATION

A ▶ **PRACTICE.** Listen. Then listen and repeat.

Do you have this sweater in a lárge?

It's a gift for my síster.

I have a jácket.

How much is this skírt?

> **Sentence stress**
>
> We stress important words in a sentence. One word gets the most (strongest) stress.

B ▶ **APPLY.** Listen. Put a dot (•) on the word with the most stress.

1. Do you like gréen?
2. Do you need a small?
3. He wants a watch.
4. Does she like blue?
5. Here you go.
6. I'm sorry.

4 CONVERSATION

A ▶ **LISTEN AND READ.** Then listen and repeat.

A: Do you have this sweater in a large?
B: No, I'm sorry. We don't.
A: Too bad. It's for my sister, and she needs a large.

B **WORK TOGETHER.** Practice the conversation in Exercise A.

C **CREATE.** Make new conversations. Use the pictures.

A: Do you have this _____ in a(n) _____?
B: No, I'm sorry. We don't.
A: Too bad. It's for my sister, and she needs a(n) _____.

D **ROLE-PLAY.** Make your own conversations. Use different clothes and sizes.

I can ask for sizes and colors. ▮   I need more practice. ▮

For more practice, go to MyEnglishLab.

Grammar

Lesson 6: Simple present: *Yes/no* questions and short answers

Simple present: *Yes/no* questions and short answers

Do	I / we / you / they	need new shoes?	Yes,	you / we / I / they	do.	No,	you / we / I / they	don't.
Does	he / she			he / she	does.		he / she	doesn't.

Grammar Watch

Use the base form of the verb in questions with *do* or *does*. In the chart, *need* is the base form.

Contractions
don't = do not
doesn't = does not

A MATCH.

1. Do you have this shirt in gray? __d__
2. Does your son like his new jeans? ____
3. Does Ms. Cho have a backpack? ____
4. Do your sisters want new clothes? ____

a. Yes, he does.
b. No, she doesn't.
c. Yes, they do.
d. Yes, we do.

B COMPLETE. Use *do*, *does*, *don't*, or *doesn't*.

1. A: _____Do_____ you have this jacket in blue?
   B: Yes, we _____do_____. Here you go.

2. A: _____ Cindy want a new watch?
   B: No, she _____. She likes her old watch.

3. A: _____ you need these jeans in a size 14?
   B: No, I _____. I need a size 12.

4. A: _____ you have this shirt in an extra small?
   B: No, we _____. But we have it in a small.

5. A: _____ the customer like that green sweater?
   B: No, he _____. He likes the blue sweater.

C WORK TOGETHER. Practice the conversations in Exercise B.

Grammar

D WRITE. Complete the questions. Use *do* or *does* and the verbs in parentheses. Then look at the pictures. Answer the questions.

1. A: __Does__ Ben __have__ an extra-large white T-shirt?
   (have)
   B: Yes, he does.

2. A: _____ Ben and Tina _____ blue shirts?
   (have)
   B: _____

3. A: _____ Tina _____ a large red jacket?
   (need)
   B: _____

4. A: _____ Ben and Tina _____ red sweaters?
   (need)
   B: _____

5. A: _____ Tina _____ a small green sweater?
   (have)
   B: _____

6. A: _____ Ben and Tina _____ blue jeans.
   (have)
   B: _____

Show what you know!

1. **TALK ABOUT IT.** Ask and answer *yes/no* questions. Use the words in the box.

   | like / red ties | have / a favorite color |
   | need / new clothes | want / new jeans |

   A: Do you like red ties?
   B: Yes, I do. Do you like red ties?
   A: No, I don't.

2. **WRITE ABOUT IT.** Now write a new question to ask about a classmate's clothes.

   Does _____?

I can ask and answer *yes/no* questions in the simple present. ■   I need more practice. ■

For more practice, go to MyEnglishLab.

Unit 5, Lesson 6   **97**

Lesson 7 Reading
Read about credit cards and debit cards

1 BEFORE YOU READ

A LABEL. Write the vocabulary words under the pictures.

cash   a credit card bill   plastic

1. _____   2. _____   3. _____

B MAKE CONNECTIONS. When you go to the store, how do you pay for things? What are some other ways to pay?

2 READ

▶ Listen and read.

Academic Skill: Make inferences

You make inferences about things the writer is thinking but doesn't say. For example, this writer says, "That is expensive!" You can infer that the writer thinks, "Paying interest is a bad idea."

SHOPPING WITHOUT CASH

Do you have cash in your wallet? Maybe you do, and maybe you don't. Some people almost never use cash.

In 2011, 36% of Americans used cash for shopping most or all of the time. Today, that number is down. People are using other ways to pay. The most common ways are debit cards and credit cards.

5 Let's say you are buying a new jacket at a store. You use a debit card. That card is connected to your account at a bank. When you use the card, the money comes out of your account that same day.

Let's say you buy the jacket with a credit card instead. A credit card lets you borrow money from the credit card company. Later, the company sends you a bill. You need to pay the money back. It is better to pay it all back on time. After the payment due date, the company charges interest on the
10 money. That is expensive!

Some people never use credit cards. They like using cash. In the U.S., people often spend more money when they shop with a credit card. Why? A credit card is a piece of plastic. Maybe it doesn't seem like real money.

An average of 3.7 credit cards, **71%**

No credit cards, **29%**

Most Americans Have Credit Cards

Source: Gallup

98 Unit 5, Lesson 7

Reading

3 CLOSE READING

A **CITE EVIDENCE.** Complete the sentences. Where is the information? Write the line number.

Lines

1. Debit cards and credit cards are _____ in the U.S.
   a. common
   b. new
   c. hard to find
   _____

2. When you use a debit card in a store, you _____.
   a. borrow money from your bank
   b. use money you have in the bank
   c. pay more money
   _____

3. When you use _____, sometimes you need to pay interest.
   a. a credit card
   b. a debit card
   c. cash
   _____

4. Credit card companies charge you interest when you pay your bill _____.
   a. before the payment due date
   b. on time
   c. late
   _____

5. When Americans shop with credit cards, not cash, they often _____.
   a. get better prices
   b. don't pay tax
   c. spend more money
   _____

B **INTERPRET.** Complete the sentences about the pie chart.

1. The pie chart shows that most Americans have _____.
   a. cash
   b. debit cards
   c. credit cards

2. _____ of Americans don't have a credit card.
   a. 19%
   b. 29%
   c. 69%

3. An American with credit cards usually has _____.
   a. 1 card
   b. 3 or 4 cards
   c. 71 cards

4 SUMMARIZE

Complete the summary with the words in the box.

| bank account | cash | credit card | due date | interest |

Many Americans don't shop with (1) _____. They often use debit cards or credit cards. A debit card takes money out of your (2) _____. But when you use a (3) _____, you are borrowing money. Pay it back by the payment (4) _____, or you will need to pay (5) _____.

Show what you know!

1. **TALK ABOUT IT.** Ask your partner, "Do you like to shop with cash? Debit cards? Credit cards?" Ask why or why not.

2. **WRITE ABOUT IT.** Now write about how you like to pay when you shop and why.

   I (like/don't like) to shop with _____ *because* _____.

I can make inferences. ■   I need more practice. ■

To read more, go to MyEnglishLab.

Lesson 8 Listening and Speaking

Return something to a store

1 BEFORE YOU LISTEN

CHOOSE. Look at the pictures. Write the sentence under the correct picture.

> The zipper doesn't work.   ~~It doesn't look good.~~   They don't fit.   They don't match.

Reasons People Return Clothes

a. _It doesn't look good._
I don't like it.

b. _____
They're too big.

c. _____
The colors don't look good together.

d. _____
It's broken.

2 LISTEN

A ▶ **LISTEN.** Two customers are talking to a sales assistant. Why are they at the store?

They want to _____ something.
a. buy   b. return

B ▶ **LISTEN FOR DETAILS.** Complete the sentences.

1. The _____ pants are the wrong size.
   a. woman's   b. man's

2. You need a _____ to get your money back at this store.
   a. credit card   b. receipt

a receipt   a credit card

Listening and Speaking

3 CONVERSATION

A **PREDICT.** Look at the picture. A customer is returning a shirt. What is she looking for?

a. her money   b. her receipt   c. her credit card

B ▶ **LISTEN AND READ.** Then listen and repeat.

Lesson 9 Grammar

Simple present negative

I				He			
You	don't	like	this color.	She	doesn't	like	this color.
We				The customer			
They							

A IDENTIFY. Cross out the incorrect words.

1. The zipper on my jacket ~~don't~~ / **doesn't** work.
2. Your new jeans **don't** / **doesn't** fit.
3. I **don't** / **doesn't** have my receipt.
4. The customers **don't** / **doesn't** like their new shoes.
5. Ms. Wong **don't** / **doesn't** like her new skirt.
6. The manager **don't** / **doesn't** need a tie.

Grammar Watch

Use the base form of the verb after *don't* or *doesn't*.

B WORK TOGETHER. Look at the picture. Find the problems. Tell your partner. There is more than one correct answer.

A: What's the problem in A?
B: The jeans don't fit. They're too big.

C WRITE. Write three problems from Exercise B.

I can make negative statements in the simple present. ☐   I need more practice. ☐

For more practice, go to MyEnglishLab.

Lesson 10 Writing

Write about clothes

1 STUDY THE MODEL

READ. Answer the questions.

> Sue Wong
> My Clothes
>
> At work, I wear a black skirt, a white blouse, and black shoes. At home, I wear jeans, a T-shirt, and sneakers. At school, I wear nice pants, a blouse, and a sweater.

1. What does Sue wear at work?
2. What does Sue wear at home?
3. What does Sue wear at school?

2 PLAN YOUR WRITING

WORK TOGETHER. Ask and answer the questions.

1. What do you wear at work?
2. What do you wear at home?
3. What do you wear at school?

Writing Skill: Use commas in a list

Use commas between words in a list. For example:
I wear a black skirt, a white blouse, and black shoes.

3 WRITE

Now write about the clothes you wear. Use the frame, the model, the Writing Skill, and your ideas from Exercise 2 to help you.

> At work, I wear ____, ____, and ____.
> At home, I wear ____, ____, and ____. At school, I wear ____, ____, and ____.

4 CHECK YOUR WRITING

WORK TOGETHER. Read your writing aloud with a partner.

WRITING CHECKLIST

☐ The writing answers the questions in Exercise 2.

☐ Each sentence begins with a capital letter.

☐ There are commas between words in a list.

☐ Each sentence ends with a period.

I can use commas between words in a list. ■   I need more practice. ■

For more practice, go to MyEnglishLab.

Lesson 11 Soft Skills at Work

Be professional

1 MEET LOC

Read about one of his workplace skills.

I'm professional. For example, I take care of customers. When a customer is angry, I'm calm.

2 LOC'S PROBLEM

READ. Circle *True* or *False*.

Loc works at a store. He is a cashier. He helps customers every day. He wants the customers to be happy.

One day, there are many customers. They are waiting in line to check out. One customer is angry. The customer says, "Why is there only one cashier? I don't want to wait!"

1. Loc is a manager at a store.   True   False
2. Two customers are waiting in line. True   False
3. A customer is angry.   True   False

3 LOC'S SOLUTION

A WORK TOGETHER. Loc is professional. What is the professional thing to do? Explain your answer.

1. Loc asks the customer, "Do you want to talk to the manager?"
2. Loc tells the customer, "I'm sorry. We're very busy now. I'll be with you in a minute."
3. Loc tells the customer, "If you can't wait, you can come back later."
4. Loc says, "_____."

B ROLE-PLAY. Look at your answers to 3A. Role-play Loc's conversation.

Show what you know!

1. **THINK ABOUT IT.** How are you professional at work? Give examples.

2. **WRITE ABOUT IT.** Now write your example in your Skills Log.

   I say "Please" and "Thank you" at work.

3. **PRESENT IT.** Give a short presentation to show how you are professional.

I can give an example from my life of being professional. ☐

Unit Review: Go back to page 85. Which goals can you check off?

6 Home, Sweet Home

PREVIEW
Look at the picture. Where are the people? Why are they there?

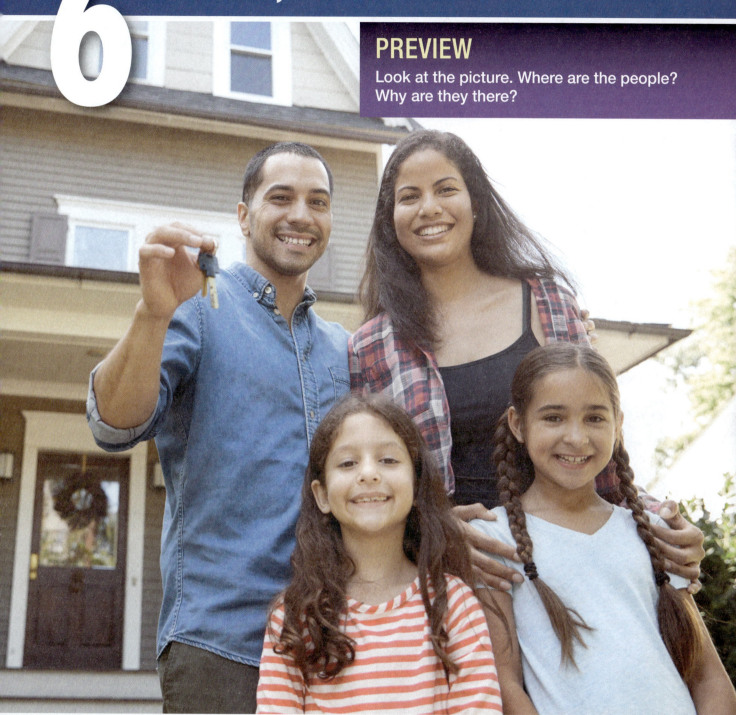

UNIT GOALS

- Name the rooms and things in a home
- Talk about a house for rent
- Ask about an apartment for rent
- Read, write, and give addresses
- Read housing ads
- Give directions
- **Academic skill:** Read again and again to understand a reading better
- **Writing skill:** Use details in your writing
- **Workplace soft skill:** Find information

105

Lesson 1

Vocabulary

Rooms and things in a home

A **PREDICT.** Look at the pictures. What do you see? What are the rooms and things in a home?

D is a bedroom.
Number 14 is a bathtub.

B ▶ **LISTEN AND POINT.** Then listen and repeat.

106 Unit 6, Lesson 1

Vocabulary

Rooms and things in a home

A. kitchen	B. dining room	C. living room	D. bedroom	E. bathroom
1. refrigerator	5. chair	7. lamp	10. closet	13. shower
2. microwave	6. table	8. sofa	11. bed	14. bathtub
3. stove		9. coffee table	12. dresser	15. toilet
4. sink				

C GIVE EXAMPLES. Student A, look at the pictures on page 106. Name the things in a room. Student B, guess the room.

A: A table and chairs.
B: Is it the living room?
A: No.
B: Is it the dining room?
A: Yes.

D DRAW A PICTURE. Student A, look at the pictures and the list of things in a home. Draw a picture of one thing. Students B and C, guess.

B: A dresser.
A: No.
C: A refrigerator.
A: Right.

Study Tip

Use sticky notes

Write words on sticky notes. Put the notes on the things in your home. Look at the notes and say the words.

Show what you know!

1. **THINK ABOUT IT.** Think about your dream home. Write a list of rooms.

2. **TALK ABOUT IT.** Talk about your dream home.

   My dream home has two bathrooms. It has a living room, a dining room, a kitchen, and three bedrooms.

   My dream home
   two bathrooms
   a living room
   a dining room

3. **WRITE ABOUT IT.** Now write a sentence about your dream home.

   My dream home has _____.

I can name the rooms and things in a home. ■   I need more practice.

For more practice, go to MyEnglishLab.

Lesson 2

Listening and Speaking

Talk about a house for rent

1 BEFORE YOU LISTEN

CHOOSE. Write the words under the pictures.

| new | old | large | small |

a _new_ kitchen   an _____ kitchen   a _____ bathroom   a _____ bathroom

| dark | sunny | expensive | inexpensive |

a _____ bedroom   a _____ bedroom   an _____ house   an _____ house

2 LISTEN

Dan   Emily

A   PREDICT. Look at the picture. Dan and Emily are looking at an ad for a house. What are they talking about?

B   ▶ LISTEN. Complete the sentence.

Dan says the house looks _____.

a. inexpensive   b. great   c. large

C   ▶ LISTEN FOR DETAILS. Complete the sentence.

The house has two bedrooms and a _____.

a. large kitchen   b. dining room

D   ▶ EXPAND. Listen to the whole conversation. What's wrong with the house?

It's _____.

a. old   b. very expensive   c. not in the U.S.

Listening and Speaking

3 CONVERSATION

A ▶ **LISTEN AND READ.** Then listen and repeat.

A: Oh, wow! This house looks great!
B: Really?
A: Yes. There are two bedrooms and a large kitchen.
B: What about a dining room?
A: Well, no. There's no dining room.

B **WORK TOGETHER.** Practice the conversation in Exercise A.

C **CREATE.** Make new conversations. Use the information in the boxes.

A: Oh, wow! This house looks great!
B: Really?
A: Yes. There are two bedrooms and a _____.
B: What about a _____?
A: Well, no. There's no _____.

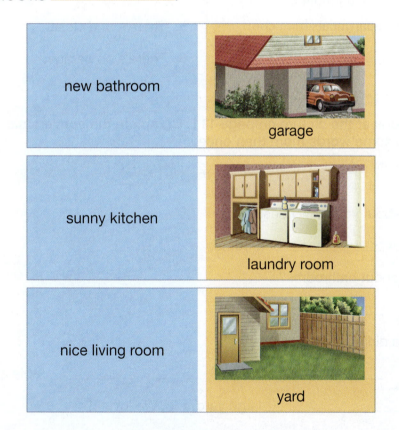

new bathroom	garage
sunny kitchen	laundry room
nice living room	yard

D **ROLE-PLAY.** Make your own conversations about a home.

I can talk about a house for rent. ☐   I need more practice. ☐

For more practice, go to MyEnglishLab.

Lesson 3 Grammar

There is/There are

There is/There are					
There is / There's	a / one	bathroom.	There is / There's	no	dining room.
There are	two	bedrooms.	There are		closets.

Grammar Watch

Contraction
There's = There is

A INTERPRET. Read the apartment ad. Circle *True* or *False*. Correct the false sentences.

FOR RENT

Large one-bedroom apartment with dining room, new bathroom, and new kitchen. Five closets! Garage. $700/month.

email Tom at tom@apartments4rent.com

1. ~~There are two bedrooms.~~ *There's one bedroom.*   True   (False)
2. There's one bathroom.   True   False
3. There's no dining room.   True   False
4. There's a new kitchen.   True   False
5. There's one closet.   True   False
6. There's no garage.   True   False

B COMPLETE. Look at the picture on page 111. Complete the conversation. Use the words in the box. Use some words more than once.

| there's a | there are two | there's no |

A: So, tell me about your new house!

B: Well, __there are two__ bedrooms.
                1.

A: Nice! What about bathrooms?

B: _____ bathrooms.
       2.

A: Great. And a dining room?

B: _____ dining room, but _____ table and chairs in the
       3.   4.
   kitchen. _____ large yard, too. We love it!
              5.

110 Unit 6, Lesson 3

Grammar

C WRITE. Look at the picture of the house. What's in each room? What's *not* in each room? Write sentences. Use *there is*, *there are*, *there's no*, and *there are no*.

In the parents' bedroom, there's a bed, a table, and a lamp. There are no pictures.

In the children's bedroom,

In the upstairs bathroom,

In the living room,

In the kitchen,

In the downstairs bathroom,

Show what you know!

1. TALK ABOUT IT. Talk about things in the rooms of your home.

A: In my bedroom, there's a bed and a dresser.
B: What about closets?
A: No, there are no closets.
C: In my bathroom . . .

2. WRITE ABOUT IT. Now write two sentences about a room in your home.

In my bedroom, there is a _____.
There is no _____.

I can use *there is/there are*. □   I need more practice. □

For more practice, go to MyEnglishLab.

Unit 6, Lesson 3 **111**

Lesson 4 Reading

Read about smoke alarms

1 BEFORE YOU READ

A   LABEL. Write the vocabulary words from the box on the lines.

| the ceiling | a landlord | a smoke alarm | renters |

1. _____
2. _____
3. _____
4. _____

B   MAKE CONNECTIONS. Are there smoke alarms in your home? What rooms are they in?

2 READ

▶ Listen and read.

> **Academic Skill: Read again and again**
>
> Read the article. Then read it again and again. Every time you read it, you learn more. One time is not enough.

Smoke Alarms

Home fires are dangerous. Every year in the U.S., about 2,500 people die from home fires. Smoke alarms save lives. They make a loud noise when a fire starts. Smoke alarms give people time to leave their homes before a fire gets too big.

5   **Which parts of the home need smoke alarms?**
Every bedroom needs a smoke alarm. Every floor of a home needs a smoke alarm. When there is no bedroom on a floor, the living room needs a smoke alarm. It is good to have a smoke alarm near the stairs, too. Smoke alarms go on or near the ceiling.

10 **Which parts of the home do not need smoke alarms?**
Most kitchens do not need smoke alarms. A smoke alarm should not be close to the stove or microwave. Then it will go off when someone cooks! A smoke alarm should never be near a window or door.

15 **Who buys the smoke alarms?**
People who own a home need to buy smoke alarms. But renters do not need to buy them. The law says their landlord needs to put smoke alarms in their home to make sure they are safe.

A smoke alarm going off

FLOOR PLAN

SMOKE ALARMS

112   Unit 6, Lesson 4

Reading

3 CLOSE READING

CITE EVIDENCE. Answer the questions. Where is the information? Write the line numbers.

Lines

1. How do smoke alarms help people?
   a. They stop fires from starting.
   b. They pour water on fires.
   c. They let people know when a fire starts.   _____

2. What's a good place for a smoke alarm?
   a. near a door
   b. near stairs
   c. near a window   _____

3. Which place needs a smoke alarm?
   a. the kitchen
   b. the bedroom
   c. the yard   _____

4. What can make the smoke alarm go off?
   a. a refrigerator
   b. a stove
   c. a sink   _____

5. Who needs to buy smoke alarms for an apartment or a house?
   a. the person who owns it
   b. the person who rents it
   c. any person with children   _____

4 SUMMARIZE

Complete the summary with the words in the box.

| bedroom | fire | landlords | smoke alarms |

Every home needs (1) _____. A smoke alarm can save your life when there is a (2) _____. There needs to be a smoke alarm in every (3) _____ of a house or apartment. Renters do not need to buy them. All (4) _____ need to put them in the right places in their buildings.

Show what you know!

1. **DRAW A PICTURE.** Draw a floor plan of your home. Draw your smoke alarms on the plan.

2. **TALK ABOUT IT.** Show your plan to your partner. Are the smoke alarms in good places? Explain.

3. **WRITE ABOUT IT.** Now write about your floor plan.

   One smoke alarm is in the _____. Another smoke alarm is in the _____.

I can read again and again to understand a reading better. ☐   I need more practice. ☐

To read more, go to MyEnglishLab.

Unit 6, Lesson 4   **113**

Lesson 5: Listening and Speaking

Ask about an apartment for rent

1 BEFORE YOU LISTEN

IDENTIFY. Look at the pictures. Complete the sentences with the words from the box. You will not use every word.

| appliances | furnished | unfurnished |

1. The _____ room has a sofa, two armchairs, and a coffee table.
2. The two kitchen areas have new _____.

Studio apartments for rent

furnished

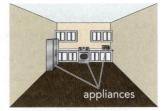
unfurnished

2 LISTEN

Amy   Lei

A PREDICT. Look at the picture. Amy and Lei are talking to a building manager. What are they talking about?

B ▶ LISTEN. Complete the sentence.

There's a _____ apartment for rent.
a. one-bedroom   b. two-bedroom

C ▶ LISTEN FOR DETAILS. Cross out the incorrect words.

1. The apartment is on the **second / seventh** floor.
2. The apartment has **beds / a dresser**.
3. The apartment has a **stove / refrigerator**.

D ▶ EXPAND. Listen to the whole conversation. Complete the sentences.

1. Amy _____ interested in the apartment.
   a. is   b. is not

2. Lei _____ interested in the apartment.
   a. is   b. is not

Listening and Speaking

3 PRONUNCIATION

A ▶ **PRACTICE.** Listen. Then listen and repeat.

• floor lamp   There's a floor lamp.

• dining room   It's in the dining room.

Stress in compound nouns

In two-word nouns, the first word is stressed.

B ▶ **APPLY.** Listen to the sentences. Mark (•) the stress.

1. There's a coffee table.
2. There are two desk lamps.
3. There's a smoke alarm.
4. It's in the living room.

4 CONVERSATION

A ▶ **LISTEN AND READ.** Then listen and repeat.

A: Excuse me. Is there an apartment for rent in this building?
B: Yes, there is. There's a one-bedroom apartment on the second floor.
A: Oh, great. Is it furnished?
B: Well, yes and no. There's a dresser, but no beds.
A: Oh. Well, are there appliances?
B: Uh, yes and no. There's a stove, but no refrigerator.

B **WORK TOGETHER.** Practice the conversation in Exercise A.

C **CREATE.** Make new conversations. Use the words in the boxes.

A: Excuse me. Is there an apartment for rent in this building?
B: Yes, there is. There's a _____ apartment on the second floor.
A: Oh, great. Is it furnished?
B: Well, yes and no. There's a _____, but no _____.

studio	sofa	coffee table
two-bedroom	desk	lamp
three-bedroom	table	chairs

D **ROLE-PLAY.** Make your own conversations. Student A, you are looking for an apartment. Student B, you are the building manager.

I can ask about an apartment for rent. ▪   I need more practice. ▪

For more practice, go to MyEnglishLab.

Unit 6, Lesson 5 **115**

Lesson 6 Grammar

Is there/Are there

Is there/Are there		Yes,		No,	
Is there	a table?		there is.		there isn't.
Are there	lamps?		there are.		there aren't.

A **IDENTIFY.** Cross out the incorrect words.

1. **A: Is there / ~~Are there~~** a bathtub in the bathroom?
   B: No, **there is / there isn't**. There's a shower.

2. **A: Is there / Are there** closets in the bedrooms?
   B: Yes, **there is / there are**. There's a closet in each bedroom.

3. **A: Is there / Are there** table lamps in the living room?
   B: No, **there are / there aren't**. There are floor lamps.

4. **A: Is there / Are there** a coffee table in the living room?
   B: Yes, **there is / there isn't**. There's a small coffee table and a sofa.

5. **A: Is there / Are there** a dining room in the apartment?
   B: No, **there isn't / there aren't**.

6. **A: Is there / Are there** a sunny kitchen?
   B: Yes, **there is / there are**. The kitchen is very sunny.

7. **A: Is there / Are there** a table in the kitchen?
   B: Yes, **there is / there are**. There's a table and four chairs.

B ▶ **SELF-ASSESS.** Listen and check your answers.

C **WORK TOGETHER.** Practice the conversations in Exercise A.

Grammar

D **WRITE.** Make questions. Then look at the picture and write short answers.

1. there / two / are / tables
   A: *Are there two tables?*
   B: *Yes, there are.*

2. lamps / are / on the tables / there
   A: _____
   B: _____

3. a sofa / in the room / there / is
   A: _____
   B: _____

4. book / on the sofa / is / there / a
   A: _____
   B: _____

5. pictures / there / are / in the room
   A: _____
   B: _____

Show what you know!

1. **THINK ABOUT IT.** Write three questions about your partner's home. Use *Is there* and *Are there*.

   Is there a lamp in your living room?
   _____
   _____
   _____

2. **TALK ABOUT IT.** Ask your questions. Answer your partner's questions.

   A: *Is there a lamp in your living room?*
   B: *Yes, there is. There's a lamp near the sofa.*

3. **WRITE ABOUT IT.** Now write about your partner's home.

   There's a lamp near the sofa in Ed's living room.
   _____
   _____

I can ask and answer questions with *Is there* and *Are there*. ◼   I need more practice. ◼

For more practice, go to MyEnglishLab.

Lesson 7: Workplace, Life, and Community Skills

Read addresses and housing ads

1 SAY ADDRESSES

A ▶ **LISTEN AND READ.** Then listen and repeat.

- ★ 6103 Lake Drive, Apartment 27
- ★ 98 East High Street
- ★ 45720 Foothill Road
- ★ 3095 Sunset Boulevard
- ★ 1463 2nd Avenue, Apartment 10
- ★ 852 Mission Street, Apartment 903

B **WORK TOGETHER.** Ask about addresses. Use the addresses in Exercise 1A.

A: What's the address, please?
B: It's 6103 Lake Drive, Apartment 27.

2 WRITE ADDRESSES

A **LOCATE.** Find the words in Exercise 1A for each abbreviation below.

1. St. _Street_
2. Ave. _____
3. Dr. _____
4. Rd. _____
5. Blvd. _____
6. Apt. _____

B **USE ABBREVIATIONS.** Write the addresses in Exercise 1A with abbreviations.

1. _____
2. _____
3. _____
4. _____
5. _____
6. _____

C **WORK TOGETHER.** Ask three classmates for an address in their neighborhood. Write the addresses. Use abbreviations.

1451 Pine St., Apt. 3

A: What's the address?
B: It's 1451 Pine Street, Apartment 3.

D **GO ONLINE.** Find the address of a home for rent in or near your neighborhood.

I can read, write, and give addresses. ■   I need more practice. ■

Workplace, Life, and Community Skills

3 READ HOUSING ADS

A **LABEL.** Write the words under the pictures.

air conditioning   cable   heat   Internet   parking   pets

1. _____   2. _____   3. _____

4. _____   5. _____   6. _____

B **INTERPRET.** Read the housing ads. Answer the questions.

A New 3 bedroom 2 bathroom apartment
Air conditioning and heat included. In unit laundry. High speed internet. Pets. 2 parking spaces.
● $3,000/mo

B Large 3 bedroom 1 bathroom apartment
Large closets. Laundry in the building. Cable and Internet ready. No pets. Street parking.
● $2,000/mo

Which apartment . . .

1. has two bathrooms? ____
2. has good closets? ____
3. has air conditioning? ____
4. is $2,000 a month? ____
5. has laundry in the apartment? ____
6. has no parking? ____
7. has cable? ____
8. is pet friendly? ____

C **TALK ABOUT IT.** Which apartment do you like?

A: Which apartment do you like?
B: I like A.
A: Why?
B: It is new. It has two bathrooms.

D **PRESENT.** Tell your class which apartment your partner likes and why.

I can read housing ads. ▪   I need more practice. ▪

For more practice, go to MyEnglishLab.

Unit 6, Lesson 7   **119**

Lesson 8

Listening and Speaking

Give directions

1 BEFORE YOU LISTEN

A **MAKE CONNECTIONS.** How do you get directions to a store? Do you use a GPS, call the store, or look at a map?

a. I use a GPS.   b. I call the store.   c. I look at a map.

B **LOCATE.** Look at the map in Exercise A. Point to North, South, East, and West.

2 LISTEN

A ▶ **LISTEN.** A couple wants to go to Joe's Furniture Store. What are they talking about?

a. the prices at Joe's
b. the directions to Joe's
c. the furniture at Joe's

B ▶ **LISTEN FOR DETAILS.** Complete the directions to Joe's Furniture Store.

1. Go _____ on Route 1.
   a. north   b. south

2. Turn _____ on Fifth Avenue.
   a. right   b. left

3. Continue for one _____.
   a. block   b. mile

4. It's _____ a park.
   a. across from   b. next to

C ▶ **EXPAND.** Listen to the whole conversation. Complete the sentence.

Joe's Furniture Store is _____.
a. closed on Sundays
b. open on Sundays until 5:00
c. open on Sundays until 7:00

Listening and Speaking

3 CONVERSATION

A ▶ **LISTEN AND READ.** Then listen and repeat.

A: How do we get to Joe's Furniture Store?
B: Let me check on my phone. OK. First, go north on Route 1 for three miles.
A: North?
B: Uh-huh. Then turn left on Fifth Avenue. Continue for one block. It's on the left, across from a park.
A: That sounds easy!

B **WORK TOGETHER.** Practice the conversation in Exercise A.

C **CREATE.** Make new conversations. Use the words in the boxes.

A: How do we get to _____?
B: Let me check on my phone. OK. First, go _____ on Route 1 for three miles.
A: _____?
B: Uh-huh. Then turn left on Fifth Avenue. Continue for one block. It's on the left, across from a _____.
A: That sounds easy!

Sam's Appliances	south	computer store
Ali's Air Conditioners	east	school
Ken's Kitchen	west	hospital

D **MAKE CONNECTIONS.** Make your own conversations. Ask for directions from your school to your partner's favorite store.

A: What's your favorite store?
B: I like Computer World.
A: How do you get there from here?
B: Go north on ...

I can give directions. ■

I need more practice. ■

For more practice, go to MyEnglishLab.

Unit 6, Lesson 8 121

Lesson 9 Grammar
Prepositions of direction and location

Prepositions of direction and location						
You're coming	from	home.		The store is	in	Riverside.
				Turn left	at	the second light.
				The store is	on	Fifth Avenue.
You're going	to	Joe's Furniture Store.		It's	at	231 Fifth Avenue.
				It's	on	the corner.

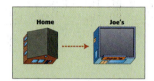 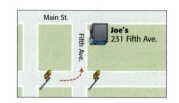

A **IDENTIFY.** Cross out the incorrect words.

Directions to Our New Apartment
- Our apartment is **on / in** Tenth Avenue **in / at** Greenville.
- If you're coming **from / to** the school, go **from / to** the first light.
- Turn right **at / on** the light. You're now **on / in** Tenth Avenue.
- Our apartment is **on / to** the corner of Tenth Avenue and Elm Street. It's **in / at** 3245 Tenth Avenue.

B **COMPLETE.** Use the words in the box.

~~at~~   at   from   in   on   to

A: Where is Eric's office?

B: It's ___*at*___ 649 Second Avenue _____ Greenville.
                 1.   2.

A: OK. How do I get there _____ here?
                                 3.

B: It's easy. Go _____ First Street and turn right _____ the light.
                      4.   5.
Continue for three blocks. Eric's office is on the right.

A: Is there a coffee shop near his office?

B: Yes. There's a nice coffee shop _____ Second Avenue.
                                         6.

I can use prepositions of direction and location.   I need more practice.

For more practice, go to MyEnglishLab.

Lesson 10 Writing

Write about your favorite room at home

1 STUDY THE MODEL

READ. Answer the questions.

> Amy Krupin
> My Favorite Room
>
> My favorite room at home is the living room. It's large and sunny. There are three big windows. There's a new sofa and a coffee table. There's a lamp next to the sofa. There's a large TV. The best part is the wall with all my family photos.

1. What is Amy's favorite room?
2. What's the room like?
3. What furniture is in the room?
4. What does Amy think is the best part?

2 PLAN YOUR WRITING

WORK TOGETHER. Ask and answer the questions.

1. What's your favorite room at home?
2. What's the room like?
3. What furniture is in the room?
4. What's the best part?

Writing Skill: Use details
Put details in your writing. For example:
No details: There are windows.
With details: There are (three) (big) windows.

3 WRITE

Now write about your favorite room at home. Use the frame, the model, the Writing Skill, and your ideas from Exercise 2 to help you.

> My favorite room at home is the ____.
> It's ____ and ____. There are ____.
> There's a ____ and a ____. There's a ____ next to the ____. The best part is ____.

4 CHECK YOUR WRITING

WORK TOGETHER. Read your writing aloud with a partner.

WRITING CHECKLIST
☐ The writing answers the questions in Exercise 2.
☐ There are details.

I can use details in my writing. ■   I need more practice. ■

For more practice, go to MyEnglishLab.

Lesson 11: Soft Skills at Work

Find information

1 MEET MILOS

Read about one of his workplace skills.

I'm good at finding information. When I can't answer a question, I find an answer. For example, I go online or I ask a co-worker.

2 MILOS'S PROBLEM

READ. Circle *True* or *False*.

Milos is an assistant building manager. He takes care of problems in the building. Sometimes he shows apartments to renters.

One day a family looks at an apartment. They ask about the neighborhood schools and stores. Milos doesn't live in the neighborhood. He can't answer their question.

1. Milos shows apartments to renters every day.   True   False
2. Milos lives in the building.   True   False
3. Milos knows the answer to the family's questions.   True   False

3 MILOS'S SOLUTION

A WORK TOGETHER. Milos is good at finding information. What is the right thing to say? Explain your answer.

1. Milos says, "I'm sorry. I don't know. I don't live in the neighborhood."
2. Milos says, "Ask the building manager. He knows the neighborhood."
3. Milos says, "I'm sorry. I don't know. Let me ask the building manager."
4. Milos says, "_____."

B ROLE-PLAY. Look at your answer to 3A. Role-play Milos's conversation.

Show what you know!

1. **THINK ABOUT IT.** What do you do when you don't know the answer to a question at school? At work? At home? Give examples.

2. **WRITE ABOUT IT.** Now write your example in your Skills Log.

   Sometimes I don't know a new word. I ask my teacher.

I can give an example from my life of finding information. ■

Unit Review: Go back to page 105. Which goals can you check off?

7 Day After Day

PREVIEW
Look at the picture. What do you see? Where are the people?

UNIT GOALS

- ☐ Name daily activities
- ☐ Make plans with someone
- ☐ Talk about work schedules
- ☐ Read and complete a time sheet
- ☐ Talk about weekend activities
- ☐ Talk about ways to relax
- ☐ **Academic skill:** Make predictions
- ☐ **Writing skill:** Use a capital letter for days of the week
- ☐ **Workplace soft skill:** Be a team player

125

Lesson 1 Vocabulary
Daily activities

A **PREDICT.** Look at the pictures. What do you see? What are the activities?

Number 4 is "eat breakfast."

B ▶ **LISTEN AND POINT.** Then listen and repeat.

C ▶ **LISTEN AND POINT.** Listen and point to the time in each picture. Then listen and repeat.

126 Unit 7, Lesson 1

Vocabulary

Daily activities

1. get up
2. take a shower
3. get dressed
4. eat breakfast
5. go to work
6. get home
7. exercise
8. cook dinner
9. eat dinner
10. wash the dishes
11. do homework
12. watch TV
13. go to bed

D **WORK TOGETHER.** Look at the pictures on page 126. Student A, ask about an activity. Student B, say the time.

A: What time does he go to work?
B: At 8:00.
A: Right!
B: What time does he . . . ?

E **ACT IT OUT.** Student A, look at the pictures and the word list. Act out an activity. Student B, guess.

B: Wash the dishes?
A: No.
B: Cook dinner?
A: Right!

> **Study Tip**
>
> **Write personal sentences**
>
> Write sentences about your daily activities. Include a time for each activity.

Show what you know!

1. **THINK ABOUT IT.** Think about your daily activities. Write the activities in the chart.

Morning	Afternoon	Evening

2. **TALK ABOUT IT.** Talk about your daily activities.

A: What do you do in the morning?
B: I get up at 5:30, and I go to work at 7:00.
A: What do you do in the afternoon?

3. **WRITE ABOUT IT.** Now write a sentence about your daily activities.

I _____ at _____.

I can name daily activities. ◼   I need more practice. ◼

For more practice, go to MyEnglishLab.

Unit 7, Lesson 1

Lesson 2

Listening and Speaking

Make plans with someone

1 BEFORE YOU LISTEN

GIVE EXAMPLES. What do you do in your free time? Check (✓) the activities. What other activities do you do?

☐ go to the movies   ☐ go to the mall   ☐ play soccer   ☐ go to the park

2 LISTEN

A PREDICT. Look at the picture. What are they doing?

B ▶ LISTEN. Complete the sentence.

The women are making plans for _____.
a. tomorrow   b. tonight   c. Sunday

C ▶ LISTEN FOR DETAILS. Complete the sentences.

1. On Saturdays, Mia _____.
   a. works   b. goes to school   c. babysits for her cousin

2. Mia gets home at _____ on Saturdays.
   a. 6:00   b. 7:00   c. 8:00

D ▶ EXPAND. Listen to the whole conversation. What does Sue want to do on Saturday?

a.    b.

Listening and Speaking

3 PRONUNCIATION

A ▶ **PRACTICE.** Listen. Then listen and repeat.

When do you get home?   Where do you work?
What do you mean?   What do you do?

> **The weak pronunciation of *do you* in questions**
>
> In conversation, *do you* often sounds like "d'ya."

B ▶ **COMPLETE.** Listen. Complete the sentences.

1. _What do you_ do in your free time?
2. _____ have English class?
3. _____ go to work?
4. _____ exercise?

4 CONVERSATION

A ▶ **LISTEN AND READ.** Then listen and repeat.

A: Are you free tomorrow? How about a movie?
B: Sorry, I'm busy. I work on Saturdays.
A: Oh. Well, when do you get home?
B: At 8:00.

B **WORK TOGETHER.** Practice the conversation in Exercise A.

C **CREATE.** Make new conversations. Use the information in the boxes.

A: Are you free tomorrow?
   How about a movie?
B: Sorry, I'm busy.
   I _____
   on _____.
A: Oh. Well, when do you get home?
B: At _____.

D **MAKE CONNECTIONS.** Make your own conversations. Use different activities, days, and times.

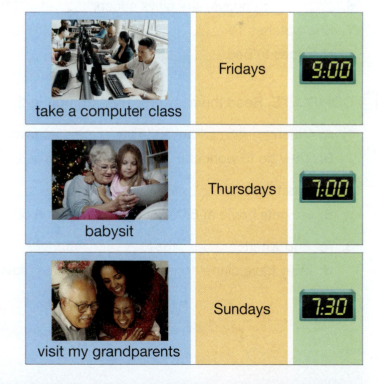

take a computer class | Fridays | 9:00
babysit | Thursdays | 7:00
visit my grandparents | Sundays | 7:30

I can make plans with someone. ▪   I need more practice. ▪

For more practice, go to MyEnglishLab.

Unit 7, Lesson 2   129

Grammar

Lesson 3: Simple present: *When* and *What time*; Prepositions of time

Simple present: Questions with *When* and *What time*

When	does	he	work?
What time	do	you	

Prepositions of time

He works **on** Mondays.

He works **from** 9:00 **to** 5:00.

He gets home **at** 6:00.

Grammar Watch

- on Mondays = every Monday
- Use *from . . . to . . .* with days and times. This shows when an activity starts and ends.
- For more prepositions of time, see page 259.

A COMPLETE. Use *on*, *at*, *from*, or *to*.

1. Ava starts work ___at___ 8:00 ___on___ Mondays.
2. She works _____ Monday _____ Friday.
3. _____ Fridays, she has dinner with her father. They eat _____ 7:00.
4. Ava has English class _____ 10:00 _____ 12:00 _____ Saturdays.
5. She meets her friends at the mall _____ 3:00.
6. _____ Sundays, she plays soccer _____ 11:00.
7. She watches TV _____ 9:00 _____ 11:00, and she goes to bed _____ 11:30.

B COMPLETE. Read the answers. Then complete the questions.

1. **A:** When ___do___ Paul and Ella ___go___ to work?
   B: They go to work at 9:00. They work from Monday to Friday.

2. **A:** What time _____ Paul _____ _____?
   B: He gets home at 6:00. Ella gets home at 6:30.

3. **A:** And when _____ they _____ dinner?
   B: They have dinner together at 7:00. It's their favorite time of the day.

Grammar

C **INTERPRET.** Look at Ben's schedule. Write questions about his activities. Use the words in parentheses.

Fri	Sat	Sun
work—8:00	soccer game—9:00 study with Maria—1:00–3:00	exercise—2:00–3:00 dinner with Mom—6:00

1. *What time does Ben start work on Fridays?*
   (What time / Ben / start work on Fridays)

2. _____
   (What time / he / play soccer on Saturdays)

3. _____
   (What time / he and Maria / study on Saturdays)

4. _____
   (When / he / exercise)

5. _____
   (When / he and his mother / have dinner)

D **WORK TOGETHER.** Ask and answer the questions in Exercise C.

Show what you know!

1. **THINK ABOUT IT.** What time do you do each activity? Complete the "You" columns.

	Friday			Saturday		
	get up	eat dinner	watch TV	get up	eat dinner	watch TV
You						
Partner						

2. **TALK ABOUT IT.** What time does your partner do each activity? Complete the chart.

   A: *What time do you get up on Fridays?*
   B: *I get up at 7:00. What about you?*

3. **WRITE ABOUT IT.** Now write about the time you and your partner do the activities.

   I get up at 7:00 on Fridays. Paul gets up at 7:30.

I can ask questions with *when* and *what time* and use prepositions of time. ☐   I need more practice. ☐

For more practice, go to MyEnglishLab.

Lesson 4: Workplace, Life, and Community Skills

Read work schedules and time sheets

1 TALK ABOUT WORK SCHEDULES

A MAKE CONNECTIONS. Look at the calendar. Which days do you work? Which days do you go to school?

December
Mon	Tue	Wed	Thu	Fri	Sat	Sun
3	4	5	6	7	8	9

B LOCATE. Write the abbreviations for the days.

Monday _Mon_   Tuesday _____   Wednesday _____   Thursday _____
Friday _____   Saturday _____   Sunday _____

C WORK TOGETHER. Look at the work schedules. Ask and answer questions. Take turns.

A: When does Ming work?
B: She works from Tuesday to Saturday, from 11:00 to 5:00.

The Computer Store
Work Schedule: December 3–9

Schedule | My Account | Help?

Employee	12/3 MON	12/4 TUE	12/5 WED	12/6 THU	12/7 FRI	12/8 SAT	12/9 SUN
Ming Chu		11:00 A.M.–5:00 P.M.	11:00 A.M.–5:00 P.M.	11:00 A.M.–5:00 P.M.	11:00 A.M.–5:00 P.M.	11:00 A.M.–5:00 P.M.	
Pedro Molina	2:30 P.M.–8:30 P.M.	2:30 P.M.–8:30 P.M.	2:30 P.M.–8:30 P.M.	2:30 P.M.–8:30 P.M.	2:30 P.M.–8:30 P.M.		
Maya Kabir		7:00 A.M.–4:00 P.M.		7:00 A.M.–4:00 P.M.		7:00 A.M.–4:00 P.M.	
Danny Costa			6:30 A.M.–10:30 A.M.	6:30 A.M.–10:30 A.M.	6:30 A.M.–10:30 A.M.		
Dawit Alemu			3:00 P.M.–10:00 P.M.	3:00 P.M.–10:00 P.M.	3:00 P.M.–10:00 P.M.	3:00 P.M.–10:00 P.M.	3:00 P.M.–10:00 P.M.

I can talk about work schedules. ■   I need more practice. ■

For more practice, go to MyEnglishLab.

Workplace, Life, and Community Skills

2 READ AND COMPLETE A TIME SHEET

A **MATCH.** Look at Nancy's time sheet. Match the words and definitions. Write the letter.

___ 1. employee
___ 2. ID #
___ 3. Time In
___ 4. Time Out

a. identification number
b. the time you finish work
c. worker
d. the time you start work

TIME SHEET

EMPLOYEE NAME — **EMPLOYEE I.D. #** 987-65-4321
Last: Johnson   First: Nancy

Week ending 7/15

DAY	TIME IN	TIME OUT	HOURS
Mon	8:30 A.M.	1:00 P.M.	4.5
Tue	9:00 A.M.	5:00 P.M.	8
Wed	8:30 A.M.	3:30 P.M.	7
Thu			
Fri			
Sat	12:00 P.M.	5:00 P.M.	5
Sun			

TOTAL HOURS: 24.5

B **INTERPRET.** Look at the time sheet in Exercise 2A. Complete the sentences.

1. Nancy worked on _Monday, Tuesday, Wednesday, and Saturday_.
2. On Tuesday, she started work at _____.
3. On _____, she finished work at 3:30.
4. She didn't work on _____.
5. She worked _____ hours on Monday.

C **APPLY.** Read the information. Complete your time sheet for the week.

You work from 7:00 A.M. to 3:00 P.M. from Tuesday to Saturday. Your employee I.D. number is 00312. Today is Monday, March 11.

D **GO ONLINE.** Find the next event on your calendar. What day is it?

_____
_____

TIME SHEET

EMPLOYEE NAME — **EMPLOYEE I.D.** _____
First: ____ Last: ____

Week ending _____

DAY	TIME IN	TIME OUT	HOURS
Mon			
Tue			
Wed			
Thu			
Fri			
Sat			
Sun			

TOTAL HOURS:

I can read and complete a time sheet. ▮   I need more practice. ▮

For more practice, go to MyEnglishLab.

Lesson 5 Listening and Speaking
Talk about weekend activities

1 BEFORE YOU LISTEN

GIVE EXAMPLES. In the U.S. and Canada, many people work from Monday to Friday. They are free on the weekend (Saturday and Sunday). Are you free on the weekend? What do you do? Check (✓) the activities. What other activities do you do?

☐ clean

☐ spend time with my family

☐ shop for food

2 LISTEN

A ▶ **LISTEN.** Look at the picture. Ling and Tony are leaving work. Listen to the conversation. What are they talking about?

   a. homework   **b.** weekend activities   **c.** work

B ▶ **LISTEN FOR DETAILS.** Complete the schedules.

Ling | Saturday | Sunday
_____ | _____

Tony | Saturday | Sunday
_____ | _____

C ▶ **EXPAND.** Listen to the whole conversation. Complete the sentence.

In Tony's home, they call Sunday _____.
a. "work day"   **b.** "play day"   **c.** "fun day"

Listening and Speaking

3 CONVERSATION

A ▶ **LISTEN AND READ.** Then listen and repeat.

A: Gee, I'm so glad it's Friday!
B: Me, too. What do you usually do on the weekend?
A: Well, I always clean the house on Saturdays, and I always spend time with my family on Sundays. What about you?
B: I usually shop for food on Saturdays, and I sometimes go to the park on Sundays.

B **WORK TOGETHER.** Practice the conversation in Exercise A.

C **CREATE.** Make new conversations. Use the pictures.

A: Gee, I'm so glad it's Friday!
B: Me, too. What do you usually do on the weekend?
A: Well, I always _____ on Saturdays, and I always _____ on Sundays. What about you?
B: I usually _____ on Saturdays, and I sometimes _____ on Sundays.

cook

ride my bike

stay home

play basketball

read

go dancing

do the laundry

go to the beach

wash my car

play cards

play video games

go swimming

D **MAKE CONNECTIONS.** Make your own conversations. Talk about your weekend activities.

I can talk about weekend activities. ▪   I need more practice. ▪

For more practice, go to MyEnglishLab.

Lesson 6 Grammar

Adverbs of frequency

Adverbs of frequency	
I	always / usually / sometimes / never clean on Saturdays.

Grammar Watch

always 100%
usually
sometimes
never 0%

A INTERPRET. David is a student at Greenville Adult School. Look at his schedule. Complete the email with *always, usually, sometimes,* or *never,* and the correct form of the verb.

	Mon	Tue	Wed	Thu	Fri	Sat	Sun
7:00	exercise	exercise	exercise	exercise	exercise		
8:00–12:00	class	work	class	work	class		
12:30	lunch	lunch	lunch	lunch	lunch	lunch	lunch
1:00–5:00	work		work		work	work	soccer?

Hi Nicole,

How are you? I'm fine. My new job is great. I __usually__ __work__ in
                                              1. (work)
the afternoon, but I _____ _____ in the morning, too. In my free
                              2. (work)
time, I do a lot of things. I _____ _____ at 7:00 A.M. Then on
                                    3. (exercise)
Mondays, Wednesdays, and Fridays, I _____ _____ class. I
                                              4. (have)
_____ _____ lunch at 12:30. I _____ _____
    5. (have)   6. (work)
on Sundays. It's my only day off! I _____ _____ soccer in the
                                              7. (play)
afternoon. I love Sundays!

Write soon,

David

136 Unit 7, Lesson 6

Grammar

B WRITE. Look at the pictures. Write about David's Sunday activities.

1. *David always visits his family on Sundays.*
   (David / always / on Sundays)

2. _____
   (They / always / at 12:30)

3. _____
   (He and his brothers / sometimes / in the park)

4. _____
   (His father and his sister / usually)

5. _____
   (His mother / usually / after lunch)

6. _____
   (His mother / never / on Sundays)

Show what you know!

1. **TALK ABOUT IT.** Tell your partner two things you always do and one thing you never do on Sundays.

   A: I always eat a big breakfast on Sundays. I always visit my mother on Sundays. I never work on Sundays.
   B: I always ...

2. **WRITE ABOUT IT.** Now write what you and your partner *always do* and *never do* on Sundays.

   I always _____ on Sundays.
   My partner always _____ on Sundays.
   I never _____.
   My partner never _____.

I can use adverbs of frequency. ▪   I need more practice. ▪

For more practice, go to MyEnglishLab.

Lesson 7 Reading

Read about how Americans spend their free time

1 BEFORE YOU READ

A MATCH. Find the meanings for the vocabulary words. Write the letters.

___ 1. chores   a. usually
___ 2. communicate   b. jobs you do at home (like cleaning, cooking)
___ 3. on average   c. talk to other people
___ 4. relax   d. spend time with other people for fun
___ 5. socialize   e. do something fun or just rest

B TALK ABOUT IT. How much free time do you have? What do you do in your free time?

2 READ

▶ Listen and read.

> **Academic Skill: Make predictions**
>
> Before you read an article, guess what it will say. Then read to find out: Were your predictions correct?

FREE TIME

What do American men and women do with their free time? Here are four common activities.

They spend time with family and friends. This is common for both men and women in the U.S. On average, men spend about 38 minutes a day with their family and friends. Women spend about 40 minutes a day with theirs.

They communicate. Many people spend time texting, using email, and talking on the phone. Men spend about 44 minutes a day on these activities. Women spend about 47 minutes a day on them.

They exercise. On average, men exercise or play sports for about 23 minutes a day. Women exercise only 15 minutes a day.

They watch TV. Men watch about 3 hours of TV a day. Women watch less TV. They watch about 2 hours and 30 minutes.

On average, American men have about 5 hours and 30 minutes of free time a day. American women have about 4 hours and 48 minutes. What's one reason American men have more free time? They don't do as many chores at home. They cook and clean for only 36 minutes a day. Women cook and clean for 1 hour and 41 minutes a day!

Source: U.S. Bureau of Labor Statistics

Free Time on an Average Day

- Other (12 minutes)
- Relaxing and thinking (17 minutes)
- Sports, games, and exercise (18 minutes)
- Reading (19 minutes)
- Computer games and other computer activities (25 minutes)
- Communicating and socializing (41 minutes)
- Watching TV (2 hours and 47 minutes)

Total free time = 4 hours 59 minutes
*Americans age 15 and older
Source: U.S. Bureau of Labor Statistics

Reading

3 CLOSE READING

A **CITE EVIDENCE.** Complete the sentences. Where is the information? Write the line number.

                                                                                                          Lines

1. On average, American men _____ for about 3 hours a day.
   a. have free time   b. watch TV   c. spend time with their families   _____

2. On average, women _____ more than men in the U.S.
   a. watch TV   b. exercise or play sports   c. communicate by phone and computer   _____

3. On average, American men have more _____ than American women.
   a. free time   b. ways to relax   c. hours at work   _____

4. On average, American women spend more time _____ than American men.
   a. doing chores   b. sleeping   c. working   _____

B **INTERPRET.** Complete the sentences about the chart.

1. On an average day, Americans watch TV for _____.
2. On an average day, Americans spend _____ communicating and socializing.
3. On an average day, Americans spend 17–19 minutes on each of these activities: _____; _____; and _____.

4 SUMMARIZE

Complete the summary with the words in the box.

| chores | communicate | on average | sports |

Americans often use their free time in these four ways: (a) they spend it with family and friends, (b) they (1) _____ by phone or by computer, (c) they exercise or play (2) _____, and (d) they watch TV. (3) _____, American men have more free time than American women. The men don't do as many (4) _____ at home.

Show what you know!

1. **TALK ABOUT IT.** Talk about the four common activities in the reading. How much time do you spend doing these things?

2. **WRITE ABOUT IT.** Now write about how you spend your free time.

   In my free time, I sometimes _____. I spend about _____ (a day/a week) doing this.

I can make predictions. ☐   I need more practice. ☐

To read more, go to MyEnglishLab.

Lesson 8 — Listening and Speaking

Talk about ways to relax

1 BEFORE YOU LISTEN

MAKE CONNECTIONS. Look at ways to relax. Which activities do you do? How often?

Ways to Relax

- ☐ take a hot bath
- ☐ do puzzles
- ☐ go running
- ☐ knit
- ☐ listen to music
- ☐ take a long walk

2 LISTEN

A ▶ IDENTIFY. Listen to Dr. Sue Miller's podcast about relaxing. Look at the pictures in Exercise 1. Check (✓) the four activities she talks about.

B ▶ LISTEN FOR DETAILS. Complete the sentence. Check (✓) all the correct answers.

Sue Miller says we need to relax. It helps us be better _____.

- ☐ runners
- ☐ students
- ☐ teachers
- ☐ friends
- ☐ workers
- ☐ family members

Listening and Speaking

3 PRONUNCIATION

A ▶ **PRACTICE.** Listen. Then listen and repeat.

wash	I **wash** the dishes after dinner.
washes	He **washes** the dishes in the morning.
relax	We **relax** at night.
relaxes	She **relaxes** on Sundays.
watch	They **watch** TV every night.
watches	He never **watches** TV.

> **Extra syllable in -es endings**
>
> Sometimes the **-es** ending on verbs adds an extra syllable.

B ▶ **APPLY.** Practice saying the sentences. Then listen and repeat.

I **use** a laptop at work.
My brother **uses** a laptop at school.

They **exercise** on the weekend.
He **exercises** in the park.

4 CONVERSATION

A ▶ **LISTEN AND READ.** Then listen and repeat.

A: You look stressed.
B: I *am* stressed. I really need to relax. How do *you* relax?
A: Well, I listen to music.
B: Really? How often?
A: Every day.
B: That's great.

B WORK TOGETHER. Practice the conversation in Exercise A.

C CREATE. Make new conversations. Use the activities on page 140.

D ROLE-PLAY. Make your own conversations. Tell your partner how you relax and how often.

I can talk about ways to relax. ☐   I need more practice. ☐

For more practice, go to MyEnglishLab.

Unit 7, Lesson 8   141

Grammar

Lesson 9
Questions with *How often*; expressions of frequency

Simple present: Questions with *How often*

How often	do	you / we / they	play soccer?
	does	he / she	

Expressions of frequency

Every day.
Once a week.
Twice a week.
Three times a week.

A WRITE. Look at Adam's schedule. Write questions. Use *How often* and the activities in the schedule.

Sun	Mon	Tue	Wed	Thu	Fri	Sat
ride my bike play soccer	have class ride my bike	ride my bike see friends go food shopping	have class ride my bike	ride my bike see friends do laundry	have class ride my bike	ride my bike play soccer

1. *How often does Adam ride his bike?*
2. *How often does he ...?*
3. _____
4. _____
5. _____
6. _____

B WORK TOGETHER. Ask and answer the questions in Exercise A. Give two answers for every question.

A: *How often does Adam play soccer?*
B: *Twice a week. Every Saturday and Sunday.*
A: *Right.*
B: *How often does Adam ...?*

I can ask questions with *How often* and use expressions of frequency. ▪

I need more practice. ▪

For more practice, go to MyEnglishLab.

Lesson 10 Writing

Write about a favorite day of the week

1 STUDY THE MODEL

READ. Answer the questions.

> Ahmed Ali
> My Favorite Day
>
> My favorite day of the week is Sunday. I never work on Sundays. On Sundays, I spend time with my friends and family. We usually go to the park. We bring a lot of food. We sit and talk. We play soccer. It's a lot of fun.

1. What is Ahmed's favorite day of the week?
2. Why is it his favorite day?
3. Who does he spend time with on his favorite day?
4. What does he do on his favorite day?

2 PLAN YOUR WRITING

WORK TOGETHER. Ask and answer the questions.

1. What's your favorite day of the week?
2. Why is it your favorite day?
3. Who do you spend time with on your favorite day?
4. What do you do on your favorite day?

Writing Skill: Use a capital letter for days of the week

Days of the week begin with a capital letter. For example:

My favorite day of the week is Sunday.

3 WRITE

Now write about your favorite day of the week. Use the frame, the model, the Writing Skill, and your ideas from Exercise 2 to help you.

> My favorite day of the week is ____. I ____ on ____. On ____, I spend time with ____. We usually go to ____. We ____. We ____. It's a lot of fun.

4 CHECK YOUR WRITING

WORK TOGETHER. Read your writing aloud with a partner.

WRITING CHECKLIST

☐ The writing answers all the questions in Exercise 2.

☐ Each day of the week begins with a capital letter.

I can use a capital letter for days of the week. ■   I need more practice. ■

For more practice, go to MyEnglishLab.

Lesson 11: Soft Skills at Work

Be a team player

1 MEET RITA

Read about one of her workplace skills.

I'm a team player. For example, I help my co-workers when they need help. I help them when I finish my work.

2 RITA'S PROBLEM

READ. Circle *True* or *False*.

Rita is an office assistant. She makes a lot of copies. Sometimes the copy machine doesn't work. Rita can fix it.

One day, she sees her co-worker at the copy machine. Her co-worker says, "I need these copies now, but the machine doesn't work!" Rita wants to leave. She is meeting her friend after work.

1. Rita works in an office.   True   False
2. The copy machine sometimes doesn't work.   True   False
3. Rita's co-worker can fix the copy machine.   True   False

3 RITA'S SOLUTION

A WORK TOGETHER. Rita is a team player. What is the right thing to say? Explain your answer.

1. Rita says, "I need to leave now, but I can help you tomorrow."
2. Rita says, "Sorry. I can't help you now. Ask Tom."
3. Rita says, "I can help you. Let me show you."
4. Rita says, "_____."

B ROLE-PLAY. Look at your answer to 3A. Role-play Rita's conversation.

Show what you know!

1. **THINK ABOUT IT.** How are you a team player at school? At work? At home? Give examples.

2. **WRITE ABOUT IT.** Now write your example in your Skills Log.

   Sometimes my classmates and I study together after class. I help them. They help me.

3. **PRESENT IT.** Give a short presentation to show how you are a team player.

I can give an example from my life of being a team player.

Unit Review: Go back to page 125. Which goals can you check off?

8 From Soup to Nuts

PREVIEW
Look at the picture. Who are the people? Where are they?

UNIT GOALS

- [ ] Name common foods
- [ ] Talk about foods you like and don't like
- [ ] Order a meal in a restaurant
- [ ] Compare food prices
- [ ] Talk about healthy food
- [ ] Plan a healthy meal
- [ ] **Academic skill:** Read captions before reading an article
- [ ] **Writing skill:** Choose the correct verb
- [ ] **Workplace soft skill:** Take action

Lesson 1 Vocabulary

Common foods

A PREDICT. Look at the pictures. What do you see? What are the foods?

Number 14 is eggs.

B ▶ LISTEN AND POINT. Then listen and repeat.

Source: www.choosemyplate.gov

146 Unit 8, Lesson 1

Vocabulary

Common foods

A. Vegetables	B. Fruit	C. Grains	D. Proteins	E. Dairy
1. potatoes	5. apples	8. bread	11. chicken	16. milk
2. onions	6. oranges	9. cereal	12. fish	17. cheese
3. cabbage	7. bananas	10. rice	13. beef	18. yogurt
4. lettuce			14. eggs	
			15. beans	**F. Oils**
				19. vegetable oil
				20. butter

C **GIVE EXAMPLES.** Student A, say a food group. Student B, say two foods in the group.

A: Vegetables.
B: Cabbage and lettuce.

D **ASK AND ANSWER.** Student A, look at the pictures and the list of foods. Choose a food, but don't say it. Students B, C, and D, ask *yes/no* questions and guess the food.

B: Do you eat it for breakfast?
A: Sometimes.
C: Is it a fruit?
A: Yes.

D: Is it red?
A: No.
B: Is it a banana?
A: Yes!

Study Tip

Practice online
Use the flashcards in MyEnglishLab.

Show what you know!

1. **THINK ABOUT IT.** Look at page 146. Write a food you usually eat on each part of the plate. Write how often you eat the food outside the plate.

2. **TALK ABOUT IT.** Talk about the foods you eat and how often you eat them. Write your partner's information.

   A: What vegetables do you eat?
   B: Potatoes.
   A: How often do you eat potatoes?
   B: Twice a week.

3. **WRITE ABOUT IT.** Now write a sentence about a food you eat and how often you eat it.

   I eat a banana every day.
   _____

I can name common foods. ■　　　　　　　　　　I need more practice. ■

For more practice, go to MyEnglishLab.

Unit 8, Lesson 1 **147**

Lesson 2

Listening and Speaking

Talk about foods you like and don't like

1 BEFORE YOU LISTEN

A LABEL. Write the words under the pictures.

| hamburger | ~~hungry~~ | pizza | taco |

a. _hungry_   b. _____   c. _____   d. _____

B MAKE CONNECTIONS. Check (✓) the foods you like.

☐ pizza ☐ tacos ☐ hamburgers

2 LISTEN

A ▶ LISTEN. Look at the picture. Listen to the conversation. Answer the question.

What are they talking about?
a. breakfast   b. lunch   c. dinner

B ▶ LISTEN FOR DETAILS. Answer the questions.

1. Who is hungry?
   a. Mark   b. Rosa   c. Mark and Rosa

2. What does Mark want for lunch?
   a. pizza   b. tacos   c. a hamburger

3. What does Rosa want for lunch?
   a. pizza   b. tacos   c. a hamburger

C ▶ EXPAND. Listen to the whole conversation. Complete the sentence.

Rosa says, "Let's have pizza and tacos for _____."
a. breakfast   b. lunch   c. dinner

148 Unit 8, Lesson 2

Listening and Speaking

3 CONVERSATION

A ▶ **LISTEN AND READ.** Then listen and repeat.

A: Wow, I'm hungry!
B: Yeah, me too. What do you want for lunch?
A: Pizza. I love pizza! What about you?
B: I don't really like pizza, but I love tacos!

B **WORK TOGETHER.** Practice the conversation in Exercise A.

C **CREATE.** Make new conversations. Use the information in the boxes.

A: What do you want for _____?
B: _____. I love _____! What about you?
A: I don't really like _____, but I love _____!

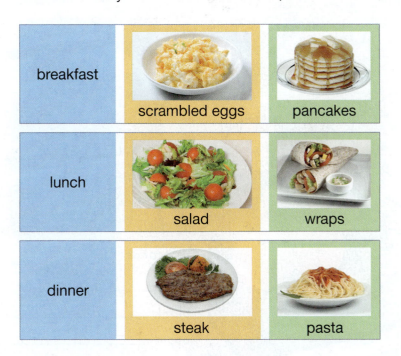

breakfast	scrambled eggs	pancakes
lunch	salad	wraps
dinner	steak	pasta

D **MAKE CONNECTIONS.** Make your own conversations. Use different foods.

I can talk about foods I like and don't like. ■   I need more practice. ■

For more practice, go to MyEnglishLab.

Unit 8, Lesson 2 149

Lesson 3

Grammar

Count and non-count nouns

Count nouns		Non-count nouns	
Rosa wants	**a potato.**	I want	**rice.**
She loves	**potatoes.**	I love	**rice.**

Grammar Watch

- **Count nouns** are nouns you can count: *one apple, two apples.*
- **Non-count nouns** are nouns you can't count: ~~one rice, two rices~~
- For a list of more non-count nouns, see page 260.
- For spelling rules for plural count nouns, see page 260.

A IDENTIFY. Complete the shopping list.

TO BUY

4 _oranges_
6 _____
black _____
apple _____
2 large _____
banana _____
3 _____
5 green _____

150 Unit 8, Lesson 3

Grammar

B **COMPLETE.** Look at the pictures. Complete the conversations.

1.  **A:** _____Apples_____ are good for you.

   B: I know. I eat an _____ every day.

2.  **A:** I love _____.

   B: Me, too! I often have two _____ for breakfast.

3.  **A:** Do you have _____?

   B: Of course! I always have _____ in the house. It's in the refrigerator.

4.  **A:** I eat _____ every day.

   B: Me, too. I love _____!

Show what you know!

1. **THINK ABOUT IT.** Name foods of the same color.
   - yellow: _bananas_____
   - white: _____
   - red: _____
   - green: _____

2. **WRITE ABOUT IT.** Now write 2 sentences about foods and colors.
   _Bananas are yellow._____
   _____ green.
   _____

I can use count and non-count nouns. ☐   I need more practice. ☐

For more practice, go to MyEnglishLab.

Lesson 4 Reading

Read about food safety

1 BEFORE YOU READ

A **LABEL.** Write the words under the pictures.

a cabinet   a counter   a freezer   a refrigerator

1. _____ 2. _____ 3. _____ 4. _____

B **MAKE CONNECTIONS.** In your kitchen, where do you keep these foods?

canned beans, oranges, cereal, milk, chicken, eggs, ice cream, potatoes, frozen vegetables, bananas

Academic Skill: Read captions

The words you see above or below a picture are **captions**. They often add important information about the picture. Before you read an article, look at any pictures and read their captions.

2 READ

▶ Listen and read.

A careful shopper always checks the date on food.

Eat Fresh!

Do you buy fresh food? Are you sure it is fresh? Be careful! Stores sometimes sell old food. Check the date on food before you buy it.

How long can you keep your food at home?

Milk is usually safe to drink for two to ten days after its sell-by date. Be
5 sure to keep it cold.

Eggs are good for three to five weeks after their sell-by date. Keep them in the refrigerator, too.

Chicken is different. You cannot keep chicken in your refrigerator for weeks after the sell-by date.
10 The refrigerators in stores are very cold. Your home refrigerator isn't as cold. Freeze chicken or cook it a day or two after you buy it. You can keep chicken in the freezer for twelve months. You can keep cooked chicken in the refrigerator for a week.

15 Some food, like **canned food**, doesn't have a sell-by date. But it isn't good forever. Keep canned food in a cool, dry place. Try to use it in twelve months.

Sometimes canned food or **frozen food** has a best-before date or a use-by date. The food will
20 taste better before that date.

Stores cannot sell food after its sell-by date.

Reading

3 CLOSE READING

CITE EVIDENCE. Complete the sentences. Where is the information? Write the line number.

Lines

1. When you go food shopping, don't buy _____.
   a. canned food
   b. frozen chicken
   c. food after its sell-by date

   _____

2. You can usually drink milk for 2 to _____ days after its sell-by date.
   a. 3
   b. 10
   c. 14

   _____

3. It is important to keep _____ in the refrigerator.
   a. frozen foods
   b. canned foods
   c. milk and eggs

   _____

4. When you buy fresh chicken, _____ in the next 1 to 2 days.
   a. cook it or freeze it
   b. put it in the refrigerator
   c. eat it

   _____

5. _____ doesn't have a sell-by date.
   a. Canned food
   b. Chicken
   c. Milk

   _____

6. It is a good idea to _____.
   a. eat food before its use-by date
   b. keep canned food for many years
   c. keep canned food in a warm place

   _____

4 SUMMARIZE

Complete the summary with the words in the box.

| buy | canned foods | safe | sell-by date | use-by date |

Most food in the supermarket has a (1) _____. Don't (2) _____ food after that date. Food is (3) _____ to eat after its sell-by date, but every food is different. Some foods are safe for a few weeks but others for only a day or two. (4) _____ don't have a sell-by date, but they have a best-before or (5) _____.

Show what you know!

1. **THINK ABOUT IT.** How do you make sure your food is fresh?

2. **WRITE ABOUT IT.** Now write about how you make sure your food is fresh.

   I always check the _____ on _____. I keep _____ in the _____.

I can read captions before reading an article. ■   I need more practice. ■

To read more, go to MyEnglishLab.

Unit 8, Lesson 4 **153**

Lesson 5 Listening and Speaking
Order a meal in a restaurant

1 BEFORE YOU LISTEN

MAKE CONNECTIONS. Look at the pictures. Check (✓) the foods you eat or drink.

 tomato soup
 coffee
 turkey sandwich
 fries
 soda
 baked potato

 hamburger
 iced tea
 salad
 fruit cup
 apple pie
 ice cream

2 LISTEN

A ▶ **LISTEN.** Look at the picture. Listen to the conversation. What is Greg doing? Complete the sentence.

He's _____ a meal.
a. ordering   b. eating   c. serving

B ▶ **LISTEN FOR DETAILS.** What does Greg want? Complete the sentence.

Greg wants a hamburger, _____.
a. a small soda, and a large order of fries
b. a large soda, and a large order of fries
c. a large soda, and a small order of fries

C ▶ **EXPAND.** Listen to the whole conversation. Complete the sentence.

For fruit, Greg orders _____.
a. an apple   b. apple juice   c. apple pie

154 Unit 8, Lesson 5

Listening and Speaking

3 PRONUNCIATION

A ▶ **PRACTICE.** Listen. Then listen and repeat.

Is that a large soda or a small soda?

Would you like coffee or tea?

> **Intonation of choice questions with *or***
>
> In choice questions with *or*, the voice goes up ↗ on the first choice and down ↘ on the last choice.

B ▶ **APPLY.** Practice saying the sentences. Then listen and repeat.

Do you want steak or pasta?
Would you like pizza or tacos?

4 CONVERSATION

A ▶ **LISTEN AND READ.** Then listen and repeat.

Server: Can I help you?
Customer: Yes. I'd like a hamburger and a soda.
Server: Is that a large soda or a small soda?
Customer: Large, please.
Server: OK, a large soda. Anything else?
Customer: Yes. A small order of fries.

B **WORK TOGETHER.** Practice the conversation in Exercise A.

C **CREATE.** Make new conversations. Use the menu.

A: Can I help you?
B: Yes. I'd like _____ and _____.
         (food)   (drink)
A: Is that a large _____ or a small
                        (drink)
_____?
  (drink)
B: Large, please.
A: OK, a large _____. Anything else?
                    (drink)
B: Yes. _____.
            (food)

Starters
tomato soup
onion soup
green salad

Sides
baked potato
fries
rice
vegetables

Desserts
apple pie
ice cream
fruit cup

Sandwiches
turkey sandwich
cheese sandwich
hamburger
black bean taco

Drinks
soda
iced tea
coffee
orange juice

D **ROLE-PLAY.** Make your own conversations. Use the menu.

I can order a meal in a restaurant. ▪   I need more practice. ▪

For more practice, go to MyEnglishLab.

Lesson 6 Grammar

Choice questions with *or*

Choice questions with *or*			
Would you like **coffee**	or	**tea**?	Tea, please.
Do you want **an apple**		**a banana**?	An apple, please.

Grammar Watch

Questions with *or* give choices. Answer with your choice. Do not say *yes* or *no*.

A COMPLETE. Use the words in parentheses with *or*.

1. Do you want ___chicken soup or salad___?
   (chicken soup / salad)
2. Would you like _____?
   (a fish sandwich / a hamburger)
3. Do you want _____?
   (fries / a baked potato)
4. Do you want _____?
   (soda / juice)
5. Would you like _____?
   (ice cream / apple pie)

B ▶ SELF-ASSESS. Listen and check your answers. Then listen and repeat.

Show what you know!

1. **WRITE ABOUT IT.** Student A, you're a server. Student B, you're a customer. Student A, write two choice questions for your partner.

   Would you like meat or fish?
   _____
   _____

2. **ROLE-PLAY.** Ask your questions from Exercise 1. Write your partner's order.

   A: *Would you like meat or fish?*
   B: *Fish, please.*

3. **PRESENT IT.** Now report to the class.

   Maria wants fish.

I can ask choice questions with *or*.   I need more practice.

For more practice, go to MyEnglishLab.

Lesson 7: Workplace, Life, and Community Skills

Compare food prices; Talk about healthy food

1 COMPARE FOOD PRICES

A ▶ **LISTEN.** Look at the ad for Farmer Tom's. Listen and repeat the prices and amounts.

B ▶ **APPLY.** Look at the ad for Country Market. Listen and fill in the prices.

C **COMPARE.** Look at the prices in the ads again. Where is each food cheaper? Circle the cheaper price.

D ▶ **LISTEN AND READ.** Then listen and repeat.

A: Where are **onions** cheaper, Farmer Tom's or Country Market?
B: Farmer Tom's. They're **79 cents a pound**.
A: Where is **bread** cheaper, Farmer Tom's or Country Market?
B: Country Market. It's **$2.59**.

E **ROLE-PLAY.** Make new conversations. Use different foods from the ads.

I can compare food prices. ▪   I need more practice. ▪

Unit 8, Lesson 7   157

Workplace, Life, and Community Skills

2 TALK ABOUT HEALTHY FOOD

A **TALK ABOUT IT.** Read the tips. Do you eat healthy food?

Tips to Stay Healthy

- Don't eat a lot of fat.
- Don't eat a lot of sodium.
- Don't eat a lot of sugar.
- 12 calories
- 300 calories

Eat the right number of calories. How many calories can you eat? Every person is different. Talk to a doctor or nurse.

B **ASSESS.** Look at the pictures. Check (✓) the foods that you think are healthy.

C **WORK TOGETHER.** Talk about your answers in Exercise 2B.

A: Green beans are good for you.
B: Why?
A: Because they don't have fat.

A: Ice cream isn't good for you.
B: Why not?
A: Because it has a lot of fat and sugar.

D **MAKE CONNECTIONS.** Which healthy foods do you usually eat?

A: I eat a lot of beans.
B: Really? Well, I eat rice every day.
C: I eat...

Workplace, Life, and Community Skills

E MATCH. Look at this label for bread. Match the words and definitions. Write the letter.

____ 1. g   a. how much you eat at one time
____ 2. mg   b. gram(s)
____ 3. Net Wt.   c. milligram(s)
____ 4. Serving size   d. how much food is in the container

F LOCATE. Look at the label in Exercise 2E. Answer the questions.

1. How much is one serving? _____1 slice_____
2. How many servings are in the package? _____
3. How many calories are in one serving? _____
4. How much fat is in one serving? _____
5. How much sodium is in one serving? _____
6. How much sugar is in one serving? _____

G INTERPRET. Look at the labels. Which drink is better for your health? Why?

_____ is better for your health because _____
_____.

H GO ONLINE. Look up the number of calories in your favorite food.

I can talk about healthy food. ▪   I need more practice. ▪

For more practice, go to MyEnglishLab.

Lesson 8: Plan a healthy meal

Listening and Speaking

1 BEFORE YOU LISTEN

GIVE EXAMPLES. Look at the pictures. What other foods are steamed, grilled, or fried?

steamed vegetables   grilled chicken   fried fish

2 LISTEN

A ▶ LISTEN FOR DETAILS. Listen to the radio talk show. Check (✓) all the correct answers.

1. What does Greg like to eat?
   - ☐ fruit and vegetables
   - ☐ meat and potatoes
   - ☐ chicken

2. What does Greg's wife think is good for Greg?
   - ☐ meat
   - ☐ fruit
   - ☐ vegetables

3. What does Hanna think is good for Greg?
   - ☐ meat
   - ☐ fruit
   - ☐ vegetables

B ▶ LISTEN FOR DETAILS. Complete the chart.

Fried chicken	_____ calories
Grilled chicken	_____ calories
Fries (small)	_____ fat (in grams)
Baked potato	_____ fat (in grams)

C WORK TOGETHER. Look at the pictures. Plan a healthy meal for Greg. Choose from the pictures.

A: How about salad, a hamburger, and fruit?
B: The hamburger isn't really healthy. It has a lot of fat! How about . . . ?

Listening and Speaking

3 CONVERSATION

A **MAKE CONNECTIONS.** Look at the pictures. Which of these foods do you like?

B ▶ **LISTEN AND READ.** Then listen and repeat.

A: Let's have **chicken** for dinner.
B: OK. How much **chicken** do we need?
A: Two pounds.
B: OK. And let's have salad with it.
A: Good idea. We have lettuce, but we need **onions**.
B: How many **onions** do we need?
A: Just one.

C **WORK TOGETHER.** Practice the conversation in Exercise B.

D **CREATE.** Make new conversations. Use the pictures in Exercise A.

E **DECIDE.** Plan an interesting salad.

A: Let's put nuts in the salad.
B: OK. And how about an avocado?
A: Oh, I don't like avocados. Let's put a mango in it.

shrimp

tomatoes

turkey

red peppers

salmon

cucumbers

roast beef

avocados

F **PRESENT.** Tell your classmates about the salad.

Our salad has nuts, mango. . . .

spinach

carrots

scallions

mango

nuts

watermelon

I can plan a healthy meal. ▪ I need more practice. ▪

For more practice, go to MyEnglishLab.

Grammar

Lesson 9: Questions and short answers with *How many* and *How much*

Questions and short answers with *How many* and *How much*

How many	eggs	do we have?	A lot.	Not many.
How much	milk	is there?	A lot.	Not much.

Grammar Watch
- Use *how many* with plural count nouns.
- Use *how much* with non-count nouns.

A COMPLETE. Look at the picture. Read the answers. Complete the questions with *How many* or *How much* and a noun.

1. **A:** _How many oranges_ do we have?
   B: Not many. We only have three.
2. **A:** _____ do we have?
   B: Not much. Just one container.
3. **A:** _____ are there?
   B: Twelve. We don't need more.
4. **A:** _____ is there?
   B: There is no cheese! Put it on the shopping list.
5. **A:** _____ are there?
   B: Six. And they're big!
   A: Great. Let's have them tonight.

B WORK TOGETHER. Look at the picture again. Ask about other food in the refrigerator.

A: How much orange juice do we have?
B: There's a lot. We don't need orange juice.
A: How many apples . . . ?

I can use questions and short answers with *How many* and *How much*. ◼

I need more practice. ◼

For more practice, go to MyEnglishLab.

Lesson 10 Writing

Write about food

1 STUDY THE MODEL

READ. Answer the questions.

> Maya Black
> My Food
>
> I always have cereal and a large coffee for breakfast. I usually eat a sandwich and a salad for lunch. In the afternoon, I usually have a cookie and a glass of milk for a snack. I sometimes eat pasta or rice for dinner.

1. What does Maya have for breakfast?
2. What does she usually eat for lunch?
3. What does she usually have for a snack?
4. What does she sometimes eat for dinner?

2 PLAN YOUR WRITING

WORK TOGETHER. Ask and answer the questions.

1. What do you have for breakfast?
2. What do you usually eat for lunch?
3. What do you usually have for a snack?
4. What do you eat for dinner?

Writing Skill: Choose the correct verb

Use the verb *eat* when you talk about food. Use the verb *drink* when you talk about drinks. You can use *have* with food or drinks. For example:
I (eat) scrambled eggs for breakfast.
I (drink) coffee for breakfast.
I (have) scrambled eggs and coffee for breakfast.

3 WRITE

Now write about the food you usually eat. Use the frame, the model, the Writing Skill, and your ideas from Exercise 2 to help you.

> I always have ____ for breakfast. I usually eat ____ for lunch. I usually have ____ for a snack. I sometimes eat ____ for dinner.

4 CHECK YOUR WRITING

WORK TOGETHER. Read your writing aloud with a partner.

WRITING CHECKLIST
- ☐ The writing answers all the questions in Exercise 2.
- ☐ Each sentence has a verb.
- ☐ The verbs *eat, drink,* and *have* are used correctly.

I can choose the correct verb. ▪   I need more practice. ▪

For more practice, go to MyEnglishLab.

Lesson 11: Soft Skills at Work

Take action

1 MEET NASIR

Read about one of his workplace skills.

I take action. When I see a problem, I do something.

2 NASIR'S PROBLEM

READ. Circle *True* or *False*.

Nasir works in a restaurant. He is a dishwasher. He washes dishes and cleans the restaurant.

One day, the restaurant is very busy. The cooks make a lot of food. Nasir sees there are not many onions or potatoes on the shelves. There is not much milk in the refrigerator. There is no bread.

1. Nasir is a server. True False
2. The restaurant is very busy. True False
3. There is a lot of milk in the refrigerator. True False

3 NASIR'S SOLUTION

WORK TOGETHER. Nasir takes action. What does Nasir do? Explain your answer.

1. Nasir writes a note for the manager with the food they need.
2. Nasir tells the cooks that they need to order food.
3. Nasir says nothing. It is not his job to order food.
4. Nasir _____.

Show what you know!

1. **THINK ABOUT IT.** How do you take action at school? At work? At home? Give examples.

2. **WRITE ABOUT IT.** Now write your example in your Skills Log.

   I tell my manager when something doesn't work.

I can give an example from my life of taking action. ◼

Unit Review: Go back to page 145. Which goals can you check off?

9 Rain or Shine

PREVIEW
Look at the picture. What do you see?

UNIT GOALS

- Name seasons and weather
- Talk about what you are doing now
- Plan for an emergency
- Ask what someone is doing now
- Understand a weather report
- **Academic skill:** Focus on details
- **Writing skill:** Use *because* to give a reason
- **Workplace soft skill:** Be ready to learn new skills

165

Lesson 1

Vocabulary

Seasons and weather

A **PREDICT.** Look at the pictures. What are the seasons and weather words?

C is spring. Number 8 is sunny.

B ▶ **LISTEN AND POINT.** Then listen and repeat.

Vocabulary

Seasons and weather

A. Fall	B. Winter	C. Spring	D. Summer
1. cool	3. cold	5. warm	7. hot
2. cloudy	4. snowy	6. rainy	8. sunny

C **ASK AND ANSWER.** Student A, point to a picture and ask about the weather. Student B, answer.

A: How's the weather?
B: It's hot and sunny.

D **TALK ABOUT IT.** Look at the pictures and the list of weather words. Talk about the weather in your native country.

A: I'm from Colombia. It's usually cool and cloudy in spring.
B: Oh, really? In Korea, it's usually . . .

Study Tip

Write and spell

Write the words. Spell the words aloud when you write.

Show what you know!

1. **SURVEY.** Ask three classmates about their favorite season here. Write their answers in the chart.

Name	Favorite Season	Reason
Paul	spring	warm, not hot

   A: What's your favorite season?
   B: I like spring.
   A: Why?
   B: Because it's warm but not hot.

2. **PRESENT IT.** Tell your class about your classmates' favorite seasons.

   Paul likes spring because it is warm but not hot.

3. **WRITE ABOUT IT.** Now write a sentence about your favorite season.

   I like _____ because _____.

I can name seasons and weather. ■   I need more practice. ■

For more practice, go to MyEnglishLab.

Lesson 2 — Listening and Speaking

Talk about what you are doing now

1 BEFORE YOU LISTEN

READ. Then answer the question.

Green Bay, Wisconsin, is in the north of the United States. Winter is usually cold and snowy there. Tampa, Florida, is in the south of the United States. Winter there is usually warm and sunny.

How is winter in your area?

2 LISTEN

A ▶ **LISTEN.** Laura is in Tampa, Florida. She is calling her friend David in Green Bay, Wisconsin. Complete the sentence.

Laura is _____ in Tampa.
- a. working
- b. studying
- c. visiting family

B ▶ **LISTEN FOR DETAILS.** Complete the sentences.

1. Laura's family is _____ now.
   - a. at home
   - b. at work
   - c. at school

2. The weather in Tampa is _____.
   - a. warm and sunny
   - b. warm and rainy
   - c. cold and rainy

C ▶ **EXPAND.** Listen to the whole conversation. Complete the sentences.

1. The weather in Green Bay is _____.
   - a. warm and sunny
   - b. cold and rainy
   - c. sunny, but not warm

2. Laura is watching _____.
   - a. her friend
   - b. the rain
   - c. TV

3. Laura sounds _____.
   - a. happy
   - b. unhappy
   - c. stressed

Listening and Speaking

3 CONVERSATION

A ▶ **LISTEN AND READ.** Then listen and repeat.

A: Hello?
B: Hi! It's me. How are you doing?
A: I'm fine, thanks. Where are you?
B: I'm in Tampa. I'm visiting family, but they're at work now.
A: Tampa! That's great! How's the weather there?
B: Well, it's cold and rainy.

B **WORK TOGETHER.** Practice the conversation in Exercise A.

C **CREATE.** Make new conversations. Use the information in the boxes.

A: Hello?
B: Hi! It's me. How are you doing?
A: I'm fine, thanks. Where are you?
B: I'm in _____. I'm visiting _____, but they're at work now.
A: _____! That's great! How's the weather there?
B: Well, it's _____ and _____.

Dallas	San Francisco	Boston
friends	my aunt and uncle	my cousins
hot	cool	cold
humid	foggy	windy

D **ROLE-PLAY.** Make your own conversations. Use different cities, people, and weather.

I can talk about what I am doing now. ▪   I need more practice. ▪

For more practice, go to MyEnglishLab.

Lesson 3 Grammar

Present continuous: Statements

Present continuous: Statements

Affirmative		
I	am	
You		
We	are	reading.
They		
He	is	
She		
It	is	raining.

Negative			
I	am		
You			
We	are	not	working.
They			
He	is		
She			
It	is	not	snowing.

Grammar Watch

- Use the present continuous for things that are happening now.
- Remember: We usually use contractions with *be* in conversations.
- For spelling rules for the present continuous, see page 260.

A COMPLETE. Use contractions.

A: What are you doing?

B: I <u>'m watching</u> TV. What are *you* doing?
      1. (watch)

A: I _____ to you!
    2. (talk)

B: Very funny. How's the weather there?

A: Well, it _____, but it's cold. How's the weather in Chicago?
    3. (not rain)

B: It _____ here.
    4. (snow)

A: Oh. Is it cold?

B: Yes. I _____ two sweaters.
    5. (wear)

A: Is Jason home?

B: Yes. He _____ today.
    6. (not work)

A: What about the kids? What are they doing?

B: They're outside. They _____ a snowman!
    7. (make)

Grammar

B COMPARE. Look at the pictures. Find 10 differences. Talk about them.

A: In Picture 1, a woman is eating an apple.
B: Right. But in Picture 2, she isn't eating an apple. She's eating a banana.

Show what you know!

1. **THINK ABOUT IT.** Find a photo of yourself.

2. **TALK ABOUT IT.** Show your photo to your partner. What are you doing? Tell your partner.

   A: I'm visiting my cousin. We're eating dinner.
   B: That's a nice picture.

3. **WRITE ABOUT IT.** Now write a sentence about your photo.

   My cousin and I are eating dinner.

I can make statements in the present continuous. ■   I need more practice. ■

For more practice, go to MyEnglishLab.

Lesson 4: Workplace, Life, and Community Skills

Plan for an emergency

1 TALK ABOUT BAD WEATHER AND EMERGENCIES

A LABEL. Which words for bad weather and emergencies do you know? Write the words under the pictures.

an earthquake	a snowstorm
a flood	a thunderstorm
~~a landslide~~	a tornado
a hurricane	a wildfire

1. _a landslide_   2. _____   3. _____   4. _____

5. _____   6. _____   7. _____   8. _____

B ▶ SELF-ASSESS. Listen and check your answers. Then listen and repeat.

C ▶ LISTEN AND READ. Then listen and repeat.

A: What do you do in a flood?
B: I leave my home.

D ROLE-PLAY. Make new conversations. Use the information in the chart.

Emergency	What to do
fire, flood, landslide	leave your home
snowstorm, thunderstorm, hurricane	stay home
tornado	go downstairs
earthquake	go under a piece of furniture

172 Unit 9, Lesson 4

Workplace, Life, and Community Skills

2 PLAN FOR AN EMERGENCY

A **TALK ABOUT IT.** Read the email. What information do employees need to know for an emergency?

> TO: employees@smbus.com
> FROM: Management
> SUBJECT: Emergency plan
>
> All Employees,
>
> We have a new emergency system.
> - New exit maps: Know the exit doors.
> - New alarm system: We will test the system on Friday, 10/28 at 10:00 A.M.
> - Put emergency numbers in your phone: Police, Fire
>
> In an emergency:
> - Leave quickly. Be calm.
> - Listen for instructions from your emergency leader.
> - Do not use elevators.
> - Go to an exit near you.
> - Go to safe areas.
>   - Parking lot next to office
>   - Sidewalk in front of office
> - Do not go back in the building.

B **INTERPRET.** Read the sentences about the email in Exercise 2A. Circle *True* or *False*.

1. There are new exit doors.   True   False
2. The alarm system test is on October 25.   True   False
3. Go out of the building quickly.   True   False
4. Use an exit near you.   True   False
5. Use the elevators in an emergency.   True   False

C **REWRITE.** Correct the false sentences in Exercise 2B.

D ▶ **LISTEN AND READ.** Then listen and repeat.

A: Where is the emergency exit near our classroom?
B: It's next to the restrooms.

E **ROLE-PLAY.** Make new conversations. Use the emergency exit maps at your school.

F **GO ONLINE.** Add emergency phone numbers to your phone.

I can plan for an emergency. ■   I need more practice. ■

For more practice, go to MyEnglishLab.

Lesson 5 Listening and Speaking

Ask what someone is doing now

1 BEFORE YOU LISTEN

LABEL. What do you need in an emergency? Write the words under the pictures.

| batteries | a first aid kit | a flashlight | matches |

1. _____ 2. _____ 3. _____ 4. _____

2 LISTEN

A ▶ **LISTEN.** Look at the picture. Ron is calling his wife Emma. Why is Ron at the supermarket?

B ▶ **LISTEN FOR DETAILS.** Read the sentences. Circle *True* or *False*.

1. Emma is watching TV.   True   False
2. Emma is doing the laundry.   True   False
3. Ron is working late.   True   False
4. A big storm is coming.   True   False

C ▶ **EXPAND.** Listen to the whole conversation. Complete the sentences. Check (✓) the correct answers.

1. Ron is buying _____. (Check more than one answer.)
   ☐ water   ☐ food   ☐ a flashlight   ☐ batteries   ☐ clothes

2. Emma wants _____.
   ☐ candles   ☐ matches   ☐ a first-aid kit

3. Emma and Ron need _____.
   ☐ good friends   ☐ a good TV   ☐ good weather

Listening and Speaking

3 CONVERSATION

A ▶ **LISTEN AND READ.** Then listen and repeat.

A: Are you watching the news?
B: No, I'm not. I'm doing the laundry.
A: Turn on the TV. A big storm is coming.
B: Really?
A: Yes. I'm coming home early. I'm at the supermarket now.

B **WORK TOGETHER.** Practice the conversation in Exercise A.

C **CREATE.** Make new conversations. Use the information in the boxes.

A: Are you watching the news?
B: No, I'm not. I'm _____.
A: Well, turn on the TV. A _____ is coming.
B: Really?
A: Yes. I'm coming home early. I'm at the _____ now.

checking email	making lunch	cleaning the apartment
hurricane	thunderstorm	snowstorm
		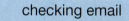
hardware store	grocery store	shopping center

D **ROLE-PLAY.** Make your own conversations. Use different activities and locations.

I can ask what someone is doing now. ▪   I need more practice. ▪

For more practice, go to MyEnglishLab.

Grammar

Lesson 6
Present continuous: *Yes/no* questions and short answers

Present continuous: *Yes/no* questions and short answers

Are	you	working?	Yes,	I am.	No,	I'm not.
	they			they **are**.		they**'re not**. / they **aren't**.
Is	he			he **is**.		he**'s not**. / he **isn't**.

A **APPLY.** Look at the picture. Answer the questions. Use short answers.

1. **A:** Are they working?

   B: <u>No, they're not. (No, they aren't.)</u>

2. **A:** Is it raining?

   B: _____

3. **A:** Is the man wearing a blue uniform?

   B: _____

4. **A:** Are they reading?

   B: _____

5. **A:** Is the woman listening to music?

   B: _____

6. **A:** Is the man eating a sandwich?

   B: _____

7. **A:** Is the man playing a game?

   B: _____

Grammar

B **WRITE.** Use the words in parentheses to write *yes/no* questions.

1. (they / eating pizza) _Are they eating pizza?_
2. (they / text) _____
3. (she / wear a hat) _____
4. (he / listen to music) _____
5. (they / wear jackets) _____

C **WORK TOGETHER.** Look at the picture on page 176. Ask and answer the questions in Exercises A and B.

A: _Are they eating pizza?_
B: _No, they're not._

Show what you know!

1. LIST. Make a list of activities.

_____

_____

_____

_____

2. ACT IT OUT. Student A, act out one activity from Exercise 1. Students B and C, guess the activity.

B: _Are you checking email?_
A: _No, I'm not._
C: _Are you texting?_
A: _Yes, I am._

3. WRITE ABOUT IT. Now write two *yes/no* questions from Exercise 2.

_____

_____

I can ask and answer *yes/no* questions in the present continuous. ■   I need more practice. ■

For more practice, go to MyEnglishLab.

Lesson 7 Reading

Read about hurricanes

1 BEFORE YOU READ

A LABEL. Write the vocabulary words from the box on the map.

| Northeast | Northwest | Southeast | Southwest |

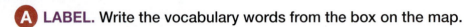

Regions of the U.S.

A compass.

B TALK ABOUT IT. Where do hurricanes happen? What happens during a hurricane?

2 READ

▶ Listen and read.

Academic Skill: Focus on details

The first time you read an article, read for the main idea. Then read again and focus on the details. The details answer questions such as *who*, *what*, *when*, *where*, *how*, and *why*.

Facts about Hurricanes

Hurricanes are big storms. A hurricane can be 600 miles across! The winds can be as strong as 200 mph (miles per hour). The winds move in a circle. The center of the circle is called the eye.

5　Hurricanes form only over warm ocean water. The water needs to be 80 degrees or higher. Warmer water makes a storm stronger. When the storm hits land, it brings both strong winds and heavy rain.

10　A hurricane also brings a storm surge. It pushes ocean water on land. The water moves at 10 to 15 mph. It can be several feet high. A one-foot storm surge can push a car off the road.

Most big storms happen during hurricane
15　season. In the Atlantic Ocean, it goes from June 1 to November 30. During hurricane season, people listen for news of storms. A hurricane watch means a bad storm might come in the next 36 hours. A hurricane warning means a hurricane is coming in
20　the next 24 hours. On average, hurricane season brings five or six hurricanes, but sometimes there are more. Usually only two are major hurricanes.

In the U.S., hurricanes most often hit the South and the Southeast. They do the most damage in
25　Florida, Texas, and Louisiana. But they cause problems in other states, too.

Source: U.S. National Weather Service Climate Prediction Center

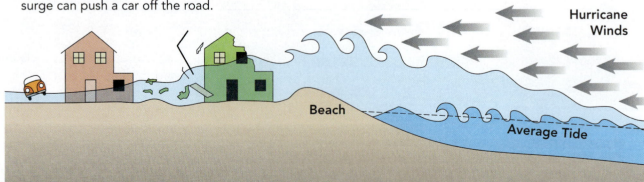

178　Unit 9, Lesson 7

Reading

3 CLOSE READING

CITE EVIDENCE. Complete the sentences. Where is the information? Write the line number.

Lines

1. A hurricane can be up to _____ miles wide.
   a. 60   b. 200   c. 600   _____

2. Hurricane winds can blow up to _____ mph (miles per hour).
   a. 100   b. 150   c. 200   _____

3. Hurricanes get started only _____.
   a. during hurricane season   b. over warm ocean water   c. in the Atlantic Ocean   _____

4. _____ means that a hurricane is coming in the next 24 hours.
   a. A storm surge   b. A hurricane watch   c. A hurricane warning   _____

5. A storm surge can be _____ high.
   a. only one foot   b. several feet   c. over 25 feet   _____

6. In the U.S., hurricanes are most common in _____.
   a. the Southwest   b. the South and Southeast   c. the 14 states on the Atlantic Ocean   _____

4 SUMMARIZE

Complete the summary with the words in the box.

| Hurricanes | ocean | Southeast | storm surges | winds |

(1) _____ are big storms. They bring dangerous (2) _____ of up to 200 mph, heavy rain, and (3) _____. Hurricanes form only over warm (4) _____ water (80° or higher). Hurricane season in the Atlantic Ocean goes from June to November. In the U.S., hurricanes most often hit places in the South and (5) _____.

Show what you know!

1. **THINK ABOUT IT.** What do people do when there is a hurricane watch?

2. **WRITE ABOUT IT.** Now write about what people do before a hurricane.

   Before a hurricane, people _____.

I can focus on details. ■   I need more practice. ■

To read more, go to MyEnglishLab.

Lesson 8: Understand a weather report

Listening and Speaking

1 BEFORE YOU LISTEN

LABEL. Write the words under the pictures.

| boots | earmuffs | gloves | a hat | ~~light clothes~~ | a raincoat |
| a scarf | shorts | sunblock | sunglasses | an umbrella | a bottle of water |

Weather! Do you have the right clothes, accessories, and supplies?

1. _light clothes_

2. _____

3. _____

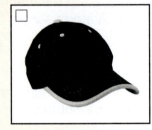
4. _____

5. _____

6. _____

7. _____

8. _____

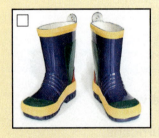
9. _____

10. _____

11. _____

12. _____

Listening and Speaking

2 LISTEN

A ▶ **RECALL.** Listen to the weather report. What clothes, accessories, and supplies do you hear? Check (✓) the pictures on page 180.

B ▶ **LISTEN FOR DETAILS.** Write the temperature for each city on the map.

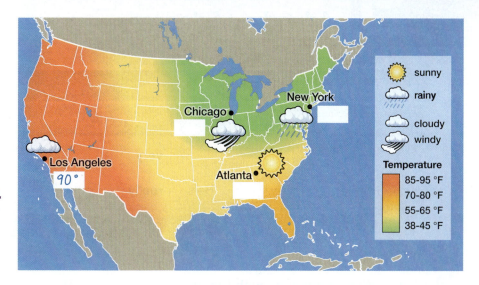

3 CONVERSATION

A **PREDICT.** Look at the picture. How is the weather?

B ▶ **LISTEN AND READ.** Then listen and repeat.

A: Are you going out?
B: Yes. Why?
A: Well, it's really **cold**, and it's pretty **windy**.
B: That's OK. I have a **scarf** and **gloves**!

C **WORK TOGETHER.** Practice the conversation in Exercise B.

D **CREATE.** Make new conversations. Use different weather words and clothes, accessories, or supplies from page 180.

E **ROLE-PLAY.** Make your own conversations. Talk about today's weather.

I can understand a weather report. ■   I need more practice. ■

For more practice, go to MyEnglishLab.

Unit 9, Lesson 8

Lesson 9 Grammar

Adverbs of degree

Adverbs of degree: *Very, really, pretty*

	Adverb	Adjective		Adverb	Adjective
It's	very	windy.	He's	very	cold.
	really			really	
	pretty			pretty	

Grammar Watch

Use *very*, *really*, or *pretty* before an adjective to make it stronger.

A APPLY. Write sentences with the words in parentheses. Then match the sentences with the pictures.

1. _It's really cold._   D
   (really / it's / cold)
2. _____ ____
   (pretty / it's / hot)
3. _____ ____
   (very / it's / windy)
4. _____ ____
   (foggy / really / it's)

B APPLY. Read the conversation. Find the three adjectives in blue. Add the word *very*, *really*, or *pretty* before each adjective. Use each word only once.

A: How's the weather?
B: It's **nice**.
A: Then let's take a walk!
B: OK. But I'm **hungry**. Let's eat first.
A: Well, there's a **good** restaurant on Main Street.
B: Great. Let's go there.

C WORK TOGETHER. Perform your conversation for the class.

D WRITE. Now write sentences about today's weather. Use *very*, *really*, or *pretty* in your sentences.

I can use adverbs of degree. ■   I need more practice. ■

For more practice, go to MyEnglishLab.

Lesson 10 Writing

Write about weather

1 STUDY THE MODEL

READ. Answer the questions.

> Pedro Melez
> The Weather in Cuba
>
> I am from Havana, Cuba. In the summer, it is hot and humid. It rains a lot. In the winter, it is sunny and warm. Winter is my favorite season in Cuba because it is warm in the day and cool at night.

1. Where is Pedro from?
2. How is the weather in Cuba in the summer?
3. How is the weather in Cuba in the winter?
4. What is Pedro's favorite season in Cuba? Why?

2 PLAN YOUR WRITING

WORK TOGETHER. Ask and answer the questions.

1. Where are you from?
2. How is the weather in your native country in the summer?
3. How is the weather in your native country in the winter?
4. What is your favorite season in your native country? Why?

Writing Skill: Use *because* to give a reason

The word *because* gives a reason. It explains why. For example:

Why is winter his favorite season? Winter is his favorite season because it is warm in the day and cool at night.

3 WRITE

Now write about the weather in your native country. Use the frame, the model, the Writing Skill, and your ideas from Exercise 2 to help you.

I'm from ____, ____. In the summer, it ____. In the winter, it ____. My favorite season is ____ because it ____.

4 CHECK YOUR WRITING

WORK TOGETHER. Read your writing aloud with a partner.

WRITING CHECKLIST

☐ The writing answers the questions in Exercise 2.

☐ The writer uses *because* to explain why.

I can use *because* to give a reason. ☐   I need more practice. ☐

For more practice, go to MyEnglishLab.

Lesson 11: Soft Skills at Work

Be ready to learn new skills

1 MEET YEFIM

Read about one of his workplace skills.

I am ready to learn new skills. For example, sometimes my work changes. Sometimes, I need to do my work in a different way. I like to learn new things.

2 YEFIM'S PROBLEM

READ. Circle *True* or *False*.

Yefim is a teacher. He learns new things in his job. Sometimes he teaches different classes. Sometimes the school has new technology.

One day he goes to a meeting. He learns about a new mobile app for emergencies at the school. All teachers need to learn the app. He's worried because he isn't good at technology. After the meeting, he talks to a co-worker.

1. The school has a new app for emergencies.   True   False
2. Teachers don't have to learn the new app.   True   False
3. Yefim is good at technology.   True   False

3 YEFIM'S SOLUTION

A WORK TOGETHER. Yefim is ready to learn new skills. What is the right thing to say to his co-worker? Explain your answer.

1. Yefim says, "I know the new mobile app is important, but I don't think I can learn it."
2. Yefim says, "I'm not good at technology. Can you help me learn the new mobile app?"
3. Yefim says, "I don't need to learn the new app. I can call 911."
4. Yefim says, "_____."

B ROLE-PLAY. Look at your answer to 3A. Role-play Yefim's conversation.

Show what you know!

1. **THINK ABOUT IT.** How are you ready to learn new things at school? At work? At home? Give examples.

2. **WRITE ABOUT IT.** Now write your example in your Skills Log.

   I can learn a new way to do my work from my co-workers.

I can give an example of how I'm ready to learn new skills.

Unit Review: Go back to page 165. Which goals can you check off?

10 Around Town

PREVIEW
Look at the picture. Where are the people? What are they doing?

UNIT GOALS

- Name places in the community
- Give locations of places in the community
- Talk about kinds of transportation
- Read traffic signs
- Read bus signs and schedules
- Ask about bus routes and costs
- Talk about weekend plans
- **Academic skill:** Give your own examples
- **Writing skill:** Use prepositions
- **Workplace soft skill:** Be reliable

Lesson 1

Vocabulary

Places in the community

A PREDICT. Look at the pictures. What do you see? What are the places?

Number 3 is a post office.

B ▶ LISTEN AND POINT. Then listen and repeat.

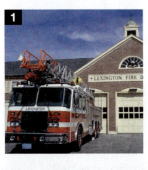

Vocabulary

Places in the community

1. a fire station
2. a bus stop
3. a post office
4. a police station
5. a supermarket
6. a drugstore
7. a gas station
8. a park
9. a bank
10. an ATM
11. a farmers' market
12. a laundromat
13. a gym
14. a clothing store
15. a café
16. a salon

C WORK TOGETHER. Look at the pictures and the list of places. Student A, choose a place. Say something you do there. Student B, guess the place.

A: I buy fruit there.
B: The supermarket?
A: No.
A: The farmers' market?
B: Right!

D CATEGORIZE. Look at the pictures and list of places. Complete the chart. Then compare answers.

Words with *station*	Words with *market*	Words with *store*

Study Tip

Count syllables

Mark the number of syllables in each word. Listen to the audio and check your work.

Show what you know!

1. **DRAW A PICTURE.** Draw a map of the streets near your school. Write the places on the map.

2. **TALK ABOUT IT.** Talk about the places around your school.

   A: Is there a café near here?
   B: Yes, it's across the street.
   C: Right. And there's a bank on King Street, next to the drugstore.

3. **WRITE ABOUT IT.** Now write a sentence about places in your community.

   There is _____ on _____ , _____ .

I can name places in the community. ■   I need more practice. ■

For more practice, go to MyEnglishLab.

Unit 10, Lesson 1   **187**

Lesson 2 — Listening and Speaking

Give locations of places in the community

1 BEFORE YOU LISTEN

IDENTIFY. Look at the ad. Complete the sentences with the words in the box.

| ~~gas station~~ | library | post office |

1. Foodsmart is near the _____gas station_____.
2. It is between the bank and the _____.
3. It is around the corner from the _____.

2 LISTEN

A ▶ **LISTEN.** Look at the picture. Listen to the conversation. Brenda is asking a man a question. What does she want?

a. a map
b. a good supermarket
c. directions

B ▶ **LISTEN FOR DETAILS.** Where is the new supermarket?

a. 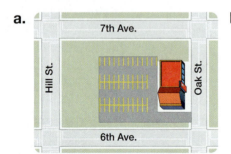   b. 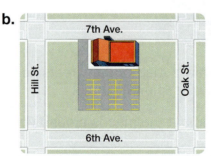   c.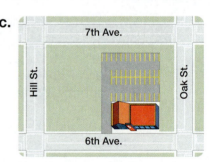

C ▶ **EXPAND.** Listen to the whole conversation. Answer the questions.

1. Are there many people at the supermarket?   a. no   b. yes
2. When is the grand opening?   a. today   b. tomorrow

Listening and Speaking

3 PRONUNCIATION

A ▶ **PRACTICE.** Listen. Then listen and repeat.

a **round**   **o** pen   to **day**   po **lice**   **sta** tion

> **Stressed syllable**
>
> In a two-syllable word, one syllable is stressed. The other syllable is not stressed.

B ▶ **APPLY.** Listen to the words. Mark (•) the stressed syllable.

sa lon   be tween   cor ner   se venth

4 CONVERSATION

A ▶ **LISTEN AND READ.** Then listen and repeat.

A: Excuse me. Can you help me? I'm looking for Foodsmart.
B: Sure. It's on Seventh between Hill and Oak.
A: Sorry?
B: It's on Seventh Avenue between Hill Street and Oak Street.
A: Thanks.

B **WORK TOGETHER.** Practice the conversation in Exercise A.

C **CREATE.** Make new conversations. Use the pictures and map.

A: Excuse me. Can you help me? I'm looking for _____.
   (place)
B: Sure. It's on _____
   (Avenue)
   between _____ and
   (Street)
   _____.
   (Street)
A: Sorry?
B: It's on _____
   (Avenue)
   between _____ and
   (Street)
   _____.
   (Street)
A: Thanks.

the DMV

the library

the courthouse

D **MAKE CONNECTIONS.** Make your own conversations. Use places and streets near your school.

I can give locations of places in the community. ▢   I need more practice. ▢

For more practice, go to MyEnglishLab.

Unit 10, Lesson 2   **189**

Lesson 3 Grammar

Prepositions of place

Prepositions of place		
The supermarket is	around	the corner from the bank.
	down	the street / the block.
	between	Hill and Oak Streets.
	on	the corner of 10th and Pine.
	near	the library.

Grammar Watch

For more prepositions of place, see page 260.

COMPLETE. Use *around*, *down*, *between*, *on*, or *near*.

1. The library is _____on_____ the corner of Oak and Elm Streets.
2. The police station is _____ Park _____ 9th and 10th Streets.
3. There's a bank _____ the corner from the police station.
4. There's a fire station _____ the street from the police station.
5. There's a post office _____ the library.
6. There's a café _____ the corner of 9th and Elm Streets.

Show what you know!

1. **IDENTIFY.** Read the sentences above again. Write the names of the places on the map.

2. **WRITE ABOUT IT.** Now write two sentences about the location of your school.

   My school is _____.
   It _____.

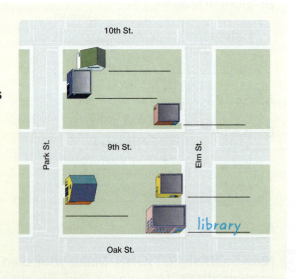

I can use prepositions of place. ■   I need more practice. ■

For more practice, go to MyEnglishLab.

Lesson 4 — Workplace, Life, and Community Skills

Talk about transportation

1 TALK ABOUT KINDS OF TRANSPORTATION

A ▶ **LISTEN AND POINT.** Then listen and repeat.

a bus

a subway

a train

a car

a bike

a taxi

B **TALK ABOUT IT.** Ask your classmates how they get to work or school. Complete the chart.

A: How do you get to work or school?
B: I take the bus.

Names	Take the bus	Take the train	Walk	Drive	Other
Susan	✓				

C **PRESENT.** Now report to the class.

Susan takes the bus.

I can talk about kinds of transportation. ■   I need more practice. ■

Unit 10, Lesson 4   191

Workplace, Life, and Community Skills

2 READ TRAFFIC SIGNS

A **LABEL.** Look at the signs. Write the meanings under the signs.

| Don't turn left. | ~~Stop.~~ | Two-way traffic. Drive on the right. |

1. _Stop._ 2. _____ 3. _____

| Drive slowly. People often cross the street here. | Drive slowly. Wait for other cars. | Right lane ends ahead. Stay to the left. |

4. _____ 5. _____ 6. _____

| Be ready to stop for trains. | Don't drive here. | Drive slowly. People often cross the street here. |

7. _____ 8. _____ 9. _____

B **IDENTIFY.** Listen to the conversations. Which signs are the people talking about? Write the number of the sign.

1. _____ 2. _____ 3. _____

I can read traffic signs. ■   I need more practice. ■

For more practice, go to MyEnglishLab.

192 Unit 10, Lesson 4

Workplace, Life, and Community Skills

3 READ BUS SIGNS AND SCHEDULES

A **WORK TOGETHER.** Look at the buses. Ask and answer questions. Take turns.

A: Which bus goes to Pine Street?
B: The Number 51. Which...?

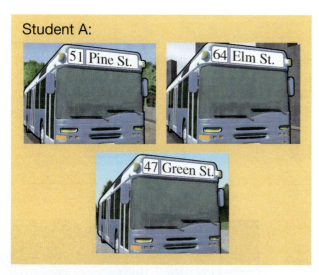
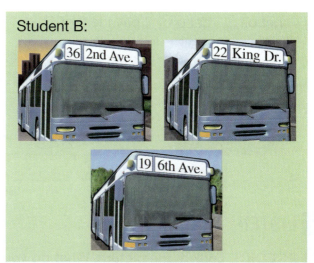

B ▶ **COMPLETE.** Look at the bus schedules. Listen and fill in the missing times.

GREENVILLE BUS SCHEDULES

BUS 36		BUS 47		BUS 51	
39th Ave.	_____	39th Ave.	8:14	King Dr.	8:15
River Rd.	8:16	Clay St.	8:23	State St.	8:22
16th Ave.	8:24	Park Ave.	_____	Oak St.	8:31
2nd Ave.	8:35	Green St.	8:40	Pine St.	_____

C **INTERPRET.** Look at the schedules in Exercise 3B. Answer the questions.

1. What time does Bus 36 leave 16th Avenue?   _8:24_
2. What time does Bus 47 leave 39th Avenue?   _____
3. What time does Bus 51 leave State Street?   _____

D **GO ONLINE.** Use a transportation website or app to find public transportation to a supermarket.

I can read bus signs and schedules. ■   I need more practice. ■

For more practice, go to MyEnglishLab.

Unit 10, Lesson 4 **193**

Lesson 5 — Listening and Speaking
Ask about bus routes and costs

1 BEFORE YOU LISTEN

LABEL. Write the words under the pictures.

get off   get on   pay the fare

a. _____

b. _____

c. _____

2 LISTEN

A PREDICT. Look at the picture. What do you see?

B ▶ LISTEN. Where do Matt and Tina want to go?

a. a supermarket
b. Adams College
c. Second Street

C ▶ LISTEN FOR DETAILS. Read the sentences. Circle *True* or *False*. Make the false sentences true.

1. They need the Number 5̵ 4 bus.   True   (False)
2. They get on at Second Street.   True   False
3. The fare is $2.00.   True   False
4. It is OK to give the driver a five-dollar bill.   True   False

D ▶ EXPAND. Listen to the second part of the conversation. Complete the sentences.

1. Matt asks the woman for _____.
   a. exact change   b. directions   c. a map
2. The woman _____ directions to Adams College.
   a. gives   b. doesn't give   c. gets
3. The woman says, "_____"
   a. It's over there. b. It's on Second Street.   c. Study, study, study!

Listening and Speaking

3 PRONUNCIATION

A ▶ **PRACTICE.** Listen. Then listen and repeat.

How **do you** get **to** Adams College?
Take **the** bus, **and** get off **at** Second Street.

> **Unstressed words**
>
> Words like *do*, *the*, *to*, and *at* are usually not stressed.

B ▶ **APPLY.** Practice saying each sentence. Then listen and repeat.

Here we are at Second Street.
We want to go to Adams College.
How do we get there?

4 CONVERSATION

A ▶ **LISTEN AND READ.** Then listen and repeat.

A: Excuse me. How do you get to Adams College?
B: Take the Number 4 bus, and get off at Second Street. It's not far from there.
A: Thanks. Oh, and how much does the bus cost?
B: Two dollars, but you need exact change.

B WORK TOGETHER. Practice the conversation in Exercise A.

C CREATE. Make new conversations. Use the information in the boxes.

A: Excuse me. How do you get to _____?
B: Take the _____, and get off at Second Street. It's not far from there.
A: Thanks. Oh, and how much does the bus cost?
B: _____, but you need exact change.

Pine Hill Park

$2.50

Green's

$3.00

the main post office

$3.50

D MAKE CONNECTIONS. Make your own conversations. Ask for directions from school to places in town.

| I can ask about bus routes and costs. ■ | I need more practice. ■ |

For more practice, go to MyEnglishLab.

Lesson 6 Grammar

Simple present questions with *How*, *How much*, and *Where*

Simple present: Questions with *How*, *How much*, and *Where*			Grammar Watch
How	do you get to Adams College?	Take the Number 4 bus.	Remember: For questions in the simple present, use **does** with *he*, *she*, and *it*.
How much	does it cost?	$2.00.	
Where	do you get off?	Second Street.	

A PUT IN ORDER. Maria is going shopping. Put the pictures in the correct order (1–4).

B WRITE. Unscramble the words to ask questions about Maria.

1. (Maria / does / shop for food / where) <u>Where does Maria shop for food?</u>
2. (get there / how / she / does) _____
3. (does / cost / how much / the milk) _____
4. (she / does / get home / how) _____
5. (the bus / where / she / does / wait for) _____

C WORK TOGETHER. Ask and answer the questions in Exercise B.

A: Where does Maria shop for food?
B: At Bob's supermarket. How . . . ?

Grammar

D **COMPLETE.** Use *How*, *How much*, or *Where* and the words in parentheses. Add *do* or *does*.

A: Excuse me. _____How do you get to_____ Pine Hill Park?
1. (you / get to)

B: Take the Number 4 train.

A: OK. _____ the train?
2. (you / get)

B: The train station is down the block. Do you see it?

A: Oh, yes. And _____ a ticket?
3. (you / buy)

B: In the station.

A: _____?
4. (it / cost)

B $2.00.

A: OK. Sorry, one more question. _____ for the park?
5. (you / get off)

B: Park Avenue. There's a big sign for the park. You can't miss it.

E ▶ **SELF-ASSESS.** Listen and check your answers.

Show what you know!

1. **THINK ABOUT IT.** Look at the pictures. Where do you buy these things? Write the places.

   __milk—DVS Drugstore__   _____

   _____   _____

2. **TALK ABOUT IT.** Talk about your answers in Step 1.

   A: Where do you buy milk?
   B: At DVS Drugstore.
   A: Oh? How much does it cost there?

3. **WRITE ABOUT IT.** Now write a note to your partner. Ask where your partner buys something. Ask how much it costs there.

   Where _____?
   _____?

I can use simple present questions with *How, How much,* and *Where*. ■

I need more practice. ■

For more practice, go to MyEnglishLab.

Unit 10, Lesson 6 **197**

Lesson 7 Reading: Read about public libraries

1 BEFORE YOU READ

A LABEL. Write the words under the pictures.

> an e-book on a tablet   a library card   a receipt with a due date

1. _____   2. _____   3. _____

B MAKE CONNECTIONS. Where is your public library? What can people do there?

2 READ

▶ Listen and read.

Academic Skill: Give your own examples

Writers often give examples to help the reader understand their ideas, like the examples in this article of library activities for children. Try to think of examples of your own when you read.

Your Public Library

The U.S. has more than 16,000 public libraries. They are open to everyone, and they are free.

You can do many things at a public library. You can read newspapers and magazines. You can study or do
5 homework. You can use Wi-Fi to go online. Many libraries have computer and English classes. Some have information about jobs. All libraries have activities for children. For example, some have summer programs. Some have homework help after school.

10 With a library card, you can borrow books, tablets, and more! How long can you keep them? Check the due date on your receipt. Don't be late, or you will need to pay a fine. The fine might be only five cents or a lot more. To get a card, fill out an application.
15 You will need to show something with your name and address. For example, show an ID, your driver's license, or a credit card bill.

An event for children at a public library.

Your public library has a website. You can find out library hours. You can read about events. You can
20 borrow e-books and watch movies online. You can renew books so you can keep them longer.

These are only a few reasons to use your public library. Go online or visit to learn more.

Reading

3 CLOSE READING

CITE EVIDENCE. Complete the sentences. Where is the information? Write the line number.

Lines

1. There are more than _____ public libraries in the U.S.
   a. 1,600   b. 16,000   c. 16,000,000   _____

2. Public libraries _____.
   a. are open all day every day   b. are free to use   c. sell books   _____

3. Children can sometimes go to the library for _____ after school.
   a. help with homework   b. free child-care   c. something to eat   _____

4. Before you can borrow things from the library, you need to _____.
   a. have a school or work ID   b. show a credit card   c. get a library card   _____

5. When you return something to the library after the due date, you _____.
   a. lose your library card   b. need to pay a fine   c. fill out an application   _____

6. Go to your public library's website to _____.
   a. take computer classes   b. pay a fine   c. renew books   _____

4 SUMMARIZE

Complete the summary with the words in the box.

| for free | library card | online | programs | public library |

You can do many things at your (1) _____. You can read, do homework, go (2) _____, and take classes (3) _____. There are activities and (4) _____ for children. You can borrow books, tablets, e-books, and movies. You just need a (5) _____. Visit your public library to get a card and learn more.

Show what you know!

1. **THINK ABOUT IT.** What are some reasons to go to a public library? What are some reasons to visit the library website?

2. **WRITE ABOUT IT.** Now write about good reasons to go to your public library.

   At my public library, I can _____.

I can give my own examples. ☐   I need more practice. ☐

To read more, go to MyEnglishLab.

Lesson 8 Listening and Speaking

Talk about weekend plans

1 BEFORE YOU LISTEN

A MAKE CONNECTIONS. Look at the pictures. Do you go to events like these in your community?

B TALK ABOUT IT. Where do you get information about events in your community? Do you look in the newspaper? Do you look online? Do you watch TV?

grand opening

concert

baseball game

yard sale

2 LISTEN

A ▶ LISTEN FOR DETAILS. Look at the Greenville Weekend Community Schedule. Listen to the radio show and complete the information.

The Greenville Weekend Community Schedule

Grand Opening

Place: Foodsmart

Day: _____

Time: _____

Baseball Game

Place: Greenville _____

Day: _____

Time: 1:00 P.M.

Concert

Place: Greenville Community College

Day: _____

Time: _____

Yard Sale

Place: the Community Center across from the _____ station

Day: _____

Time: 10:00 A.M. to _____

Listening and Speaking

B ▶ **LISTEN FOR DETAILS.** Which events are free? Check (✓) all the correct answers.

☐ the grand opening ☐ the baseball game
☐ the concert ☐ the yard sale

C **GIVE EXAMPLES.** Are there free events in your community? What are some examples?

There are free movies at the library.

3 CONVERSATION

A **PREDICT.** Look at the picture. What are they talking about?

a. the new supermarket
b. a weekend concert
c. the community college

B ▶ **LISTEN AND READ.** Then listen and repeat.

A: What are you doing this weekend?
B: I'm going to **a concert**.
A: Oh? Where's **the concert**?
B: At **the community college**. Do you want to go?
A: Sounds great.

C **WORK TOGETHER.** Practice the conversation in Exercise B.

D **CREATE.** Make new conversations. Use the events in the Greenville Weekend Community Schedule on page 200.

E **MAKE CONNECTIONS.** Make your own conversations.

I can talk about weekend plans. ■ I need more practice. ■

For more practice, go to MyEnglishLab.

Lesson 9 Grammar
Present continuous for future plans

Present continuous for future plans				
What	**are** you **doing**	next weekend?	I'm going	to a concert.
How	**are** you **getting**	there?	I'm taking	the bus.
Who	**are** you **going**	with?	I'm going	with Ana.

A **DECIDE.** Read each sentence. Is the sentence about the present or the future? Check (✓) the correct box.

	Present	Future
1. I'm working next weekend.	☐	✓
2. I'm doing my English homework now.	☐	☐
3. Are you coming with us to the movie tomorrow?	☐	☐
4. When are you visiting your grandparents?	☐	☐
5. I'm sorry, but I can't talk now. I'm cooking dinner.	☐	☐

B **COMPLETE.** Use the present continuous form of the verbs in parentheses.

1. **A:** What ___are___ you ___doing___ (do) tomorrow?
   B: I _____ (meet) my friends at the mall.
   A: How _____ you _____ (get) there?
   B: I _____ (take) the bus.

2. **A:** Where _____ Sam _____ (go) this weekend?
   B: He _____ (go) to Riverside for a concert.

3. **A:** When _____ your children _____ (visit) you?
   B: They _____ (come) for dinner next Sunday.

I can use the present continuous for future plans. ■   I need more practice. ■

For more practice, go to MyEnglishLab.

Lesson 10: Writing — Write about your street

1 STUDY THE MODEL

READ. Answer the questions.

> Lee Chang
> My Street
>
> I live on Winter Street. There are many stores near my home. There is a drugstore, a big supermarket, and a café down the block. There is also a bus stop next to my building and a subway station across the street. I like my street because I can walk to the stores.

1. What is the name of Lee's street?
2. What stores are near his home?
3. What transportation is near his home?
4. What does Lee like about his street?

2 PLAN YOUR WRITING

WORK TOGETHER. Ask and answer the questions.

1. What's the name of your street?
2. What stores are near your home?
3. What transportation is near your home?
4. What do you like about your street?

Writing Skill: Use prepositions

Prepositions are very different in every language. Be sure you use the correct preposition in English. For example:
I live ⓞn Winter Street.

3 WRITE

Now write about your street. Use the frame, the model, the Writing Skill, and your ideas from Exercise 2 to help you.

> I live on _____. There are many _____ near my home. There is a _____, a _____, and a _____ down the block. There is also _____. I like my street because _____.

4 CHECK YOUR WRITING

WORK TOGETHER. Read your writing aloud with a partner.

WRITING CHECKLIST

☐ The writing answers all the questions in Exercise 2.

☐ The prepositions are correct.

I can use prepositions. ▪ I need more practice. ▪

For more practice, go to MyEnglishLab.

Lesson 11: Soft Skills at Work

Be reliable

1 MEET ANI

Read about one of her workplace skills.

I'm reliable. For example, I always arrive at work on time. My manager knows I will be on time every day.

2 ANI'S PROBLEM

READ. Circle *True* or *False*.

Ani works at a hospital. She is a nurse's assistant. She helps patients. She needs to arrive at work on time. She takes the train to work every day. It takes one hour.

One morning, Ani looks at the train app. She sees the train to work is thirty minutes late.

1. Ani is a nurse at a hospital.   True   False
2. Ani can arrive a little late for work. True   False
3. Ani's train is one hour late.   True   False

3 ANI'S SOLUTION

WORK TOGETHER. Ani is reliable. What is the reliable thing to do? Explain your answer.

1. Ani calls her supervisor and says, "I'm sorry. I'll be late because the train is late."
2. Ani arrives late for work. Then she says to her supervisor, "I'm sorry I'm late."
3. Ani calls her supervisor and says, "I don't feel well today. I can't come to work."
4. Ani _____.

Show what you know!

1. **THINK ABOUT IT.** How are you reliable at school? At work? At home? Give examples.

2. **WRITE ABOUT IT.** Now write your example in your Skills Log.

   I always finish my homework before class.

I can give an example from my life of being reliable.

Unit Review: Go back to page 185. Which goals can you check off?

11 Health Matters

PREVIEW
Look at the picture. What do you see? Who are the people?

UNIT GOALS

- [ ] Name parts of the body
- [ ] Call to explain an absence
- [ ] Follow a doctor's instructions
- [ ] Read medicine labels
- [ ] Talk about health problems
- [ ] Give advice
- [ ] **Academic skill:** Apply what you read
- [ ] **Writing skill:** Use a topic sentence
- [ ] **Workplace soft skill:** Make good decisions

205

Lesson 1 Vocabulary

Parts of the body

A PREDICT. Look at the pictures. What do you see? What are the parts of the body?

Number 11 is leg.

B ▶ LISTEN AND POINT. Then listen and repeat.

1. head
2. face
3. neck
4. shoulder
5. arm
6. elbow
7. wrist
8. hand
9. chest
10. stomach
11. leg
12. knee
13. ankle
14. foot/feet
15. eye
16. nose
17. mouth
18. tooth/teeth
19. ear
20. back

206 Unit 11, Lesson 1

Vocabulary

Parts of the body

1. head
2. face
3. neck
4. shoulder
5. arm
6. elbow
7. wrist
8. hand
9. chest
10. stomach
11. leg
12. knee
13. ankle
14. foot/feet
15. eye
16. nose
17. mouth
18. tooth/teeth
19. ear
20. back

C SAY AND SPELL. Student A, look at the word list. Say a part of the body. Student B, ask for the spelling.

A: Stomach.
B: How do you spell that?
A: S-T-O-M-A-C-H.
B: Thanks.

D CATEGORIZE. Look at the pictures and word list. Complete the chart. Then compare answers.

I have one . . .	I have two . . .
head	legs

Study Tip

Type and spell

Type the words in your phone. Spell the words aloud when you type.

Show what you know!

1. **IDENTIFY.** Student A, look at the pictures and word list. Say a part of the body. Student B, point to your body part.

   Ankle.

2. ▶ **LISTEN AND ACT.** Listen and follow the commands.

touch

clap

nod

shake

3. **WRITE ABOUT IT.** Now write sentences about what you do with your body.

   I clap my _____. I nod my _____.
   I point to my _____.

I can name parts of the body. ☐   I need more practice. ☐

For more practice, go to MyEnglishLab.

Lesson 2 Listening and Speaking
Call to explain an absence

1 BEFORE YOU LISTEN

IDENTIFY. Look at the pictures. The children don't feel well. They feel sick. Complete the sentences.

1. Her ____throat____ hurts.
2. Her _____ hurts.
3. His _____ hurts.
4. His _____ hurts.

1. sore throat   2. stomachache

3. toothache   4. headache

2 LISTEN

A PREDICT. Look at the picture. What do you see?

B ▶ LISTEN. Complete the sentence.

Mrs. Lee is calling _____.
a. her son's school because he's sick.
b. the doctor because her son is sick.
c. the hospital because she is sick.

C ▶ LISTEN FOR DETAILS. Complete the sentences.

1. Ms. Wong is _____.
   a. a teacher
   b. an office assistant
   c. a parent
2. Alex has a sore throat and a _____.
   a. stomachache
   b. headache
   c. toothache

D ▶ EXPAND. Listen to the whole conversation. Circle *True* or *False*.

1. Mrs. Lee's other children feel well.   True   False
2. Mrs. Lee needs to call the school again later.   True   False

Listening and Speaking

3 CONVERSATION

A ▶ **LISTEN AND READ.** Then listen and repeat.

A: Good morning. Greenville Elementary.
B: Hello. This is Terry Lee. I'm calling about my son Alex.
A: Is that Alex Lee?
B: Yes. He's sick today. He has a sore throat and a headache.
A: I'm sorry to hear that. What class is he in?
B: He's in Ms. Wong's class.

B **WORK TOGETHER.** Practice the conversation in Exercise A.

C **CREATE.** Make new conversations. Use the information in the boxes. Change *he* to *she* when necessary.

A: Good morning. Greenville Elementary.
B: Hello. This is Terry Lee. I'm calling about my ▭ Alex.
A: Is that Alex Lee?
B: Yes. **He**'s sick today. **He** has ▭ and ▭.
A: I'm sorry to hear that. What class is **he** in?
B: **He**'s in Ms. Wong's class.

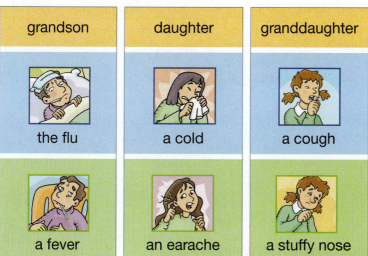

grandson	daughter	granddaughter
the flu	a cold	a cough
a fever	an earache	a stuffy nose

D **ROLE-PLAY.** Make your own conversations. Student A, you're sick. Call work.

A: Hi. This is _____. I can't come to work today. I have a . . .
B: I'm sorry to hear that.

I can call to explain an absence. ▪   I need more practice. ▪

For more practice, go to MyEnglishLab.

Unit 11, Lesson 2 **209**

Lesson 3 Grammar
Review: Simple present

Review: Simple present			
Information questions and answers		**Yes/no questions and answers**	
How **do** you **feel**?	My throat **hurts**.	**Do** you **have** a fever?	**Yes**, I **do**.
How **does** Alex **feel**?	He **doesn't feel** well.	**Does** he **have** a fever?	**No**, he **doesn't**.

COMPLETE. Use the correct form of the verbs in parentheses. Give short answers.

Mom: Doctor, I'm worried about Maria. I think she ___has___ the flu.
(1. have)

Doctor: How _____ you _____, Maria?
(2. feel)

Maria: Terrible. I _____ a cough and a stuffy nose.
(3. have)

Doctor: What about your throat? _____ it _____?
(4. hurt)

Maria: Yes, it _____. But just a little. _____ I
5.

_____ a fever?
(6. have)

Doctor: Let's see, . . . No, you _____.
7.

Mom: _____ she _____ the flu?
(8. have)

Doctor: No. She _____ the flu. It's just a bad cold.
(9. not have)

Mom: That's good. I _____ a lot better now!
(10. feel)

Show what you know!

ROLE-PLAY. Student A, you are sick. Student B, ask questions.

A: I feel terrible.
B: What's wrong?
A: My _____ hurts.
B: Do you have . . . ?

I can use the simple present. ■   I need more practice. ■

For more practice, go to MyEnglishLab.

Workplace, Life, and Community Skills

Lesson 4: Follow a doctor's instructions and read medicine labels

1 SEE THE DOCTOR

A ▶ **LISTEN AND READ.** Then listen and repeat.

A: City Clinic. Can I help you?
B: This is Viktor Petrov. I'd like to make an appointment for a check-up.
A: Sure. For what day?
B: Can I come in tomorrow?
A: No, I'm sorry. There are no openings this week. How about next Thursday afternoon at 2:00?
B: OK. Next Thursday at 2:00 is good.
A: OK, that's Thursday, March 3rd, at 2:00 P.M. See you then.

B ▶ **INTERPRET.** Listen to the conversation again. Circle the letter of the correct text message.

a. Please note this new appt for Viktor: 3/2/19 at 2:00 P.M. Text C to confirm. Questions? Call 618-555-6341. City Clinic. Text STOP to Unsubscribe. Thank you.

b. Please note this new appt for Viktor: 3/3/19 at 2:00 P.M. Text C to confirm. Questions? Call 618-555-6341. City Clinic. Text STOP to Unsubscribe. Thank you.

C **ROLE-PLAY.** Make a new conversation. Use your own name. Use different days, dates, and times. Complete the text message with your partner's information.

Please note this new appt for
_____:
_____ at _____.
Text C to confirm. Questions? Call 618-555-6341. City Clinic. Text STOP to Unsubscribe. Thank you.

Workplace, Life, and Community Skills

D **LABEL.** Look at the pictures of a check-up. Write the instructions under the pictures.

> Lie down.
> Look straight ahead.
> Make a fist.
>
> Open your mouth and say Ahh.
> Roll up your sleeve.
> Sit on the table.
>
> ~~Step on the scale.~~
> Take a deep breath.

1. Step on the scale.

2. _____

3. _____

4. _____

5. _____

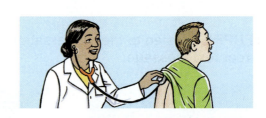

6. _____

7. _____

8. _____

E **ROLE-PLAY.** Student A, you are a doctor. Give instructions.
Student B, you are a patient. Act out the instructions.

F **GO ONLINE.** Find the phone number for a clinic in or near your neighborhood.

I can follow a doctor's instructions. ▪   I need more practice. ▪

For more practice, go to MyEnglishLab.

212 Unit 11, Lesson 4

Workplace, Life, and Community Skills

2 READ MEDICINE LABELS

A **LABEL.** Write the words under the pictures.

| operate machinery | ~~orally~~ | out of reach | tablet |

1. __orally__   2. _____   3. _____   4. _____

B ▶ **SELF-ASSESS.** Listen and check your answers.

C ▶ **LISTEN.** Complete the medicine label.

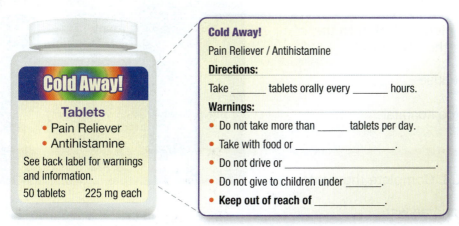

Cold Away!
Pain Reliever / Antihistamine
Directions: _____
Take _____ tablets orally every _____ hours.
Warnings: _____
• Do not take more than _____ tablets per day.
• Take with food or _____.
• Do not drive or _____.
• Do not give to children under _____.
• **Keep out of reach of** _____.

D **INTERPRET.** Look at the medicine label. Answer the questions.

1. What is this medicine for? __pain or cold__
2. How much of the medicine do you take at one time?
   _____
3. How often do you take this medicine? _____
4. How much of this medicine can you take in one day?
   _____
5. What do you take this medicine with? _____
6. What age children cannot take this medicine?
   _____

MAX-COLD AWAY

Pain Reliever / Antihistamine
Directions: Take 1 tablet orally every 4–6 hours
Warnings:
• Do not take more than 6 tablets per day.
• Take with food or milk.
• Do not drive or operate machinery.
• Do not give to children under 12.
• **Keep out of reach of children.**

I can read medicine labels. ▢   I need more practice. ▢

For more practice, go to MyEnglishLab.

Unit 11, Lesson 4

Lesson 5: Listening and Speaking

Talk about health problems

1 BEFORE YOU LISTEN

IDENTIFY. Look at the calendar. Write the words.

| the day before yesterday | last night |
| yesterday | ~~today~~ last week |

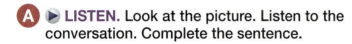

January calendar showing Jan 2–15, with Thursday Jan 12 circled.

1. Jan. 12 = _today_
2. Jan. 11 = _____
3. Jan. 11 at night = _____
4. Jan. 10 = _____
5. Jan. 2–8 = _____

2 LISTEN

A ▶ LISTEN. Look at the picture. Listen to the conversation. Complete the sentence.

Luisa wasn't at work because _____.
a. she was sick
b. her daughter was in the hospital
c. her daughter was sick

B ▶ LISTEN FOR DETAILS. Complete the sentences.

1. Luisa's daughter was home with _____.

   a.    b.    c.

2. Her daughter is now _____.

   a.    b.    c.

C ▶ EXPAND. Listen to the whole conversation. Who is sick now? _____

Listening and Speaking

3 PRONUNCIATION

A ▶ **PRACTICE.** Listen. Then listen and repeat.

She was **sick**. She **was**n't in **school**.

It was the **flu**. It **was**n't a **cold**.

They were **ab**sent. They **we**ren't **late**.

> **Pronunciation of was/were and wasn't/weren't**
>
> *Was* and *were* are often not stressed. *Wasn't* and *weren't* are stressed.

B ▶ **CHOOSE.** Listen to the sentences. Check (✓) the word you hear.

1. ☐ was ✓ wasn't
2. ☐ were ☐ weren't
3. ☐ was ☐ wasn't
4. ☐ were ☐ weren't
5. ☐ was ☐ wasn't
6. ☐ were ☐ weren't

4 CONVERSATION

A ▶ **LISTEN AND READ.** Then listen and repeat.

A: You weren't here yesterday.
B: I know. My daughter was home sick. She had a bad cold.
A: Oh, too bad. How is she now?
B: A lot better, thanks. She's back at school.

B **WORK TOGETHER.** Practice the conversation in Exercise A.

C **CREATE.** Make new conversations. Use the words in the boxes. Change *she* to *he* when necessary.

A: You weren't here _____.
B: I know. My _____ was home sick. **She** had a bad _____.
A: Oh, too bad. How is **she** now?
B: A lot better, thanks. **She**'s back at school.

| Wednesday |
| last night |
| the day before yesterday |

| son |
| grandson |
| granddaughter |

| headache |
| earache |
| stomachache |

D **ROLE-PLAY.** Make your own conversations. Use different times, people, and health problems.

I can talk about health problems. ☐   I need more practice. ☐

For more practice, go to MyEnglishLab.

Lesson 6 Grammar

Past of *be*: Statements

Past of *be*: Statements		
Affirmative		
I / He / She / We	was	sick yesterday.
You / They	were	

Negative		
I / He / She / We	wasn't	sick last week.
You / They	weren't	

Grammar Watch

Contractions
wasn't = was not
weren't = were not

A IDENTIFY. Cross out the incorrect words.

1. We **are / were** here today, but we **are / were** absent yesterday.
2. He **is / was** OK now, but he **is / was** sick last night.
3. They **are / were** in school yesterday, but they **aren't / weren't** here now.
4. She **is / was** at the doctor's office yesterday. Now she **is / was** at home in bed.
5. My brother **isn't / wasn't** here now, but he **is / was** here yesterday.
6. I **am / was** OK last week, but now I **am / was** sick.

B COMPLETE. Use *was* or *were*.

Sonia _____was_____ home sick the day before
                1.
yesterday. Her sister _____ sick, too.
                           2.
They _____ both in bed all day.
         3.
Sonia's parents _____ worried.
                      4.
Yesterday, Sonia _____ a lot
                        5.
better. Her sister _____ better,
                       6.
too. Sonia's parents _____
                          7.
very happy!

216 Unit 11, Lesson 6

Grammar

C INTERPRET. Look at yesterday's attendance sheet. Complete the sentences with *was*, *were*, *wasn't*, or *weren't*.

1. Carlos ___wasn't___ in class yesterday.
2. Carla and Min Jung _____ there, but Min Jung _____ late.
3. Tina and Sonia _____ there. They _____ both home sick.
4. Dora _____ there, but Edgar _____ there.

Student Name	Week 1				
	M	T	W	Th	F
Carla Cruz	H				
Carlos Delgado	A				
Min Jung Lee	L				
Sonia Lopez	A				
Dora Moreno	H				
Edgar Vargas	A				
Tina Wong	A				

SEMESTER: Fall   H= Here   A= Absent   L= Late

D WRITE. Look at the pictures. Write two sentences about each picture.

last week

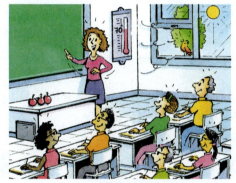
yesterday

1. _The teacher was sick last week._
2. _____
3. _____
4. _____

Show what you know!

1. **TALK ABOUT IT.** Look at the pictures again. Talk about the differences. Use *was*, *were*, *wasn't*, and *weren't*.

   A: Last week it was rainy.
   B: Right. But yesterday it was sunny.

2. **WRITE ABOUT IT.** Now write about two differences in your class.

   Last week three students were absent. Yesterday one student was absent.
   _____
   _____

I can use the past of *be*. ■   I need more practice. ■

For more practice, go to MyEnglishLab.

Unit 11, Lesson 6

Lesson 7 Reading

Read about walking and health

1 BEFORE YOU READ

A CHOOSE. Complete the sentences with the vocabulary in the box.

| energy | getting stronger | losing weight |

1. Her bones are _____.
2. He has a lot of _____.
3. She's _____.

B TALK ABOUT IT. Do you walk a lot? Do you think walking is good for you? Why or why not?

2 READ

B ▶ Listen and read.

> **Academic Skill: Apply what you read**
>
> Use what you learn from the reading to think about the world. Does the information change your ideas? Can it be useful to you, your family, or your friends?

Walk Your Way to Good Health!

Most people walk 4,000 steps every day.

It's free. It's easy. It's good for you. And guess what? You already do it every day. What is it? Walking.

When you walk every day:
5 You have a lot of energy. Your bones get strong. Your heart gets strong, too. You prevent heart disease and other health problems.

10 For good health, you should walk 10,000 steps a day (about five miles). Taking 10,000 steps a day burns about 2,000 to 3,500 calories 15 a week. There are 3,500 calories in one pound of body fat. So walking can also help you lose weight.

Most people walk 4,000 steps a day. These 4,000 steps are part of your daily routine. You walk from the bedroom to the kitchen. You walk to your car or 20 the bus stop. You walk from the entrance of your school to your classroom. So you need only 6,000 more steps a day.

Here are some ways to add steps to your daily routine:
25 • Don't take the elevator. Take the stairs.
• Walk when you talk on the phone.
• Get off the bus one stop early. Then walk the rest of the way.
• Don't park near the place you're going.
30 It's easy. So what are you waiting for? Start walking!

Reading

3 CLOSE READING

CITE EVIDENCE. Complete the sentences. Where is the information? Write the line number.

Lines

1. Walking will help you _____.
   a. prevent heart disease
   b. make friends
   c. save time
   _____

2. You need to walk _____ to help your heart and bones get strong.
   a. fast
   b. every day
   c. upstairs
   _____

3. Everyone should walk _____ steps a day for good health.
   a. 2,000
   b. 6,000
   c. 10,000
   _____

4. When you walk 10,000 steps, you are walking _____ miles.
   a. 2
   b. 5
   c. 10
   _____

5. To lose a pound of body fat, you need to use _____ calories.
   a. 2,000
   b. 3,500
   c. 3,000
   _____

6. Add steps to your day! When you take the bus, _____.
   a. don't sit down
   b. get off early and walk
   c. run to the bus stop
   _____

4 SUMMARIZE

Complete the summary with the words in the box.

| energy | health | heart | steps | weight |

Walking is good for your (1) _____. Walking every day gives you a stronger (2) _____, stronger bones, and more (3) _____. It helps prevent health problems and helps you lose (4) _____. For good health, walk 10,000 (5) _____ a day (about five miles). It's free and easy to do.

Show what you know!

1. **TALK ABOUT IT.** How can you add steps to your daily routine?

2. **WRITE ABOUT IT.** Explain how you can add steps to your daily routine.

   To add steps to my daily routine, I can _____.

I can apply what I read. ☐   I need more practice. ☐

To read more, go to MyEnglishLab.

Lesson 8 Listening and Speaking

Give advice

1 BEFORE YOU LISTEN

MAKE CONNECTIONS. What do you do for a toothache? a backache? the flu? Read the chart in 2A. Are your answers in the chart?

2 LISTEN

A ▶ **IDENTIFY.** Listen to the radio show. Number the problems in the chart in the order you hear them.

Ask the Doctor

Problem		Advice	The doctor says...	
			Do	Don't
☐ A toothache		Put heat on it.	☐	☐
		Eat a piece of onion.	☐	☐
		Drink lime juice.	☐	☐
1 A backache		Use an ice pack.	✓	☐
		Take a hot shower.	☐	☐
		Use a heating pad.	☐	☐
☐ The flu		Stay in bed.	☐	☐
		Drink a lot.	☐	☐
		Take antibiotics.	☐	☐

Important: You should see a doctor or nurse if you don't feel better soon.

Listening and Speaking

B ▶ **LISTEN FOR DETAILS.** What does the doctor say? Check (✓) *Do* or *Don't* in the chart on page 220.

3 CONVERSATION

A **PREDICT.** Look at the pictures. The woman has a sore throat. What does her friend suggest? Do you think it is a good suggestion?

B ▶ **LISTEN AND READ.** Then listen and repeat.

A: I have **a sore throat**.
B: I'm sorry to hear that. Maybe you should **drink tea and honey**.
A: That's a good idea.
B: But call the doctor if you don't feel better soon. You really shouldn't wait too long.

C **WORK TOGETHER.** Practice the conversation in Exercise B.

D **CREATE.** Make new conversations. Use the information from the chart on page 220.

E **ROLE-PLAY.** Make your own conversations. Use different problems and suggestions.

I can give advice. ■   I need more practice. ■

For more practice, go to MyEnglishLab.

Lesson 9 Grammar

Statements with *should*

Statements with *should*					
Affirmative			**Negative**		
I			I		
You			You		
He	should	rest.	He	shouldn't	work.
She			She		
We			We		
They			They		

Grammar Watch

Use the base form of the verb after *should* or *shouldn't*.

Contraction

shouldn't = should not

A IDENTIFY. Cross out the incorrect words.

1. My sister has a bad back. She ~~should~~ / **shouldn't** lift heavy things.
   She **should** / **shouldn't** ask a nurse about back exercises.
2. My friend has a stomachache. He **should** / **shouldn't** drink a lot of tea.
   He **should** / **shouldn't** eat fries.
3. My uncle has a sore throat and a cough. He **should** / **shouldn't** talk too much.
   He **should** / **shouldn't** take medicine.
4. My ankle hurts. I **should** / **shouldn't** walk. I **should** / **shouldn't** put ice on it.

B WORK TOGETHER. Read the labels. What do they mean?

A: What does this mean: "Take medication on an empty stomach"?
B: It means you shouldn't take it with food.
C: Right. You should take it before you eat.

a.   b.   c.

d.    e.

I can use *should* and *shouldn't* to give advice. ▪   I need more practice. ▪

For more practice, go to MyEnglishLab.

Lesson 10 Writing

Write about healthy habits

1 STUDY THE MODEL

READ. Answer the questions.

> Sam Sousa
> My Healthy Habits
>
> I have many healthy habits. I walk every day. I eat fresh fruit and vegetables every day. I have a check-up with the doctor every year.
>
> But I should change one habit. I only sleep six hours a night. I should sleep more.

1. What are Sam's healthy habits?
2. What habit should Sam change?
3. How should Sam change that habit?

2 PLAN YOUR WRITING

WORK TOGETHER. Ask and answer the questions.

1. What are your healthy habits?
2. What is one habit you should change?
3. How can you change that habit?

Writing Skill: Use a topic sentence

Start each paragraph with a topic sentence. A topic sentence tells the main idea of the paragraph. For example:

<u>I have many healthy habits.</u> I walk every day. I eat fresh fruit and vegetables every day. I have a check-up with the doctor every year.

3 WRITE

Now write about your healthy habits. Use the frame, the model, the Writing Skill, and your ideas from Exercise 2 to help you.

> I have many healthy habits. I ____ every day. I ____ every day. I ____ every year. But I should change one habit. I ____. I should ____ more.

4 CHECK YOUR WRITING

WORK TOGETHER. Read your writing aloud with a partner.

WRITING CHECKLIST

☐ The writing answers all the questions in Exercise 2.

☐ Each paragraph starts with a topic sentence.

I can use a topic sentence. ■   I need more practice. ■

For more practice, go to MyEnglishLab.

Lesson 11: Soft Skills at Work

Make good decisions

1 MEET AYA

Read about one of her workplace skills.

I make good decisions. I take care of myself. I know it's important to be healthy.

2 AYA'S PROBLEM

READ. Circle *True* or *False*.

Aya is an office assistant. She works Monday to Friday, 8:00 A.M. to 5:00 P.M. She takes care of herself. She eats healthy food, and she exercises.

Today, Aya is sick. She has a fever, a sore throat, and a headache. The office is very busy today. She has a lot of work to do.

1. Aya works every day from Monday to Friday.   True   False
2. Aya doesn't eat healthy food.   True   False
3. Aya doesn't have a lot of work at the office.   True   False

3 AYA'S SOLUTION

WORK TOGETHER. Aya makes good decisions. What is the right thing to do? Explain your answer.

1. Aya goes to work and goes to the doctor after work.
2. Aya doesn't go to work. She goes to the doctor.
3. Aya takes cold medicine and goes to work.
4. Aya _____.

Show what you know!

1. **THINK ABOUT IT.** How do you make good decisions at school? At work? At home? Give examples.

2. **WRITE ABOUT IT.** Now write your example in your Skills Log.

   I make good decisions about the food I buy and cook for my children. I buy a lot of fruit and vegetables.

3. **PRESENT IT.** Give a short presentation to show how you make good decisions.

I can give an example from my life of making good decisions. ▪

Unit Review: Go back to page 205. Which goals can you check off?

12 Help Wanted

PREVIEW
Look at the picture. What do you see? Where are they?

UNIT GOALS
- [ ] Name job duties
- [ ] Respond to a help-wanted sign
- [ ] Read job postings
- [ ] Talk about hours you can work
- [ ] Talk about work experience
- [ ] **Academic skill:** Mark up a text when reading
- [ ] **Writing skill:** Recognize and use a subject in a sentence
- [ ] **Workplace soft skill:** Respond well to feedback

Lesson 1

Vocabulary

Job duties

A PREDICT. Look at the pictures. What do you see? What are the job duties?

Number 2 is "use a computer."

B ▶ LISTEN AND POINT. Then listen and repeat.

Vocabulary

Job duties

1. answer the phone
2. use a computer
3. fix things
4. make food
5. serve food
6. take care of children
7. help patients
8. drive a truck
9. make copies
10. help customers
11. take care of grounds
12. use a cash register
13. supervise workers
14. work on buildings

C ASK AND ANSWER. Student A, point to a picture. Ask, "What is she or he doing?" Student B, answer.

He is using a computer.

D CATEGORIZE. Look at the verbs in the list of job duties. Write the words that go with the verbs in the chart. Then compare answers.

Use	Make	Help	Take care of
a computer			

Study Tip

Make connections

Make cards. On one side, write a job duty. On the other side, write one job with that job duty.

Show what you know!

1. **SURVEY.** Ask four classmates about their job duties. Write their answers in the chart.

   A: Min, what do you do?
   B: At work, I drive a truck. What about you?

Name	Duty	Place
Min	drives a truck	at work

2. **PRESENT IT.** Tell your class about your classmates' job duties.

   Min drives a truck at work.

3. **WRITE ABOUT IT.** Now write about your job duties.

   I _____ at _____.

I can name job duties. ■   I need more practice. ■

For more practice, go to MyEnglishLab.

Lesson 2 Listening and Speaking

Respond to a help-wanted sign

1 BEFORE YOU LISTEN

TALK ABOUT IT. Look at the picture of Dino's Diner. What do you see?

2 LISTEN

A ▶ **LISTEN.** Look at the picture. Kofi is in Dino's Diner. Listen to the conversation. Why is he there?

a. He wants a hamburger.
b. He works there.
c. He wants a job.

B ▶ **LISTEN FOR DETAILS.** Complete the sentences.

1. Kofi is a _____.

a.    b.    c.

2. He makes great _____.

a.    b.    c.

C ▶ **EXPAND.** Listen to the whole conversation. Read the sentences. Circle *True* or *False*.

1. Dino gives Kofi a job.   True   False
2. Kofi is starting his new job tomorrow.   True   False
3. Kofi answers Dino's phone.   True   False

Listening and Speaking

3 PRONUNCIATION

A ▶ **PRACTICE.** Listen. Then listen and repeat.

I can **serve**.	I **can't cook**.
She can **make pasta**.	She **can't** make **bread**.

> **Sentence stress:** *Can* and *can't* in statements
>
> *Can* is usually not stressed.
> *Can't* is stressed.

B ▶ **CHOOSE.** Listen to the sentences. Check (✓) the word you hear.

1. ☐ can ✓ can't
2. ☐ can ☐ can't
3. ☐ can ☐ can't
4. ☐ can ☐ can't
5. ☐ can ☐ can't
6. ☐ can ☐ can't

4 CONVERSATION

A ▶ **LISTEN AND READ.** Then listen and repeat.

A: I noticed the Help Wanted sign. I'd like to apply for a job.
B: OK. Which job?
A: Well, I'm a cook. I can make great hamburgers.
B: Can you make pizza?
A: No. I can't make pizza, but I can learn.

B **WORK TOGETHER.** Practice the conversation in Exercise A.

C **CREATE.** Make new conversations. Use the information in the boxes.

A: I noticed the Help Wanted sign. I'd like to apply for a job.
B: OK. Which job?
A: Well, I'm _____. I can _____.
B: Can you _____?
A: No. I can't _____, but I can learn.

a sales assistant	 use a cash register	take returns
an office assistant	 use a computer	 take inventory
a carpenter	 make cabinets	fix furniture

D **ROLE-PLAY.** Make your own conversations. Use different jobs and skills.

I can respond to a help-wanted sign. ☐   I need more practice. ☐

For more practice, go to MyEnglishLab.

Lesson 3 Grammar

Can: Statements

Can: Statements

Affirmative			Negative		
I			I		
He			He		
She	**can**	drive.	She	**can't**	cook.
We			We		
You			You		
They			They		

Grammar Watch

Use the base form of the verb after *can* or *can't*.

Contraction

can't = can not

A INTERPRET. Read Olga's job skills. Complete the sentences with *can* or *can't*.

Name: Olga Popova   **Office Jobs 4U**

Check the skills you have.

- ✓ use a computer
- ✓ answer phones
- ☐ create presentations
- ✓ make copies
- ☐ write reports
- ✓ organize things
- ☐ work with numbers
- ✓ help customers
- ☐ supervise workers

1. Olga ___can___ use a computer, and she _____ answer phones.
2. She _____ create presentations, and she _____ write reports.
3. She _____ work with numbers, but she _____ organize things.
4. She _____ supervise workers, but she _____ help customers.
5. She _____ make copies.

B WORK TOGETHER. Look at the job skills in Exercise A. What can you do? What can't you do?

A: I can use a computer, but I can't write reports.
B: I can't organize things, but I can work with numbers.

Grammar

C COMPLETE. Look at the pictures. Complete the sentences with *can* or *can't* and the verbs in the box.

| cook | drive | ~~make~~ |
| speak | take | take care of |

1.  He __can't make__ furniture.

2.  She _____ a taxi.

3.  They _____ English.

4.  We _____.

5.  I _____ messages.

6.  He _____ children.

Show what you know!

1. TALK ABOUT IT. Look at the picture. What can the people do? What can't they do?

A: The man in the green shirt can't fix the light.
B: Right. The woman in the red shirt can use a cash register.

2. WRITE ABOUT IT. Now write two sentences about the people's job skills.

The woman in the blue shirt can answer the phone.
_____
_____

| I can use *can* in affirmative and negative statements. ▪ | I need more practice. ▪ |

For more practice, go to MyEnglishLab.

Unit 12, Lesson 3 **231**

Lesson 4: Read job postings

Workplace, Life, and Community Skills

1 READ JOB POSTINGS

A **MAKE CONNECTIONS.** Read the information. Do you work? Do you work full-time or part-time?

> Full-time = 35–40 hours a week
> Part-time = less than 35 hours a week

A: I work full-time in an office. What about you?
B: I have two part-time jobs.

B **MATCH.** Find the words in the job postings. Match the words and definitions.

____ 1. experience   a. to fill out or give papers to ask for a job
____ 2. apply   b. written information about your past jobs and education
____ 3. résumé   c. when you go to a place and meet a person
____ 4. in person   d. skills you have from a job or jobs you did before

A.
DRIVERS
Deliveries Now is looking for full-time drivers
Drive a truck and deliver packages
One year of experience
$12.00/hour
Apply Now

B.
CHILD-CARE WORKER
Part-time child-care needed for two children after school
Monday to Friday 3 P.M. to 6 P.M
Help with homework and play with children
$10.00/hour

Email résumé to Ina ina.gibbs@igibbs.com

C.
COOK
Aunt Kay's Restaurant. No experience needed
Part-time: evenings
$15.00/hour

Apply in person. Monday to Friday 2:00 P.M. to 4:00 P.M.: 409 Market St., San Francisco, CA

C **INTERPRET.** Look at the job postings in Exercise 1B. Write the letter of the posting.

1. Job __A__ is full-time.
2. Job ____ pays $10 an hour.
3. Job ____ is evenings only.
4. You don't need experience for Job ____.
5. You need to go to the place to apply for Job ____.
6. You need to apply online for Job ____.
7. You can send an email for Job ____.

Workplace, Life, and Community Skills

D MAKE CONNECTIONS. Read the information. Which shift do you work?

> The first shift is usually from 7:00 A.M. to 3:00 P.M.
> The second shift is usually from 3:00 P.M. to 11:00 P.M.
> Third shift is usually from 11:00 P.M. to 7:00 A.M.

E IDENTIFY. Look at the job listings. Listen to the conversation. Which job listing are they talking about?

A.

MANAGER
IMAGINE is looking for a full-time manager for the first shift. You will supervise workers and make schedules. You need 2 years' experience.

APPLY NOW

B.

SECURITY GUARDS
SAFE PLACES is looking for part-time security guards for all shifts. We pay $12.00/hour. You don't need experience.

APPLY NOW

C.

NURSE'S ASSISTANTS   NEW
Greenville General Hospital

We're looking for full-time nurse's assistants for second and third shifts. You will take care of patients and help nurses. You need one year's experience. We pay $15.00/hour.

Email résumé to:
wendy.miller@greenvillehospital.org

F TALK ABOUT IT. Talk about the job you want. Why do you want this job?

A: I want a job as a security guard. The pay is good, and I can work the day or night shift. What about you?
B: I want a job as . . .

G GO ONLINE. Find a job listing for a job you want.

I can read job postings. ■   I need more practice. ■

For more practice, go to MyEnglishLab.

Lesson 5 — Listening and Speaking

Talk about hours you can work

1 BEFORE YOU LISTEN

LABEL. Look at the picture. Label the people. Use the words in the box.

| customer | repair person | sales assistant |

2 LISTEN

A ▶ **LISTEN.** Look at the picture below. Listen to the conversation. Who is the woman?

a. a customer
b. an employee at the store
c. a repair person

B ▶ **LISTEN FOR DETAILS.** Which questions does the woman ask the man? Check (✓) the correct questions.

☐ Can you work this Saturday?
☐ Can you work from 2:00 to 6:00?
☐ Can you work this evening?
☐ Can you work from 2:00 to 7:00?

C ▶ **EXPAND.** Listen to the whole conversation. Answer the questions.

1. Who is the man?
   a. a new sales assistant
   b. an elevator repair person

2. Who does the woman think the man is?
   a. a new sales assistant
   b. an elevator repair person

3. What does the woman want the man to do?
   a. work her shift on Saturday
   b. fix the elevator on Saturday

234 Unit 12, Lesson 5

Listening and Speaking

3 PRONUNCIATION

▶ **PRACTICE.** Listen. Then listen and repeat.

A: Can you start tomorrow?
B: Yes, I **can**.

A: Can you work Saturday?
B: No, I **can't**.

> **Sentence stress:** *Can* and *can't* in short answers
>
> In short answers, *can* and *can't* are stressed.

4 CONVERSATION

A ▶ **LISTEN AND READ.** Then listen and repeat.

A: This store is really busy.
B: I know. Listen, I need a favor. Can you work this Saturday?
A: Uh, well, yes, I can.
B: Oh, great, thanks, because I can't. Can you work from 2:00 to 7:00?
A: Um, yes. I guess so.

B **WORK TOGETHER.** Practice the conversation in Exercise A.

C **CREATE.** Make new conversations. Use the words in the boxes.

A: This  is really busy.
B: I know. Listen, I need a favor. Can you work _____?
A: Uh, well, yes, I can.
B: Oh, great, thanks, because I can't. Can you work from _____?
A: Um, yes. I guess so.

restaurant	tomorrow	6:00–11:00
hospital	Monday	8:00–3:00
hotel	June 11	4:00–10:00

D **ROLE-PLAY.** Make your own conversations. Ask someone you work with to change shifts with you.

A: Listen, I need a favor. Can you work _____?
B: _____? Yes, I can.
A: Oh, great. And can you work _____?
B: _____? Sure.
A: Thanks!

I can talk about hours I can work. ■   I need more practice. ■

For more practice, go to MyEnglishLab.

Lesson 6 Grammar

Can: Yes/no questions and short answers

Can	you / he / she / they	work	this Saturday?	Yes,	I / he / she / they	can.	No,	I / he / she / they	can't.

A APPLY. Write questions with *can*. Use the words in parentheses. Give short answers.

1. A: _Can you work nights?_
   (you / work nights)

   B: _Yes, I can._ I'm free every night.

2. A: _____
   (you / work weekends)

   B: _____ I can only work weekdays. I'm busy on weekends.

3. A: _____
   (you / come to work early tomorrow)

   B: _____ What time should I come in?

4. A: _____
   (she / start tomorrow)

   B: _____ She can be here at 9:00.

5. A: _____
   (your sister / fix the car)

   B: _____ She's good with cars.

6. A: _____
   (Bill / drive a truck)

   B: _____ He doesn't have a driver's license.

B ▶ SELF-ASSESS. Listen and check your answers.

C WORK TOGETHER. Practice the conversations in Exercise A.

Grammar

D INTERPRET. Look at the job posting. Write job interview questions with *can*. Ask about a job applicant's skills and work hours.

1. Can you answer phones?
2. _____
3. _____
4. _____
5. _____

jobs.com

Office Assistant
General Hospital, Dallas Texas

Job Skills:
Answer phones
Use a computer
Organize files
Write reports

Job Type: Full-Time

Salary: $15.00/hr

APPLY NOW

E WORK TOGETHER. Student A, ask the questions in Exercise D. Student B, answer the questions and add information.

A: Can you answer phones?
B: Yes, I can. I can take messages, too.

Show what you know!

1. **THINK ABOUT IT.** Think of a job. Write the name of the job. _____

2. **TALK ABOUT IT.** Student A, ask, "What's my job?" Other students, ask *yes/no* questions with *can* about Student A's job skills. You can ask 10 questions.

   A: What's my job?
   B: Can you use a cash register?
   A: No, I can't.
   C: Can you drive a truck?
   A: No, I can't.
   D: Can you make furniture?
   A: Yes, I can.
   E: Are you a carpenter?
   A: Yes, I am.
   B: OK, my turn. Guess my job.

3. **WRITE ABOUT IT.** Now write two questions about job skills. Use *can*.

   Can you fix things?
   Can you _____?
   _____?

I can use *can* in *yes/no* questions and short answers. ■   I need more practice. ■

For more practice, go to MyEnglishLab.

Lesson 7 Reading

Read about job interviews

1 BEFORE YOU READ

A CHOOSE. Complete the sentences with the vocabulary in the box.

| leaning forward | making eye contact | on her lap |

1. They're _____ _____.

2. She has her hands _____ _____.

3. He's _____ _____.

B TALK ABOUT IT. Your body language is the way you stand, sit, or move. All three say something about you. Why is body language important during a job interview?

2 READ

▶ Listen and read.

> **Academic Skill: Mark up a text**
>
> When you read an article for the second time, use a pencil, pen, or highlighter to mark it up. Circle important words. Underline sentences. Try using different colors.

MAKING A GOOD FIRST IMPRESSION IN A JOB INTERVIEW

When you meet someone for the first time, you quickly form an opinion about him or her. This opinion is your first impression of the person. That person forms a first impression of you, too. You want to
5 make a good impression. This is very important in a job interview.

Before Your Interview
Choose the right clothes to wear. Your clothes and hair should look
10 clean and neat. Be sure you smell good, but don't wear much perfume or cologne.

During Your Interview
When you meet the interviewer, make
15 eye contact and smile. Shake hands firmly. Stand about three feet away. When you sit down, try to look relaxed but sit up in your chair. Lean forward a little and look at the interviewer. This shows you are listening. Put your hands on
20 your lap, not in your pockets. Don't touch your face or hair.

At the End of Your Interview
When the interview is finished, shake hands again. Remember that in the
25 U.S., most people like a strong handshake. Make eye contact and smile. Say thank you.

In a job interview, the right clothes and good body language can help you
30 make a good first impression.

A good job interview starts with good body language.

Reading

3 CLOSE READING

CITE EVIDENCE. Complete the sentences. Where is the information? Write the line number.

Lines

1. Your first impression of someone is _____.
   a. the first words you say to the person
   b. the opinion you form of the person when you meet
   c. your first interview with the person
   _____

2. When you use the right body language in a job interview, it _____.
   a. helps you make a good impression
   b. means you don't need to talk
   c. saves time
   _____

3. Make eye contact, smile, and give the interviewer a _____ handshake.
   a. fast
   b. relaxed
   c. firm
   _____

4. During the interview, keep your hands _____.
   a. on the interviewer's desk
   b. on your lap
   c. moving
   _____

5. Look at the interviewer and lean forward in your chair to _____.
   a. be friendly
   b. show you are listening
   c. look excited and happy
   _____

6. At the end of your interview, _____.
   a. say you need the job
   b. ask if you can have the job
   c. say thank you
   _____

4 SUMMARIZE

Complete the summary with the words in the box.

| clean | eye contact | forward | impression | interviewer |

In a job interview, you want to make a good (1) _____. Before the interview, make sure you look (2) _____ and neat. When you meet the (3) _____, shake hands firmly and make (4) _____. Sit leaning (5) _____ with your hands on your lap. At the end, say thank you and shake hands again.

Show what you know!

1. **TALK ABOUT IT.** Talk about what you should and should not do when you have a job interview. Make a list of all your ideas.

2. **WRITE ABOUT IT.** Now write about what to do—and what not to do—when you have a job interview.

   When you have a job interview, you should _____. Don't _____.

I can mark up a text when reading. ◼︎   I need more practice. ◼︎

To read more, go to MyEnglishLab.

Unit 12, Lesson 7 **239**

Lesson 8 Listening and Speaking

Talk about work experience

1 BEFORE YOU LISTEN

PREDICT. Look at the picture in the *Greenville Reporter*. What do you see?

2 LISTEN

A ▶ **LISTEN.** Why is Tina Martins interviewing Dinh Tran and Mai Lam?

a. They have a new restaurant.   b. They were students in Greenville.

B ▶ **LISTEN FOR DETAILS.** Complete the sentences. Choose the correct words from the box.

| a hospital | a hotel | people's homes | a restaurant |

1. Dinh was a cook in _____.
2. Mai was a cook in _____.

C ▶ **LISTEN AND RECALL.** Complete the newspaper article. Use words from the radio interview.

People in the News   Greenville Reporter

Mai Lam (left) and Dinh Tran

Meet Dinh Tran and Mai Lam. They are the owners of Saigon, Greenville's first Vietnamese _restaurant_ (1). Many people here know Dinh and Mai. Dinh was a _____ (2), a server, and a _____ (3) at the Greenville Café for _____ (4) years, and Mai worked in many people's homes as a cook. Dinh and Mai were also _____ (5) at the Greenville Adult School. Their first teacher, Emily Reed, says: "They were very good _____ (6), but they were great _____ (7). Our class parties were always wonderful because of Dinh and Mai's _____ (8). I'm sure their restaurant will be a big success." Everyone in Greenville wishes the couple lots of luck.

D COMPARE. Look at your answers. Compare with a partner.

Listening and Speaking

3 CONVERSATION

A ▶ **LISTEN AND READ.** Then listen and repeat.

A: Congratulations! This place looks great!
B: Thanks.
A: So, is this your first café?
B: Yes, it is. But I worked in a café before.
A: Oh. What did you do?
B: I was a server.
A: How long were you there?
B: Two years.

B **WORK TOGETHER.** Practice the conversation in Exercise A.

C **CREATE.** Make new conversations. Use the information in the boxes.

A: Congratulations! This place looks great!
B: Thanks.
A: So, is this your first _____?
B: Yes, it is. But I worked in a _____ before.
A: Oh. What did you do?
B: I was a _____.
A: How long were you there?
B: _____ years.

salon	hair stylist	three
grocery store	cashier	four
clothing store	sales assistant	five

D **ROLE-PLAY.** Make your own conversations. Use different stores, jobs, and times.

I can talk about work experience. ▪   I need more practice. ▪

For more practice, go to MyEnglishLab.

Unit 12, Lesson 8 **241**

Lesson 9 Grammar
Past of *be*: Questions and answers

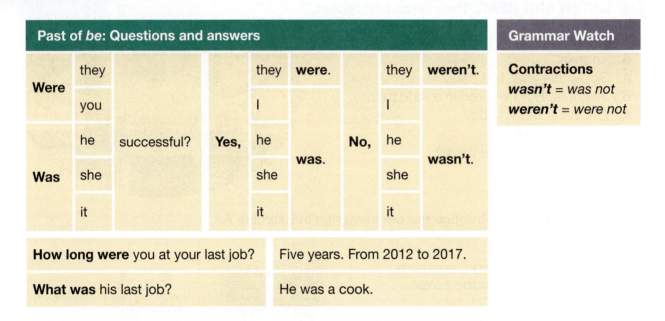

| How long were you at your last job? | Five years. From 2012 to 2017. |
| What was his last job? | He was a cook. |

A APPLY. Write questions. Use *was* or *were*.

1. What / your last job *What was your last job?*
2. the job / full-time _____
3. How long / you / there _____
4. you / happy there _____

B ▶ SELF-ASSESS. Listen and check your answers.

C ROLE-PLAY. Student A, you are a store manager. Student B, you need a job. Student B, read your job history. Student A, interview Student B.

A: *What was your last job?*
B: *I was a cashier.*

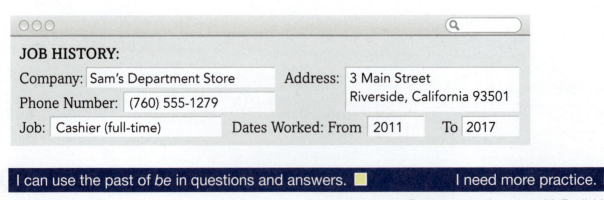

I can use the past of *be* in questions and answers. ■   I need more practice. ■

For more practice, go to MyEnglishLab.

Lesson 10 Writing

Write about job skills

1 STUDY THE MODEL

READ. Answer the questions.

> Kim Song
> An Office Assistant
>
> I want a job as an office assistant. I have some of the skills for the job. I can use a computer. I can make copies. I can't write reports in English, but I can learn!

1. What job does Kim want?
2. What skills does Kim have for the job?
3. What skill does Kim need to learn?

2 PLAN YOUR WRITING

WORK TOGETHER. Ask and answer the questions.

1. What job do you want?
2. What skills do you have for the job?
3. What skill do you need to learn?

Writing Skill: Recognize and use subjects

In English, every sentence has a subject. For example:

(He) wants to be a taxi driver.
(I) can make copies.

3 WRITE

Now write about a job you want. Use the frame, the model, the Writing Skill, and your ideas from Exercise 2 to help you.

> I want a job as a/an ____. I have some of the skills for the job. I can ____. I can ____. I can't ____, but I can learn!

4 CHECK YOUR WRITING

WORK TOGETHER. Read your writing aloud with a partner.

WRITING CHECKLIST

☐ The writing answers all the questions in Exercise 2.

☐ Each sentence has a subject.

☐ Each sentence has a verb.

I can recognize and use a subject in a sentence. ■   I need more practice. ■

For more practice, go to MyEnglishLab.

Lesson 11 — Soft Skills at Work

Respond well to feedback

1 MEET KAI

Read about one of his workplace skills.

I respond well to feedback. When I make a mistake, I listen and learn. The next time I can do a better job.

2 KAI'S PROBLEM

READ. Circle *True* or *False*.

Kai has a new job at a hospital. He is a custodian. He cleans the rooms and halls.

Today is his first day at the new job. Kai is cleaning a room. He is using a new machine. His co-worker comes in the room and says, "You are not cleaning the floor right. This isn't safe."

1. Kai is cleaning a room with his co-worker.   True   False
2. Kai knows how to use the machine.   True   False
3. Kai's co-worker tells Kai he made a mistake.   True   False

3 KAI'S SOLUTION

A WORK TOGETHER. Kai responds well to feedback. What is the right thing to say? Explain your answer.

1. Kai says, "I can do it my way. You can do it your way."
2. Kai says, "This is my first day. Can you show me how to do it?"
3. Kai says, "It's OK. I can do it."
4. Kai says, "_____."

B ROLE-PLAY. Look at your answer to 3A. Role-play Kai's conversation.

Show what you know!

1. **THINK ABOUT IT.** How do you respond well to feedback at school? At work? At home? Give examples.

2. **WRITE ABOUT IT.** Now write your example in your Skills Log.

    When my teacher corrects my writing, I write it again.

I can give an example from my life of responding well to feedback.

Unit Review: Go back to page 225. Which goals can you check off?

MY SOFT SKILLS LOG

This is a list of my soft skills. They are skills I use every day. They are important for work, school, and home. In a job interview, I can talk about my soft skills. I can give these examples from my life.

Unit 1: I'm friendly.

For example, _____

_____

_____

Unit 2: I'm a good listener.

For example, _____

_____

_____

Unit 3: I'm flexible.

For example, _____

_____

_____

Unit 4: I separate work and home life.

For example, _____

_____

_____

Unit 5: I'm professional.

For example, _____

_____

_____

Unit 6: I'm good at finding information.

For example, _____

_____

_____

MY SOFT SKILLS LOG

Unit 7: I'm a team player.
For example, _____
_____
_____
_____

Unit 8: I take action.
For example, _____
_____
_____
_____

Unit 9: I'm ready to learn new skills.
For example, _____
_____
_____
_____

Unit 10: I'm reliable.
For example, _____
_____
_____
_____

Unit 11: I make good decisions.
For example, _____
_____
_____
_____

Unit 12: I respond well to feedback.
For example, _____
_____
_____
_____

GRAMMAR REVIEW

UNIT 1 GRAMMAR REVIEW

A Complete the sentences with the correct form of *be*. Use contractions where possible.

1. I _____'m_____ in Level 2. I _____'m not_____ in Level 1.
   (be)   (be/not)
2. The book _____ hard. It _____ easy.
           (be/not)   (be)
3. My teacher _____ from the U.S. He _____ from Canada.
              (be)   (be/not)
4. Paula and I _____ from Mexico. We _____ from El Salvador.
               (be)   (be/not)
5. I _____ in Level 1. I _____ in Level 2.
     (be/not)   (be)
6. My classmates _____ helpful. My class _____ hard.
                  (be)   (be)

B PARTNERS. Look at the pictures. Complete the conversations. Use your own words.

1.
2.
3.
4.

C PARTNERS. Practice the conversations.

D ▶ DICTATION. Listen. Then listen again and complete the conversation.

Carla: This is Dinh and Mai. _____They're_____ from Vietnam.
                                       1.

Boris: Nice to _____ _____. _____ Boris Popov. Carla
                      2.   3.   4.
and I are students at the Greenville Adult School. _____ in Level 1.
                                                          5.

Grammar Review **247**

GRAMMAR REVIEW

Mai: Nice to meet you, Boris. Where _____ you _____ ?
                                        6.   7.

Boris: _____ _____ Russia.
            8.   9.

Carla: Dinh and Mai _____ students at Greenville, too. _____ in
                          10.   11.

Level 5, and _____ in Level 6.
              12.

Boris: Really? That's great.

E STEP 1. Complete the sentences. Choose the correct words.

1. My name _____ Boris Popov. I _____ from Russia.
            (is / are)   (is / am)

2. Carla is my classmate. _____ _____ from Peru.
                          (They / She) (is / are)

   _____ are in Level 1.
   (We / She)

3. Ms. Reed _____ the teacher. _____ _____ from
            (is / are)   (He / She) (are not / is not)

   my country. _____ _____ from Canada.
                (He / She) (is / are)

STEP 2. Write two or three sentences about yourself, a classmate, or your teacher. Use the sentences in Step 1 as examples.

_____

_____

_____

UNIT 2 GRAMMAR REVIEW

A Complete the conversation. Use the words in the box.

| a   an   servers   is   Is   Is   work   work   works |

A: ___Is___ that Carlos?
        1.

B: No. That's Pablo Gomez. He _____ with
                                    2.

Maria and Helena Peres. They _____ at
                              3.

Rico's Diner.

A: Oh. What do they do?

B: They're _____.
                4.

248 Grammar Review

A: Really? I _____ at a restaurant, too.
5.

I'm _____ cook. What about you?
6.

What do you do?

B: I'm _____ electrician.
7.

A: How's your job? _____ it hard?
8.

B: Yes, it _____. But it's interesting, too.
9.

Name: Meg Brown
Job: Server
Place of work: Rico's Diner
Home: Queens, New York

B **STEP 1.** Read the information about Meg Brown. Answer these questions: What does Meg do? Where does she work? Where does she live?

Meg ____is a server____.
She _____.
She _____.

STEP 2. Answer the questions about yourself. What do you do? Where do you work? Where do you live? Write complete sentences.

_____
_____
_____

UNIT 3 GRAMMAR REVIEW

A Complete these instructions. Write the correct words.

OK, class. ____Open____ your books to page 10. _____ is a picture
1. (Open / Close)   2. (This / These)

story. Now work with a partner. _____ at the picture. Ask questions. For
3. (Look / Don't look)

example, "Is _____ a marker? Are _____ tablets?" Now look at
4. (that / those)   5. (that / those)

the picture on page 11. _____ about _____ with your partner.
6. (Talk / Don't talk)   7. (it / them)

Tell _____ or _____ about the picture. _____ four
8. (he / him)   9. (she / her)   10. (Write / Don't write)

sentences about it. Show _____ to your partner.
11. (they / them)

Grammar Review **249**

GRAMMAR REVIEW

B **STEP 1.** Complete the sentences. Use words from the box. Use *Don't* when necessary. Sometimes more than one answer is correct.

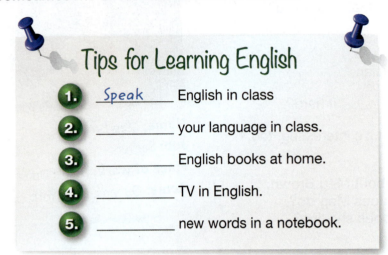

ask
listen
practice
read
speak
use
study
watch
write

STEP 2. Write four more tips for learning English. Use words from the box in Step 1.

_____
_____
_____
_____

UNIT 4 GRAMMAR REVIEW

A Complete the paragraph. Choose the correct words.

____My____ name is Tina.
1. (Our / My)

_____ husband's name is Mike.
2. (My / Her)

We _____ both 53 years old, and
3. (are / have)

we're both tall and thin. _____
4. (Our / We)

have two children. _____ son's name is Chris, and our daughter's name is
5. (Your / Our)

Kate. Chris is married. _____ wife's name is Jennie. Chris and Jennie have
6. (His / Her)

a daughter. _____ name is Amanda. She _____ ten years old.
7. (Their / Her)   8. (has / is)

Amanda is _____ first granddaughter! She _____ tall, and she
9. (our / their)   10. (is / has)

_____ long hair. Amanda looks just like _____ Aunt Kate!
11. (is / has)   12. (my / her)

B **STEP 1.** Complete the paragraph about Mel. Use *my*, *their*, and the correct form of *be* or *have*.

_____My_____ name is Mel. I _____ 75 years old. I _____
     1.   2.   3.
tall, and I _____ a beard. _____ wife's name is Anna. She
            4.   5.
_____ tall, too, and she _____ short hair. We _____
    6.   7.   8.
two daughters. _____ names _____ Tina and Cindy.
                           9.   10.

STEP 2. Write about yourself. Use the paragraph in Step 1 as an example.

My name is _____. *I* . . .

_____

_____

_____

UNIT 5 GRAMMAR REVIEW

A Complete the sentences. Use the verbs in parentheses.

A: Hi. I _____need_____ a gift for my friend.
           1. (need)

_____ you _____ this
                                  2. (have)
shirt in white?

B: No, we _____. But we _____
                3.   4. (have)
it in yellow.

A: Hmm. My friend _____ yellow.
                           5. (not/like)

B: _____ your friend _____ blue?
                                        6. (like)

A: Yes, he _____. He _____ a large.
                    7.   8. (need)

B: Oh, sorry. We _____ a large.
                       9. (not/have)

B **STEP 1.** Complete the questions. Use words from the box or your own ideas.

Do you have _____red shoes_____ ?

1. Do you have _____ ?
2. Do you want _____ ?
3. Do you need _____ ?
4. Do you like _____ ?

red	white	pink	sweater	jacket
yellow	khaki	orange	jeans	shoes
blue	black	purple	pants	shirt

Grammar Review **251**

GRAMMAR REVIEW

STEP 2. PARTNERS. Take turns. Student A, ask a question from Step 1. Student B, answer the question. Then add information.

A: Do you have red shoes?
B: No, I don't. But I have pink shoes. Do you have ... ?

STEP 3. Write sentences about your partner.

Mai has pink shoes.

1. _____
2. _____
3. _____

UNIT 6 GRAMMAR REVIEW

A Complete the conversation. Use *is there*, *there's*, *there's no*, and *there are no*.

A: This apartment is very nice. ___Is there___ a laundry room in the building?
   1.

B: Yes, _____ a laundry room on the second floor.
        2.

A: Good. _____ a garage?
         3.

B: Yes, _____ a garage, too.
        4.

A: OK. One more thing. What about furniture? There's a table in the living room, but

_____ sofa, and _____ chairs in the dining room.
     5.   6.

B: Well, _____ a furniture store in Riverside. Their furniture is good, and it's not
         7.

expensive. And _____ a good sale on now.
                     8.

B **STEP 1.** Look at the map. Complete the directions from the apartment to the furniture store.

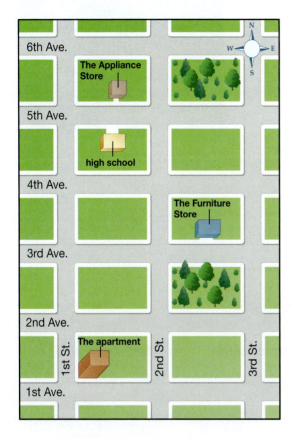

Directions ___from___ Ana's apartment
_____ Ted's Furniture Store:

Go _____ on 1st Avenue _____ 2nd Street. Turn _____ on 2nd Street.

Go _____ 3rd Avenue. Turn _____ on 3rd Avenue. The store is _____ 3rd Avenue between 2nd and 3rd Streets across from a small park.

STEP 2. Write directions from the Furniture Store to the Appliance Store.

_____
_____
_____
_____

UNIT 7 GRAMMAR REVIEW

A ▶ **DICTATION.** Listen. Then listen again and complete the conversation.

A: Hey, Brenda. You look great.

B: Thanks, Alan. I feel great! I think it's because I ride my bike a lot.

A: Oh? ___How___ often _____ you ride your bike?
      1.   2.

B: Four or five _____ a week.
                    3.

A: Really? _____?
              4.

B: I _____ ride before work, _____ 6:00 to 7:00, and I
         5.   6.

_____ ride on Saturdays from 9:00 to 10:00.
7.

A: Good for you!

B **PARTNERS.** Practice the conversation in Exercise A.

Grammar Review **253**

GRAMMAR REVIEW

C **STEP 1. PARTNERS.** Talk about free-time activities.

A: What do you do in your free time?
B: I play soccer.
A: Oh. How often do you play?
B: Once a week. I play on Thursdays from 5:00 to 7:00.

STEP 2. Write three sentences about your partner's free-time activities.

David plays soccer once a week. He plays on Thursdays. He plays from 5:00 to 7:00.

UNIT 8 GRAMMAR REVIEW

A ▶ **DICTATION.** Two friends are talking about a recipe. Listen. Then listen again and complete the conversation.

A: This omelet is really good. What's in it?

B: _____Eggs_____ and cheese. Oh, and there's
1.
_____, but not much.
2.

A: Eggs? How _____ eggs?
3.

B: Three.

A: And how _____ cheese?
4.

B: Just one slice.

A: What do you cook it in? Do you use butter _____ oil?
5.

B: I use _____, but it's good with _____, too.
6.   7.

B **STEP 1.** You are planning a meal. What do you want? Circle one food or drink in each pair.

1. soup or salad
2. meat or fish
3. rice or potatoes
4. carrots or green beans
5. coffee or tea
6. ice cream or cake

STEP 2. GROUPS OF 5. Ask your classmates about their choices. Count the students. Write the number next to each food.

How many people want soup?

soup __2__ salad __3__

1. soup ____ salad ____
2. meat ____ fish ____
3. rice ____ potatoes ____
4. carrots ____ green beans ____
5. coffee ____ tea ____
6. ice cream ____ cake ____

STEP 3. Write six sentences about your group's choices.

Two students want soup, and three students want salad.

STEP 4. Tell the class about your group's meal.

Our group wants salad, fish, ...

UNIT 9 GRAMMAR REVIEW

A ▶ **DICTATION.** Listen. Then listen again and complete the conversation.

A: Hi, Sandy. It's me, Gail. Are you at work?

B: _____(1)_____, I _____(2)_____ today. I'm home. There's a _____(3)_____ bad snowstorm here. Schools are closed again.

A: Wow! So, what _____(4)_____ the kids _____(5)_____?

B: Well, Tony and Dino are outside in the snow. They _____(6)_____ pictures.

A: That's nice. What about Maria? _____(7)_____ she _____(8)_____ in the snow?

B: _____(9)_____, she _____(10)_____. She _____(11)_____ computer games with my dad.

A: And you?

B: Well, I _____(12)_____. And my mom and I _____(13)_____ laundry. I'm not at work, but I'm _____(14)_____ busy. And I'm _____(15)_____ tired.

Grammar Review **255**

GRAMMAR REVIEW

B **STEP 1. PARTNERS.** Look at the picture. What are the people doing?

A: In Apartment 1, the man is sleeping.
B: Right. And in Apartment 2 . . .

STEP 2. Choose six apartments. Write sentences about the people.

In Apartment 1, the man is sleeping.

_____
_____
_____
_____
_____

UNIT 10 GRAMMAR REVIEW

A Complete the conversation. Cross out the incorrect words.

A: What ~~do you do~~ / **are you doing** tomorrow?
B: I **go** / **'m going** to the library in Greenville. I **go** / **'m going** every Friday.
A: Every Friday! **How** / **Where** do you get there?
B: Well, I always **take** / **am taking** the Number 2 bus. The library is on Oak **near** / **between** 7th and 8th Avenues. The bus stops **down** / **near** the block from the library.
A: Oh, really? **What** / **When** are you going?
B: At noon. Why?
A: I **go** / **'m going** to the DMV. It's right **around** / **between** the corner from the library. We can go together!

B **STEP 1.** Think about your weekend plans. Fill in the "You" rows. Write two activities.

	What?	When?	Who?
You	concert	Sat. afternoon	me, Amy, Joe
Your Partner			

STEP 2. PARTNERS. Talk about your plans. Complete the chart.

A: What are you doing this weekend?
B: I'm going to a concert in the park.
A: Oh. When . . .

STEP 3. Write two sentences about your plans and two sentences about your partner's plans.

I am going to a concert on Saturday afternoon. I am going with . . .

_____

_____

UNIT 11 GRAMMAR REVIEW

A Complete the conversation. Use the words in the box.

| does | feels | has | have | hurts | should | was | was | ~~weren't~~ |

A: You ____weren't____ here last week.
   1.

B: No, I _____ home. My son _____ sick with the flu.
   2.   3.

A: Oh, I'm so sorry to hear that. _____ he feel better now?
   4.

B: Not really. He still _____ a bad headache, and his throat _____.
   5.   6.

A: Hmm. Maybe you _____ take him to the doctor.
   7.

B: We _____ an appointment for tomorrow.
   8.

A: Well, I hope he _____ better soon.
   9.

B **STEP 1. GROUPS OF 3.** Read the problems. Make suggestions.

Problem 1
Bobby, a 10-year-old boy, has a stomachache every morning before school. What should his parents do?

Problem 2
Sara has a backache. Her friend tells her to exercise. Is this a good suggestion? Sara isn't sure. What should she do?

Problem 3
Ted has a bad sore throat. He wants to go to work. His wife thinks he should stay home. What should he do?

A: OK, Problem 1. What should Bobby's parents do?
B: Hmm. Maybe they should talk to his teacher. Maybe there's a problem at school.
C: Or, maybe they should take him to the doctor.

GRAMMAR REVIEW

STEP 2. Write one suggestion for each problem.

Problem 1. _____
Problem 2. _____
Problem 3. _____

UNIT 12 GRAMMAR REVIEW

A Complete the interview with *was*, *were*, *can*, and *can't*.

A: So, I see you ____were____ a sales assistant at Creative Clothing in Smithfield.
1.
How long ____were____ you there?
2.

B: Three years. I _____ there from 2013 to 2016. Then my family moved.
3.

A: _____ you speak Korean? We have a lot of Korean customers.
4.

B: Yes, I _____ speak Korean, English, and a little Spanish. I _____
5. 6.
a cashier in a Mexican restaurant for six months.

A: Our store is always busy on weekends. _____ you work weekends?
7.

B: Well, I can work Saturdays, but I _____ work Sundays.
8.

A: That's OK. When can you start?

B: I _____ start next weekend.
9.

B STEP 1. Complete the information about a job you or a friend had.

Company: _____
Job: _____ Dates Worked: From _____ To _____
The job was ☐ full-time ☐ part-time

C STEP 2. Write three sentences about the job in Step 1.

I was a sales assistant at Creative Clothing in Smithfield. I was there for three years.

The job was . . .
_____
_____

GRAMMAR REFERENCE

Unit 2, Lesson 3, page 31

Some irregular plural nouns			
child	**children**	person	**people**
man	**men**	foot	**feet**
woman	**women**	tooth	**teeth**

Unit 2, Lesson 9, page 42

Spelling rules for simple present tense: Third-person singular (*he, she, it*)

1. Add **-s** for most verbs: *work—work**s**   play—play**s***
2. Add **-es** for words that end in **-ch, -s, -sh, -x,** or **-z**: *watch—watch**es**   relax—relax**es***
3. Change the *y* to *i* and add **-es** when the base form ends in a consonant + *y*: *study—stud**ies***
4. Add **-s** when the base form ends in a vowel + *y*: *play—play**s**   enjoy—enjoy**s***
5. Some verbs have **irregular forms**: *do—**does**   have—**has**   go—**goes***

Unit 7, Lesson 3, page 130

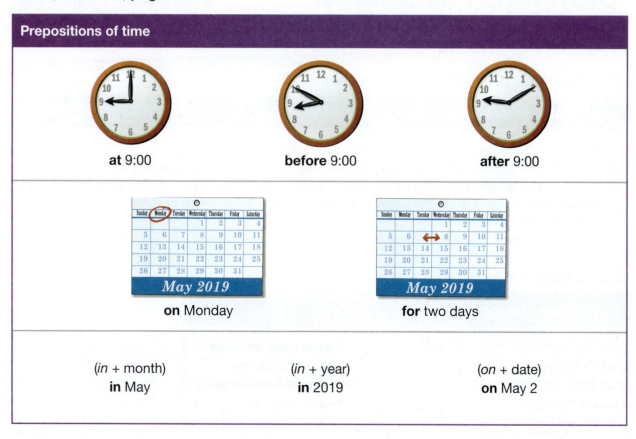

Prepositions of time

at 9:00   before 9:00   after 9:00

on Monday   for two days

(*in* + month) in May   (*in* + year) in 2019   (*on* + date) on May 2

Grammar Reference 259

GRAMMAR REFERENCE

Unit 8, Lesson 3, page 150

Some common non-count nouns
Food: beef, bread, butter, cabbage, cake, cereal, chicken, chocolate, fish, ice cream, lettuce, oil, pizza, rice, salmon, shrimp, soup, yogurt **Drinks:** coffee, juice, milk, soda, tea, water **School Subjects:** art, English, history, math, music, science **Activities:** basketball, homework, laundry, soccer **Others:** air-conditioning, chalk, electricity, furniture, hair, information, luggage, money, news, paper, transportation, weather

Remember: Non-count nouns are singular. Example: *Pizza is my favorite food.*

Spelling rules for plural count nouns		
Add *-s* to most nouns	book—book**s**	
Add *-es* to most nouns that end in *-ch, -s, -sh, -x,* or a consonant + *o*.	watch—watch**es** guess—guess**es** dish—dish**es**	box—box**es** potato—potato**es**
Change *y* to *i* and add *-es* to nouns that end in a consonant + *y*.	baby—bab**ies**	city—cit**ies**
Change *f* to *v* and add *-s* to nouns that end in *-fe*.	knife—kni**ves**	wife—wi**ves**
Change *f* to *v* and add *-es* to nouns that ends in *-f*.	loaf—loa**ves**	shelf shel**ves**

Unit 9, Lesson 3, page 170

Spelling rules for present continuous
1. Add *-ing* to the base form: cook—cook**ing**   eat—eat**ing**
2. For verbs that end in *e,* drop the final *e* and add *-ing*: take—tak**ing**   make—mak**ing**
3. For one-syllable verbs that end in a consonant, a vowel, and a consonant, double the final consonant and add *-ing*. Do not double the final consonant if it is a *w, x,* or *y*: get—get**ting**   play—play**ing**

Unit 10, Lesson 3, page 190

Prepositions of place	
in Los Angeles	*across from* the bank
on First Street	*around* the corner
at 231 First Street	*next to* the supermarket
down the block	*near* the corner
between First and Second Streets	*in/at* school

ABCs and Numbers

The Alphabet

Aa	Bb	Cc	Dd	Ee	Ff	Gg	Hh	Ii	Jj	Kk	Ll	Mm
Nn	Oo	Pp	Qq	Rr	Ss	Tt	Uu	Vv	Ww	Xx	Yy	Zz

Cardinal Numbers

1 one	2 two	3 three	4 four	5 five	6 six
7 seven	8 eight	9 nine	10 ten	11 eleven	12 twelve
13 thirteen	14 fourteen	15 fifteen	16 sixteen	17 seventeen	18 eighteen
19 nineteen	20 twenty	21 twenty-one	22 twenty-two	23 twenty-three	24 twenty-four
25 twenty-five	26 twenty-six	27 twenty-seven	28 twenty-eight	29 twenty-nine	30 thirty
40 forty	50 fifty	60 sixty	70 seventy	80 eighty	90 ninety
100 hundred					

Ordinal Numbers

1st first	2nd second	3rd third	4th fourth	5th fifth	6th sixth
7th seventh	8th eighth	9th ninth	10th tenth	11th eleventh	12th twelfth
13th thirteenth	14th fourteenth	15th fifteenth	16th sixteenth	17th seventeenth	18th eighteenth
19th nineteenth	20th twentieth	21st twenty-first	22nd twenty-second	23rd twenty-third	24th twenty-fourth
25th twenty-fifth	26th twenty-sixth	27th twenty-seventh	28th twenty-eighth	29th twenty-ninth	30th thirtieth
40th fortieth	50th fiftieth	60th sixtieth	70th seventieth	80th eightieth	90th ninetieth
100th hundredth					

WORD LIST

UNIT 1

Regions
Africa, 7
Asia, 7
Central America, 7
Europe, 7
Middle East (the), 7
North America, 7
South America, 7

Countries
Brazil, 7
Canada, 7
China, 7
Cuba, 7
El Salvador, 7
Ethiopia, 7
Iraq, 7
Mexico, 7
Peru, 7
Poland, 7
Russia, 7
Somalia, 7
South Korea, 7
Syria, 7
United State (the), 7
Vietnam, 7

absent, 12
boring, 18
bow, 8
class, 14
classmate, 12
countries, 7
easy, 16
first name, 10
friendly, 19
good, 18
great, 18
hard, 16
helpful, 19
hug, 8
Identification Card (ID Card), 15
immigrant, 16
interesting, 18
last name, 10
late, 12
regions, 7
shake hands, 8
smart, 19
regions, 7
student, 19
teacher, 19

UNIT 2

accountant, 27
assembly line worker, 41
caregiver, 41
carpenter, 41
cashier, 27
child-care worker, 27
CNA, 38
construction site, 27
cook, 27
custodian, 27
doctor, 27
driver, 27
electrician, 27
email address, 33
factory, 41
healthcare, 38
home, 27
homemaker, 27
hospital, 27
landscaper, 27
manager, 27
nurse, 27
nursing home, 38
office, 27
office assistant, 27
orderly, 38
painter, 27
phone number, 32
restaurant, 27
sales assistant, 27
server, 27
stock clerk, 41
store, 27
supermarket, 41

UNIT 3

across from, 59
backpack, 47
board, 47
book, 47
borrow, 48
cafeteria, 58
computer lab, 58
computer lab assistant, 60
custodian, 60
desk, 47
dictionary, 47
director, 60
director's office, 61
elevator, 58
eraser, 47
folder, 47
hall, 58
keyboard, 54
laptop, 47
librarian, 60
library, 58
marker, 47
mouse, 54
next to, 59
notebook, 47
office, 58
on the left, 59
on the right, 59
phone, 47
piece of paper, 47
printer, 54
projector, 47
put away, 48
restroom, 58
screen, 54
stairs, 58
sticky note, 47
tablet, 47
take out, 48
three-ring binder, 47
turn off, 48

UNIT 4

Months
January, 78
February, 78
March, 78
April, 78
May, 78
June 78
July, 78
August, 78
September, 78
October, 78
November, 78
December, 78

aunt, 69
average, 74
beard, 74
birthday, 79
blended family, 72
brother, 67
calendar, 78
children, 67
common, 73
cousin, 69
date, 78
daughter, 67
divorced, 72
family tree, 67
family, 68
father, 67
female, 67
grandfather, 67
grandmother, 67
height, 74
holiday, 78
husband, 67
look like, 68
male, 67
married, 72
month of the year, 78
mother, 67
mustache, 74
parents, 67
photo, 69
remarried, 73
short, 74
sister, 67
son, 67
step-brother, 72
step-father, 72
step-mother, 72
step-sister, 72
tall, 74
thin, 74
uncle, 69
weight, 74
wife, 67

UNIT 5

bank account, 99
bill, 98
black, 87
blouse, 87
blue, 87
brown, 87
cash, 98
clothes, 86
credit card, 98
debit card, 98
dime, 92
dress, 87
due date, 99
extra large, 94
extra small, 94
gray, 87
green, 87
handbag, 89
interest, 99
jacket, 87
jeans, 87
khaki, 87
large, 94
medium, 94
need, 88
nickel, 92
orange, 87
pants, 87

262 Word List

penny, 92
pink, 87
plastic, 98
price, 93
purple, 87
quarter, 92
receipt, 93

red, 87
return, 100
shirt, 87
shoes, 87
skirt, 87
small, 94
sneakers, 87

socks, 87
sweater, 87
T-shirt, 87
tax, 93
tight, 101
wallet, 89
want, 88

watch, 89
wear, 87
white, 87
yellow, 87
zipper, 100

UNIT 6

address, 118
air conditioning, 119
apartment, 110
appliances, 114
avenue, 118
bathroom, 107
bathtub, 107
bed, 107
bedroom, 107
boulevard, 118
cable, 119
ceiling, 112
chair, 107
closet, 107
coffee table, 107

dark, 108
dining room, 107
dresser, 107
drive, 118
east, 120
expensive, 108
fire, 113
floor lamp, 115
for rent, 108
furnished, 114
garage, 109
go off, 112
GPS, 120
heat, 119
inexpensive, 108

Internet, 19
kitchen, 107
lamp, 107
landlord, 112
laundry room, 109
living room, 107
map, 120
microwave, 107
north, 120
parking, 119
pet, 119
refrigerator, 107
renter, 112
road, 118
shower, 107

sink, 107
smoke alarm, 112
sofa, 107
south, 120
stove, 107
street, 118
studio, 115
sunny, 108
table, 107
toilet, 107
unfurnished, 114
west, 120
yard, 109

UNIT 7

Days
Monday, 132
Tuesday, 132
Wednesday, 132
Thursday, 132
Friday, 132
Saturday, 132
Sunday, 132

babysit, 129
chore, 138
clean, 134
communicate, 138
cook dinner, 127
days of the week, 132
do homework, 127
do puzzles, 140

do the laundry, 135
eat breakfast, 127
eat dinner, 127
employee, 133
exercise, 127
free time, 138
get dressed, 127
get home, 127
get up, 127
go dancing, 135
go running, 140
go swimming, 135
go to bed, 127
go to the beach, 135
go to the mall, 128
go to the movies, 128
go to the park, 128

go to work, 127
ID number, 133
knit, 140
listen to music, 140
on average, 138
play basketball, 135
play cards, 135
play soccer, 128
play sports, 139
play video games, 135
read, 135
relax, 138
ride a bike, 135
shop for food, 134
socialize, 138
spend time with
  someone, 134

stay home, 135
stressed, 141
take a (computer) class, 129
take a hot bath, 140
take a long walk, 140
take a shower, 127
time in, 133
time out, 133
time sheet, 133
visit someone, 129
wash a car, 135
wash the dishes, 127
watch TV, 127
work schedule, 132

UNIT 8

apple pie, 154
apples, 147
avocados, 161
baked potato, 154
bananas, 147
beans, 147
beef, 147
black bean taco, 155
bread, 147
butter, 147
cabbage, 147
cabinet, 152
calories, 158
canned foods, 153
carrots, 161
cereal, 147
cheese, 147
chicken, 147
coffee, 154
counter, 152
cucumbers, 161

dairy, 147
eggs, 147
fat, 158
fish, 147
freezer, 152
fresh, 152
fried, 160
fries, 154
frozen food, 153
fruit, 147
fruit cup, 154
grains, 147
gram (g), 159
green beans, 158
grilled, 160
hamburger, 148
ice cream, 154
iced tea, 154
lettuce, 147
mango, 161
milk, 147

milligram (mg), 159
net weight, 159
nuts, 161
oils, 147
onions, 147
orange juice, 155
oranges, 147
pancakes, 149
pasta, 149
pizza, 148
potatoes, 147
proteins, 147
red peppers, 161
refrigerator, 152
rice, 147
roast beef, 161
salad, 149
salmon, 161
scallions, 161
scrambled eggs, 149
sell-by date, 153

serving size, 159
shrimp, 161
soda, 154
sodium, 158
spinach, 161
steak, 149
steamed, 160
sugar, 158
taco, 148
tomatoes, 161
tomato soup, 154
turkey, 161
turkey sandwich, 154
use-by date, 153
vegetable oil, 147
vegetables, 147
watermelon, 161
wraps, 149
yogurt, 147

WORD LIST

UNIT 9

alarm system, 173
batteries, 174
boots, 180
cloudy, 167
cold, 167
cool, 167
earmuffs, 180
earthquake, 172
emergency, 172
emergency exit, 173
exit doors, 173
exit maps, 173
fall, 167
fire, 172
first aid kit, 174
flashlight, 174
flood, 172
foggy, 169
gloves, 180
hat, 180
hot, 167
humid, 169
hurricane, 172
hurricane warning, 178
hurricane watch, 178
landslide, 172
light clothes, 180
matches, 174
northeast, 178
northwest, 178
raincoat, 180
rainy, 167
scarf, 180
seasons, 167
shorts, 180
snowstorm, 172
snowy, 167
southeast, 178
southwest, 178
spring, 167
storm surges, 179
summer, 167
sunblock, 180
sunglasses, 180
sunny, 167
thunderstorm, 172
tornado, 172
umbrella, 180
warm, 167
weather, 167
wildfire, 172
winds, 179
windy, 169
winter, 167

UNIT 10

around the corner from, 190
ATM, 187
bank, 187
baseball game, 200
between, 190
bike, 191
bus, 191
bus schedule, 193
bus stop, 187
café, 187
car, 191
clothing store, 187
concert, 200
courthouse, 189
DMV, 189
down the street/block, 190
drugstore, 187
due date, 198
e-book, 198
exact change, 194
fare, 194
farmers' market, 187
fire station, 187
gas station, 187
get off/on, 194
grand opening, 200
gym, 187
laundromat, 187
library card, 198
near, 190
on the corner of, 190
park, 187
police station, 187
post office, 187
salon, 187
subway, 191
supermarket, 187
taxi, 191
traffic signs, 192
train, 191
transportation, 191
yard sale, 200

UNIT 11

ankle, 207
antibiotics, 220
arm, 207
back, 207
chest, 207
clap, 207
cold, 209
cough, 209
doctor, 208
ear, 207
earache, 209
elbow, 207
energy, 218
eye, 207
face, 207
fever, 209
flu, 209
foot/feet, 207
get strong, 218
hand, 207
head, 207
headache, 208
health, 219
heart, 219
heating pad, 220
ice pack, 220
knee, 207
leg, 207
lie down, 212
look straight ahead, 212
lose weight, 218
make a fist, 212
mouth, 207
neck, 207
nod, 207
nose, 207
open your mouth, 212
operate machinery, 213
orally, 213
out of reach, 213
patient, 212
put heat on it, 220
roll up your sleeve, 212
shake, 207
shoulder, 207
sick, 208
sit on the table, 212
sore throat, 208
stay in bed, 220
step on the scale, 212
steps, 219
stomach, 207
stomachache, 208
stuffy nose, 209
tablet, 213
take a deep breath, 212
take a hot shower, 220
take antibiotics, 220
tooth/teeth, 207
toothache, 208
touch, 207
use a heating pad, 220
use an ice pack, 220
weight, 219
wrist, 207

UNIT 12

answer the phone, 227
apply for a job, 229
carpenter, 229
cashier, 241
create presentations, 230
customer, 234
drive a truck, 227
experience, 232
fix furniture, 229
fix things, 227
full-time, 232
hair stylist, 241
help customers, 227
help patients, 227
hotel, 235
in person, 232
job interview, 238
make cabinets, 229
make copies, 227
make food, 227
office assistant, 229
organize things, 230
part-time, 232
repair person, 234
résumé, 232
sales assistant, 229
salon, 241
serve food, 227
shift, 233
supervise workers, 227
take care of children, 227
take care of grounds, 227
take inventory, 229
take returns, 229
use a cash register, 227
use a computer, 227
work on buildings, 227
work with numbers, 230
write reports, 230

AUDIO SCRIPT

UNIT 1

Page 8, Exercises 2B and 2C

Carla: Hi, I'm Carla Cruz.
Boris: Hi, I'm Boris Popov.
Carla: Nice to meet you.
Boris: Nice to meet you, too.

Page 8, Exercise 2D

Carla: Hi, I'm Carla Cruz.
Boris: Hi, I'm Boris Popov.
Carla: Nice to meet you.
Boris: Nice to meet you, too.
Carla: Where are you from, Boris?
Boris: I'm from Russia. What about you?
Carla: I'm from Peru.

Page 11, Exercise 2D

1.
A: Your name, please?
B: Michael Chen.
A: Can you spell your first name, please?
B: Sure. M-I-C-H-A-E-L.
A: M-I-C-H-A-E-L. OK, Mr. Chen. You want to take English classes, right?
B: Right.
A: Thank you, Mr. Chen.

2.
A: Your name, please?
B: Vera Kotova.
A: Can you spell your last name, please?
B: Sure. K-O-T-O-V-A.
A: K-O-T-O-V-A. OK, Miss Kotova. You want to take English classes, right?
B: Right.
A: Thank you, Miss Kotova.

3.
A: Your name, please?
B: Ana Lopez.
A: Can you spell your last name, please?
B: Sure. L-O-P-E-Z.
A: L-O-P-E-Z. OK, Ms. Lopez. You want to take English classes, right?
B: Right.
A: Thank you, Ms. Lopez.

Page 12, Exercises 2B and 2C

Carla: Who's that?
Sen: That's Boris.
Carla: No, that's not Boris.
Sen: Oh, you're right. That's Max.
Carla: Max? Where's he from?
Sen: He's from Mexico.

Page 12, Exercise 2D

Carla: Who's that?
Sen: That's Boris.
Carla: No, that's not Boris.
Sen: Oh, you're right. That's Max.
Carla: Max? Where's he from?
Sen: He's from Mexico.
Carla: So, where's Boris?
Sen: I don't know. I guess he's absent.
Boris: I'm not absent. I'm here! Sorry I'm late.

Page 13, Exercise 3B

1. She's a student.
2. He's in Level 1.
3. He's late.
4. She's Sen.
5. She's not here.
6. He's from China.

Page 18, Exercises 2A and 2B

Min Jung: Hi. So, what class are you in?
Boris: We're in Level 1.
Min Jung: Oh. How is it?
Mimi: It's good. The teacher is great.
Min Jung: How are the students?
Boris: They're great, too.

Page 18, Exercise 2C

Min Jung: Hi. So, what class are you in?
Boris: We're in Level 1.
Min Jung: Oh. How is it?
Mimi: It's good. The teacher is great.
Min Jung: How are the students?
Boris: They're great, too. There's just one problem.
Min Jung: Oh? What's the problem?
Boris: English! It's hard.

Page 22, Exercise C

1. He's not in Level 3.
2. Level 3 isn't easy.
3. We're not late.
4. They're in my class.
5. They aren't absent.
6. The teachers are helpful.

UNIT 2

Page 28, Exercise 2A

Edgar: Omar, this is Rosa. Rosa, this is Omar.
Rosa: Hi, Omar. Nice to meet you.
Omar: Hi, Rosa. Nice to meet you, too.

Page 28, Exercises 2B and 2C; Page 29, Exercise 4A

Rosa: So, what do you do?
Omar: I'm a landscaper. And I'm a student at Greenville Adult School.
Rosa: Really? I'm a student there, too. And I'm a sales assistant.
Omar: Oh, that's interesting.

AUDIO SCRIPT

Page 28, Exercise 2D

Rosa: So, what do you do?
Omar: I'm a landscaper. And I'm a student at Greenville Adult School.
Rosa: Really? I'm a student there, too. And I'm a sales assistant.
Omar: Oh, that's interesting. I think Emilio is a sales assistant, too.
Rosa: No, he's not. He's an office assistant, not a sales assistant.

Page 31, Show What You Know, Exercise 3

Which are the most common jobs in the U.S.?
Sales assistants are number 1.
Cashiers are number 2.
Food preparers and servers are number 3.
Office assistants are number 4.
Nurses are number 5.

Page 32, Exercise 1C

1. 412-960-5334
2. 619-464-2083
3. 305-576-1169
4. 323-835-4191
5. 214-847-3726
6. 773-399-2114

Page 32, Exercise 1D

1.
Hi, Ben. This is Mr. Fernandez at Center Hospital. I'm calling about the Landscaper job. Please call me back at 562-555-1349. That's 562-555-1349.

2.
Hi, Maya. This is Grace Simms at Grace's Office Supplies. I'm calling about the cashier job. Please call me back. My number is 408-555-7821. That's 408-555-7821.

3.
Hi, Nara. This is Jin Wu at Greenville Store. I'm calling about the sales assistant job. Please call me back at 773-555-9602. That's 773-555-9602.

4.
Hi, Juan. This is Ms. Rodriguez at Carla's Restaurant. I'm calling about the manager job. Please call me back at 339-555-8851. That's 339-555-8851.

Page 33, Exercise 2C

1. D-A-N dot S-I-L-V-E-R at cc mail dot edu
2. G dot Simms at h mail dot com
3. T Lopez 7-1-5 at go mail dot com
4. J-I-N dot W-U at new mail dot edu

Page 34, Exercises 2B and 2C

Marta: Who's that? Is she a teacher?
Boris: No, she's not. She's a student. And she's a cashier at Al's Restaurant.
Marta: Oh, that's interesting. And what do you do?
Boris: I'm a cook.

Page 34, Exercise 2D

Marta: Who's that? Is she a teacher?
Boris: No, she's not. She's a student. And she's a cashier at Al's Restaurant.
Marta: Oh, that's interesting. And what do you do?
Boris: I'm a cook.
Marta: A cook! I'm a cook, too.
Boris: Really?
Marta: Yes. I'm a cook, a server, a child-care worker, and a doctor.
Boris: Four jobs!
Marta: Yes. I'm a homemaker!

Page 35, Exercise 3B

1. Is she a teacher?
2. She's a student.
3. What do you do?
4. Are you a doctor?
5. Are they servers?
6. Where are you from?
7. Who's that?
8. you a cook?

Page 40, Exercises 2A and 2B

Dora: So, what do you do?
Sali: I'm a nurse.
Dora: Really? Where do you work?
Sali: I work at a school on Main Street. I'm a school nurse.
Dora: Oh. That's nice.

Page 40, Exercise 2C

Dora: So, what do you do?
Sali: I'm a nurse.
Dora: Really? Where do you work?
Sali: I work at a school on Main Street. I'm a school nurse.
Dora: Oh. That's nice. What about you, Omar?
Omar: I work at a school, too.
Dora: Are you a teacher?
Omar: No.
Dora: Are you an office assistant?
Omar: No. I'm a student.
Sali: That's not a job, Omar.
Omar: Oh, yes, it is. It's a hard job.

UNIT 3

Page 48, Exercises 2A and 2B

Ms. Reed: OK, everyone. Please put away your books. Take out a piece of paper.
Student 1: Can I borrow a pencil?
Student 2: Sure. Here you go.

Page 48, Exercise 2C

Ms. Reed: OK, everyone. Please put away your books. Take out a piece of paper.
Student 1: Can I borrow a pencil?
Student 2: Sure. Here you go.

Ms. Reed:	Uh-oh. Please turn off your phones.
Student 1:	Uhmm. Ms. Reed?
Ms. Reed:	Yes?
Student 1:	I think that's your phone.
Ms. Reed:	Oh!

Page 54, Exercises 2B and 2C

Carlos:	What's this called in English?
Mimi:	It's a mouse.
Carlos:	And these? What are these called?
Mimi:	They're printers.

Page 54, Exercise 2D

Carlos:	What's this called in English?
Mimi:	It's a mouse.
Carlos:	And these? What are these called?
Mimi:	They're printers.
Carlos:	Nope. You're wrong.
Mimi:	What? I'm not wrong. That's a mouse, and those are printers.
Carlos:	No, they're not. This is a picture of a mouse, and that's a picture of printers.
Mimi:	Very funny.

Page 55, Exercise 3B

1. ten
2. they
3. these

Page 60, Exercises 2B and 2C

Ken:	Excuse me. Is the computer lab open?
Berta:	Sorry. I don't know. Ask him.
Ken:	Oh, OK. But . . . Who is he?
Berta:	He's the computer lab assistant.

UNIT 4

Page 68, Exercises 2B and 2C

Kim:	That's a great photo. Who's that?
Gina:	My father.
Kim:	Oh, he looks nice.
Gina:	Thanks.

Page 68, Exercise 2D

Kim:	That's a great photo. Who's that?
Gina:	My father.
Kim:	Oh, he looks nice.
Gina:	Thanks.
Kim:	And is that your sister? She looks like you.
Gina:	Thanks, but that's not my sister. That's my daughter!

Page 74, Exercises 2A and 2B

Pam:	Is your family here in this country?
Leo:	My brother is here. He's a carpenter.
Pam:	Oh. What's he like?
Leo:	He's great. He's a lot of fun.
Pam:	Does he look like you?
Leo:	No. He's tall and thin and he has long hair.

Page 74, Exercise 2C

Pam:	Is your family here in this country?
Leo:	My brother is here. He's a carpenter.
Pam:	Oh. What's he like?
Leo:	He's great. He's a lot of fun.
Pam:	Does he look like you?
Leo:	No. He's tall and thin, and he has long hair. Here's a picture of him.
Pam:	Oh. He has a beard and a mustache, too.
Leo:	He has one more thing, too.
Pam:	Oh, yeah. What's that?
Leo:	He has a wife.
Pam:	Oh.

Page 78, Exercise 2B

1. January twenty-first
2. January fifth
3. January seventeenth
4. January eighth
5. January twenty-fourth
6. January eleventh
7. January thirtieth
8. January ninth

Page 79, Exercise 2E

1.
A: What's your date of birth?
B: It's March fourteenth, nineteen eighty-seven.

2.
A: When was your son born?
B: October second, two thousand eleven.

3.
A: What's your sister's date of birth?
B: It's May twenty-eighth, nineteen ninety-eight.

4.
A: When was your daughter born?
B: August thirty-first, two thousand five.

5.
A: When was your father born?
B: December seventeenth, nineteen sixty-nine.

6.
A: What's your brother's date of birth?
B: It's September second, nineteen seventy-two.

Page 80, Exercises 2B and 2C

Kofi:	Hi, Ellen. Where are you?
Ellen:	I'm at my friend's house. I'm babysitting for her kids.
Kofi:	Oh. How old are they?
Ellen:	Well, her son is in the fifth grade. I think he's eleven. And her daughter is six. She's in the first grade.

Page 80, Exercise 2D

Kofi:	Hi, Ellen. Where are you?
Ellen:	I'm at my friend's house. I'm babysitting for her kids.

AUDIO SCRIPT

Kofi: Oh. How old are they?
Ellen: Well, her son is in the fifth grade. I think he's eleven. And her daughter is six. She's in the first grade.
Kofi: What are they like?
Ellen: Well, the boy is great. His name is Ken.
Kofi: Oh. And what about the girl?
Ellen: Terry? She's really friendly, but my friend says she's Terry the terrible.
Kofi: Why?
Ellen: I really don't know.

UNIT 5

Page 88, Exercises 2A and 2B

Meg: I need a gift for my brother. It's his birthday next week.
Carlos: How about clothes?
Meg: Well, he needs clothes, but he wants a backpack.

Page 88, Exercise 2C

Meg: I need a gift for my brother. It's his birthday next week.
Carlos: How about clothes?
Meg: Well, he needs clothes, but he wants a backpack.
Carlos: So get two backpacks.
Meg: Two backpacks? Why two, Carlos?
Carlos: My birthday is next month, and I want a backpack!

Page 93, Exercise 2B

1.
Customer: Excuse me. How much is this blouse?
Assistant: It's $11.95.

2.
Customer: Excuse me. How much are these shoes?
Assistant: They're $34.99.

3.
Customer: Excuse me. How much is this watch?
Assistant: It's $23.50.

4.
Customer: Excuse me. How much are these pants?
Assistant: They're $13.49.

Page 94, Exercises 2B and 2C

Kofi: Do you have this sweater in a large?
Assistant: No, I'm sorry. We don't.
Kofi: Too bad. It's for my sister, and she needs a large.

Page 94, Exercise 2D

Kofi: Do you have this sweater in a large?
Assistant: No, I'm sorry. We don't.
Kofi: Too bad. It's for my sister, and she needs a large.

Assistant: What about this sweater? Does she like blue?
Kofi: Yes, she does.
Assistant: Well, here you go.
Kofi: Great. Thanks.

Page 100, Exercises 2A and 2B

Assistant: May I help you?
Customer 1: Yes. I need to return these pants.
Assistant: OK. What's the problem?
Customer 1: They don't fit. They're too big.
Assistant: Do you have your receipt?
Customer 1: Yes, I do. It's here somewhere! . . . Oh, here it is.
Assistant: Thank you. And here's your money . . . Next. May I help you?
Customer 2: Yes. I'd like to return this jacket.
Assistant: OK. What's the problem?
Customer 2: The zipper is broken.
Assistant: Do you have your receipt?
Customer 2: Uh, no.
Assistant: We can only give you store credit.
Customer 2: That's OK. I always shop here.
Assistant: Well, here you go.
Customer 2: Thank you.

UNIT 6

Page 108, Exercises 2B and 2C

Dan: Oh, wow! This house looks great!
Emily: Really?
Dan: Yes. There are two bedrooms and a large kitchen.
Emily: What about a dining room?
Dan: Well, no. There's no dining room.

Page 108, Exercise 2D

Dan: Oh, wow! This house looks great!
Emily: Really?
Dan: Yes. There are two bedrooms and a large kitchen.
Emily: What about a dining room?
Dan: Well, no. There's no dining room.
Emily: That's OK. The kitchen's large. How's the rent?
Dan: Not bad. It's pretty inexpensive. There is one problem, though.
Emily: Oh? What's that?
Dan: It's not in the United States. It's in Canada!

Page 114, Exercises 2B and 2C

Amy: Excuse me. Is there an apartment for rent in this building?
Manager: Yes, there is. There's a one-bedroom apartment on the second floor.
Amy: Oh, great. Is it furnished?
Manager: Well, yes and no. There's a dresser, but no beds.
Lei: Oh. Well, are there appliances?

Manager: Uh, yes and no. There's a stove, but no refrigerator.

Page 114, Exercise 2D

Amy: Excuse me. Is there an apartment for rent in this building?
Manager: Yes, there is. There's a one-bedroom apartment on the second floor.
Amy: Oh, great. Is it furnished?
Manager: Well, yes and no. There's a dresser, but no beds.
Lei: Oh. Well, are there appliances?
Manager: Uh, yes and no. There's a stove, but no refrigerator. So? Are you interested?
Amy: Well, yes.
Lei: And no.

Page 120, Exercises 2A and 2B

Woman: How do we get to Joe's Furniture Store?
Man: Let me check on my phone. OK. First, go north on Route 1 for three miles.
Woman: North?
Man: Uh-huh. Then turn left on Fifth Avenue. Continue for one block. It's on the left, across from a park.
Woman: That sounds easy.

Page 120, Exercise 2C.

Woman: How do we get to Joe's Furniture Store?
Man: Let me check on my phone. OK. First, go north on Route 1 for three miles.
Woman: North?
Man: Uh-huh. Then turn left on Fifth Avenue. Continue for one block. It's on the left, across from a park.
Woman: That sounds easy.
Man: So, let's go!
Woman: Wait a second. Today is Sunday, and it's 3:30. Is Joe's open?
Man: Good question. Let me check. They're open Monday to Saturday from 10:00 AM to 7:00 PM, and Sunday from 10:00 AM to 5:00 PM.
Woman: OK. Let's hurry. They close soon.

UNIT 7

Page 128, Exercises 2B and 2C

Sue: Are you free tomorrow? How about a movie?
Mia: Sorry, I'm busy. I work on Saturdays.
Sue: Oh. Well, when do you get home?
Mia: At 8:00.

Page 128, Exercise 2D

Sue: Are you free tomorrow? How about a movie?
Mia: Sorry, I'm busy. I work on Saturdays.
Sue: Oh. Well, when do you get home?
Mia: At 8:00. [eight o'clock]
Sue: That's not a problem.

Mia: No? What time is the movie?
Sue: What do you mean?
Mia: What time does the movie start?
Sue: It starts when we want. I have lots of movies at home.

Page 129, Exercise 3B

1. What do you do in your free time?
2. When do you have English class?
3. What time do you go to work?
4. Where do you exercise?

Page 134, Exercises 2A and 2B

Ling: Gee, I'm so glad it's Friday.
Tony: Me, too. What do you usually do on the weekend?
Ling: Well, I always clean the house on Saturdays, and I always spend time with my family on Sundays. What about you?
Tony: I usually shop for food on Saturdays, and I sometimes go to the park on Sundays.

Page 134, Exercise 2C

Ling: Gee, I'm so glad it's Friday.
Tony: Me, too. What do you usually do on the weekend?
Ling: Well, I always clean the house on Saturdays, and I always spend time with my family on Sundays. What about you?
Tony: I usually shop for food on Saturdays, and I sometimes go to the park on Sundays.
Ling: I love the weekend.
Tony: Yeah, especially Sunday.
Ling: Right. Saturday is for cleaning and shopping, and Sunday is for fun.
Tony: Exactly. In our house, we call Sunday "fun day."

Page 140, Exercises 2A and 2B

Hello. This is Dr. Sue Miller with Life Styles. Our podcast today is about relaxing.

Many people say, "Relax? I never relax." What about you? Do you relax? How often do you relax?

How often do you take a long hot bath?
How often do you go running?
How often do you listen to music?
How often do you take a long walk?

Sometimes? Never? That's not good.

We're all busy, but we all need to relax—and not just sometimes. We need to relax every day.

It helps us be better students, workers, friends, and family members.

Remember: You'll do more if you relax. So, take a bath, go for a run, listen to music, take a long walk. Thank you for listening to Life Styles. This is Dr. Sue Miller saying good-bye and relax!

AUDIO SCRIPT

UNIT 8

Page 148, Exercises 2A and 2B

Mark: Wow, I'm hungry!
Rosa: Yeah, me too. What do you want for lunch?
Mark: Pizza! I love pizza! What about you?
Rosa: I don't really like pizza, but I love tacos!

Page 148, Exercise 2C

Mark: Wow, I'm hungry!
Rosa: Yeah, me too. What do you want for lunch?
Mark: Pizza! I love pizza! What about you?
Rosa: I don't really like pizza, but I love tacos! And look! There's a taco place over there!
Mark: Sounds good! And there's a pizza place, too. But wait a minute. It's not time for lunch!
Rosa: No?
Mark: No. It's only 10:30!
Rosa: So, forget about lunch. Let's have pizza and tacos for breakfast.

Page 154, Exercises 2A and 2B

Server: Can I help you?
Greg: Yes, I'd like a hamburger and a soda.
Server: Is that a large soda or a small soda?
Greg: Large, please.
Server: OK, a large soda . . . Anything else?
Greg: Yes. A small order of fries.

Page 154, Exercise 2C

Server: Can I help you?
Greg: Yes, I'd like a hamburger and a soda.
Server: Is that a large soda or a small soda?
Greg: Large, please.
Server: OK, a large soda . . . Anything else?
Greg: Yes. A small order of fries.
Liz: A hamburger, fries, and a soda? You know, that's not very healthy! What about vegetables?
Greg: Well, there's lettuce on the hamburger.
Liz: OK . . . And what about fruit?
Greg: You're right! I need fruit. I know . . . I'll have a piece of apple pie, too.

Page 157, Exercise 1B

1.
A: How much is the chicken?
B: It's three twenty-nine a pound.

2.
A: How much are the bananas?
B: They're ninety-nine cents a pound.

3.
A: How much is the yogurt?
B: It's three eighty-five.

4.
A: How much are the apples?
B: They're one ninety-nine a pound.

5.
A: How much are the onions?
B: They're eighty-nine cents a pound.

6.
A: How much is the bread?
B: It's two fifty-nine.

Page 160, Exercises 2A and 2B

Hannah: Good morning. This is Hannah Charles with Greenville News Radio. You're listening to The Food Show. Do you have questions about food? Well, call and ask. Now here's our first caller . . .
Greg: Hi Hannah. I'm Greg Johnson. My wife says that I don't eat healthy food. She says, "Eat more fruit and vegetables." But I'm a meat and potatoes man.
Hannah: OK, Mr. Meat and Potatoes. Tell me, do you like chicken?
Greg: Sure. I eat a lot of chicken.
Hannah: And do you like grilled chicken or fried chicken?
Greg: I like grilled chicken and fried chicken.
Hannah: OK. Now let me ask you a question. How many calories are there in a piece of fried chicken?
Greg: Hmm. I don't know.
Hannah: 250 calories.
Greg: 250 calories!
Hannah: That's right, but in a piece of grilled chicken there are only about 100 calories. So, the choice is easy. The next time you have chicken, eat grilled chicken, not fried.
Greg: OK. That's not so hard.
Hannah: Now another question. This is about potatoes. How much fat is there in an order of fries? Do you know?
Greg: A lot?
Hanna: You're right. There are 15 grams of fat in a small order of fries. But there's no fat in a plain baked potato. That's 15 grams in the fries and no grams in the baked! But remember, no butter! So the next time you have potatoes, think baked, not fried.
Greg: Wow. I don't believe it!
Hannah: Yes. And one more thing, listen to your wife! She's right. Those vegetables and fruit are good for you. Thanks a lot for calling The Food Show. We have time for one more call.

UNIT 9

Page 168, Exercises 2A and 2B

David: Hello?
Laura: Hi! It's me. How are you doing?
David: I'm fine, thanks. Where are you?
Laura: I'm in Tampa. I'm visiting family, but they're at work now.

David: Tampa! That's great! How's the weather there?
Laura: Well, it's cold and rainy.

Page 168, Exercise 2C
David: Hello?
Laura: Hi! It's me. How are you doing?
David: I'm fine, thanks. Where are you?
Laura: I'm in Tampa. I'm visiting family, but they're at work now.
David: Tampa! That's great! How's the weather there?
Laura: Well, it's cold and rainy.
David: Oh, that's too bad. It's beautiful here in Green Bay. It's not warm, but it's sunny.
Laura: Don't tell me that! Here I am in Tampa, and I'm just sitting in the living room and watching the rain!

Page 174, Exercises 2A and 2B
Ron: Are you watching the news?
Emma: No, I'm not. I'm doing the laundry.
Ron: Turn on the TV. A big storm is coming.
Emma: Really?
Ron: Yes. I'm coming home early. I'm at the supermarket now.

Page 174, Exercise 2C
Ron: Are you watching the news?
Emma: No, I'm not. I'm doing the laundry.
Ron: Turn on the TV. A big storm is coming.
Emma: Really?
Ron: Yes. I'm coming home early. I'm at the supermarket now.
Emma: Oh, good. Are you getting water?
Ron: Yes. I'm getting water, food, and a lot of batteries.
Emma: Great. Get matches, too.
Ron: OK. Do we need anything else?
Emma: Yes. We need good weather!

Page 181, Exercises 2A and 2B
Good morning. This is Weather Watch on Greenville News Radio.

Here's the weather report for cities across the country.

It's cloudy and very hot in Los Angeles. The temperature is already 90 degrees. Wear light clothes and drink lots of water if you go outside.

It's a beautiful day in Atlanta! It's warm and very sunny now with a temperature of 75 degrees So, go outside, take your sunglasses, and enjoy the nice weather.

It's raining in New York City, and the temperature is 62 degrees. Take your umbrella if you go out.

It's very windy in Chicago. The temperature is only 38 degrees. So, don't forget your scarf and gloves. It's pretty cold out there.

UNIT 10

Page 188, Exercises 2A and 2B
Woman: Excuse me. Can you help me? I'm looking for Foodsmart.
Man: Sure. It's on Seventh between Hill and Oak.
Woman: Sorry?
Man: It's on Seventh Avenue between Hill Street and Oak Street.
Woman: Thanks.

Page 188, Exercise 2C
Woman: Excuse me. Can you help me? I'm looking for Foodsmart.
Man: Sure. It's on Seventh between Hill and Oak.
Woman: Sorry?
Man: It's on Seventh Avenue between Hill Street and Oak Street.
Woman: Thanks. Uh . . . is that near here?
Man: Yes. It's just around the corner.
Woman: They're having a grand opening. I guess there are a lot of people there.
Man: No, not really. Only one or two workers.
Woman: Really? I don't understand.
Man: Today is October 7. The grand opening is tomorrow, October 8!

Page 192, Exercise 2B
Conversation 1
A: Don't turn left here.
B: Oh, thanks. I'll turn at the next street.

Conversation 2
A: Be careful. There's a school near here.
B: You're right. I'll drive slowly. A lot of kids cross here.

Conversation 3
A: Be careful. There's a railroad crossing.
B: I know. Do you see a train?
A: Not right now, but be careful anyway.

Page 193, Exercise 3B
Bus 36 leaves 39th Avenue at 8:06 A.M.
Bus 47 leaves Park Avenue at 8:34 A.M.
Bus 51 leaves Pine Street at 8:36 A.M.

Page 194, Exercises 2B and 2C
Tina: Excuse me. How do you get to Adams College?
Officer: Take the Number 4 bus, and get off at Second Street. It's not far from there.
Tina: Thanks. Oh, and how much does the bus cost?
Officer: Two dollars, but you need exact change.

Page 194, Exercise 2D
Driver: Second Street.

AUDIO SCRIPT

Matt:	OK. Here we are at Second Street. Now what?
Tina:	There's a woman. Let's ask her.
Matt:	Excuse me. We want to go to Adams College. How do we get there?
Woman:	It's easy! Study, study, study.

Pages 200–201, Exercise 2A and 2B

Welcome back to Greenville News Radio. It's time for our Weekend Watch.

What are your plans for this weekend? Are you looking for something to do? Well, here's what's happening in our community.

Foodsmart is having its grand opening on Saturday, October 8. They're giving away samples at 3:00. There'll be lots of food and drinks at this free event. Saturday night, Greenville's very own Zeebees are singing at the community college. The concert begins at 8:00. Tickets are on sale now for five dollars.

There's a baseball game Sunday afternoon at one o'clock. Greenville High is playing Lincoln High in Greenville Park. Free with a student ID.

And also on Sunday there's a community yard sale at the Community Center across from the fire station. People are selling old toys, furniture, and clothes. The sale is from 10 A.M. to 4 P.M. Get there early. It doesn't cost just to look!

This is Simon Chan. Have a great weekend!

UNIT 11

Page 207, Show What You Know, Exercise 2

1. Touch your nose.
2. Clap your hands.
3. Close your eyes.
4. Shake your head.
5. Touch your arm.
6. Point to your chest.
7. Nod your head.
8. Point to your knee.

Page 208, Exercises 2B and 2C

Assistant:	Good morning. Greenville Elementary.
Mrs. Lee:	Hello. This is Terry Lee. I'm calling about my son Alex.
Assistant:	Is that Alex Lee?
Mrs. Lee:	Yes. He's sick today. He has a sore throat and a headache.
Assistant:	I'm sorry to hear that. What class is he in?
Mrs. Lee:	He's in Ms. Wong's class.

Page 208, Exercise 2D

Assistant:	Good morning. Greenville Elementary.
Mrs. Lee:	Hello. This is Terry Lee. I'm calling about my son Alex.
Assistant:	Is that Alex Lee?
Mrs. Lee:	Yes. He's sick today. He has a sore throat and a headache.
Assistant:	I'm sorry to hear that. What class is he in?
Mrs. Lee:	He's in Ms. Wong's class.
Assistant:	OK. Thank you for calling. I'll tell Ms. Wong. I hope he feels better soon.
Daughter 1:	Mom, my throat hurts!
Son:	Mom, my head hurts!
Daughter 2:	Mommy, my stomach hurts!
Mrs. Lee:	Uh-oh. Can I call you back?

Page 213, Exercise 2C

Cold Away!
Pain Reliever. Antihistamine.

Directions:
Take 2 tablets orally every 6 hours.

Warnings:
- Do not take more than 8 tablets per day.
- Take with food or milk.
- Do not drive or operate machinery.
- Do not give to children under 12.
- Keep out of reach of children.

Page 214, Exercises 2A and 2B

Tuan:	You weren't here yesterday.
Luisa:	I know. My daughter was home sick. She had a bad cold.
Tuan:	Oh, too bad. How is she now?
Luisa:	A lot better, thanks. She's back at school.

Page 214, Exercise 2C

Tuan:	You weren't here yesterday.
Luisa:	I know. My daughter was home sick. She had a bad cold.
Tuan:	Oh, too bad. How is she now?
Luisa:	A lot better thanks. She's back at school.
Tuan:	Great. And what about your other kids?
Luisa:	Well, they were sick last week, but they're OK now.
Tuan:	That's good. Well, take care, Luisa, and have a good day.
Luisa:	Oh, thanks, Tuan. I'll try.

Page 215, Exercise 3B

1. Marie wasn't here yesterday morning.
2. The students were in class.
3. The teacher was absent.
4. We weren't at work.
5. She was in school.
6. They weren't sick.

Pages 220–221, Exercises 2A and 2B

Dr. Garcia:	Good evening. This is Dr. Elias Garcia. You're listening to Ask the Doctor. I'm here to answer your health questions. Our first question is from Carl Gold. Carl?

Carl: Yes. Hello, Dr. Garcia. Here's my problem. I exercise. I know it's good to exercise, but I get these terrible backaches. What should I do? Should I use an ice pack?
Dr. Garcia: Yes, ice is good if your backache is from exercising. But only at first. Later, heat is better. And take a long hot shower.
Carl: A hot shower?
Dr. Garcia: Yes. You should use a heating pad, too.
Carl: OK, great. Thank you, Dr. Garcia.
Dr. Garcia: You're welcome. Hello, this is Ask the Doctor. Who's speaking?
Jon: Hello, Dr. Garcia. My name is Jon Kerins. I have a terrible toothache. What should I do? Should I put heat on it?
Dr. Garcia: No. You shouldn't. Heat feels good, but it isn't good for you. Here's what you should do. Eat a piece of onion.
Jon: A piece of onion?
Dr. Garcia: Yes! An onion helps the pain. Also, you should drink lime juice regularly — it helps prevent toothaches.
Jon: Wow. Lime juice. OK, thank you, Dr. Garcia.
Dr. Garcia: Thanks for calling. . . . Hello?
Dana: Hi, I'm Dana Jones. My whole family has the flu. What should we do?
Dr. Garcia: Gee, I'm really sorry to hear that. There's not much you can do. Stay in bed and drink a lot of fluids.
Dana: You mean, like water?
Dr. Garcia: Yes, water, or tea, or even juice. You should drink as much as you can.
Dana: What about antibiotics?
Dr. Garcia: No, Antibiotics don't help the flu. You shouldn't take them.
Dana: OK. Well, thanks.
Dr. Garcia: I hope you all feel better soon. And that's all the time we have for today . . .

UNIT 12

Page 228, Exercises 2A and 2B
Kofi: I noticed the Help Wanted sign. I'd like to apply for a job.
Dino: OK. Which job?
Kofi: Well, I'm a cook. I can make great hamburgers.
Dino: Can you make pizza?
Kofi: No, I can't make pizza, but I can learn.

Page 228, Exercise 2C
Kofi: I noticed the Help Wanted sign. I'd like to apply for a job.
Dino: OK. Which job?
Kofi: Well, I'm a cook. I can make great hamburgers.
Dino: Can you make pizza?
Kofi: No, I can't make pizza, but I can learn.
Dino: Good. As you can see, this place is really busy. The phone never stops.
Kofi: Well, I can answer the phone, too.
Dino: Great. Can you start now? Can you answer the phone?
Kofi: Sure. Dino's Diner. Can I help you?

Page 229, Exercise 3B
1. He can't drive.
2. He can use a computer.
3. She can fix things.
4. She can't cook.
5. I can't lift boxes.
6. I can answer phones.

Page 233, Exercise 1E
A: Hey, you're looking for a job, right?
B: That's right. Why?
A: Well, here's an online job posting. It says you don't need experience.
B: Really? What's the schedule?
A: Well, it's only part-time, but you can work any shift.
B: Oh, that's great. And how much is the pay?
A: Twelve dollars an hour.
B: Hmmmm. That's not bad. How can I apply?

Page 234, Exercises 2A and 2B
Dana: Hi, I'm Dana.
Sam: Hi, I'm Sam. Wow. This store is really busy.
Dana: I know. Listen, I need a favor. Can you work this Saturday?
Sam: Uh, well, yes, I can.
Dana: Oh, great, thanks, because I can't. Can you work from 2:00 to 7:00?
Sam: Um, yes. I guess so.

Page 234, Exercise 2C
Dana: Hi, I'm Dana.
Sam: Hi, I'm Sam. Wow. This store is really busy.
Dana: I know. Listen, I need a favor. Can you work this Saturday?
Sam: Uh, well, yes, I can.
Dana: Oh, great, thanks, because I can't. Can you work from 2:00 to 7:00?
Sam: Um, yes. I guess so . . . but, I don't understand. Why are you asking me all these questions?
Dana: Well, you're the new sales assistant, right?
Sam: No . . . I'm the elevator repair guy. I'm here to fix the elevator.

Page 240, Exercises 2A, 2B, and 2C.
Tina: Good afternoon. This is Tina Martins. You're listening to Meet Your Neighbors. Today, I'm in Saigon, Greenville's first Vietnamese restaurant, and I'm talking with Dinh Tran and Mai Lam. Hello. And congratulations! Your restaurant looks great.

Audio Script

AUDIO SCRIPT

Mai: Thank you.
Dinh: Thanks, Tina.
Tina: So, Dinh, is this your first restaurant?
Dinh: Yes, it is. But I worked in a restaurant before.
Tina: Oh. Was that here it Greenville?
Dinh: Yes. The Greenville Café.
Tina: How long were you there?
Dinh: Eight years.
Tina: And what did you do? Were you a cook?
Dinh: Oh, I did a lot of things. I was a cashier, a server, and a cook.
Tina: Wow. So, you really know the restaurant business.
Dinh: Yes, I think so.
Tina: Mai, were you in the restaurant business, too?
Mai: No. I worked in people's homes. I took care of children and I cooked for the families.
Tina: That's interesting. When did you come to this country?
Mai: Twelve years ago.
Tina: Well, your English is great.
Mai: Thanks. We were students at the Greenville Adult School. We also cooked at the school!
Tina: Really!?
Dinh: Yes, we cooked for class parties.
Mai: Right. As our first teacher, Emily Reed, says, we were good students, but we were great cooks!
Dinh: That's right! She says our class parties were always wonderful because of our food.
Mai: Actually, Dinh and I always loved to cook. And now we can cook for everyone here in Greenville. We want everyone here to visit us.
Dinh: Yes. We're right across the street from the new Foodsmart. And we're open every day from noon to 11 P.M.
Tina: Well, it's almost noon now, and people are waiting for the doors to open. So business looks good, and the food smells delicious. For those of you listening today, make a reservation for Saigon at 213-555-8775. And thank you for listening to Meet your Neighbors.

Page 247, Exercise D

Carla: This is Dinh and Mai. They're from Vietnam.
Boris: Nice to meet you. I'm Boris Popov. Carla and I are students at the Greenville Adult School. We're in Level 1.
Mai: Nice to meet you, Boris. Where are you from?
Boris: I'm from Russia.
Carla: Dinh and Mai are students at Greenville, too. He's in Level 5, and she's in Level 6.
Boris: Really? That's great.

Page 253, Exercise A

A: Hey, Brenda. You look great.
B: Thanks, Alan. I feel great! I think it's because I ride my bike a lot.
A: Oh? How often do you ride your bike?
B: Four or five times a week.
A: Really? When?
B: I usually ride before work, from 6:00 to 7:00, and I always ride on Saturdays from 9:00 to 10:00.
A: Good for you!

Page 254, Exercise A

A: This omelet is really good. What's in it?
B: Eggs and cheese. Oh, and there's salt, but not much.
A: Eggs? How many eggs?
B: Three.
A: And how much cheese?
B: Just one slice.
A: What do you cook it in? Do you use butter or oil?
B: I use oil, but it's good with butter, too.

Page 255, Exercise A

A: Hi, Sandy. It's me, Gail. Are you at work?
B: No, I'm not working today. I'm home. There's a really bad snowstorm here. Schools are closed again.
A: Wow! So, what are the kids doing?
B: Well, Tony and Dino are outside in the snow. They're taking pictures.
A: That's nice. What about Maria? Is she playing in the snow?
B: No, she isn't. She's playing computer games with my dad.
A: And you?
B: Well, I'm cooking. And my mom and I are doing laundry. I'm not at work, but I'm pretty busy. And I'm very tired.

MAP OF THE UNITED STATES AND CANADA

MAP OF THE WORLD

Map of the World

INDEX

ACADEMIC SKILLS
Critical thinking
  categorizing
    body parts, 207
    classroom items, 47
    job duties, 227
    places in community, 187
  comparing
    food prices, 157
    pictures, 77, 171, 217
  making connections
    in readings, 72
    while studying, 227
  making inferences, 98
Numeracy: graphs and charts
  of attendance, 15, 217
  of contact information, 33
  of country origins, 17
  of credit card holders, 98–99
  of daily activities, 127, 131
  of descriptions of people, 77
  of emergency plans, 172
  of favorite seasons, 167
  of free time activities, 138–139
  of health advice, 220
  of immigrant origins, 16–17
  of job duties, 227
  of job titles, 27
  of personal names, 10
  of top jobs in U.S., 38
Numeracy: math skills
  adding, 77, 92, 133, 139
  calculating age, 82
  calculating medicine doses, 213
  calculating nutrition information, 159
  calculating time, 133, 139
  comparing food prices, 157
  subtracting, 82
  using percentages, 16–17, 72, 93, 98
Reading
  article headings in, 52
  article titles in, 16
  about blended families, 72–73
  of bus signs and schedules, 193
  of captions, 152
  about credit cards and debit cards, 98–99

focusing on details in, 178
of food labels, 158–159
about food safety, 152–153
about free-time activities, 138–139
about good study habits, 52–53
of groceries ads, 157
about healthcare jobs, 38–39
about hurricanes, 178–179
about immigrants, 16–17
about job interviews, 238–239
of job postings, 232–233, 237
learning from, 218
learning new vocabulary in, 38
making connections in, 72
making inferences in, 98
making predictions in, 138
of maps
  community, 187
  U.S. and Canada, 279
  U.S. regions, 178
  weather, 181
  world, 6
marking up texts during, 238
of medicine labels, 213
more than once (re-reading), 112
about public libraries, 198–199
of receipts, 93
of rental home listings, 108–111, 118–119
about smoke alarms, 112–113
of street addresses, 118
of traffic signs, 192
about walking and health, 218–219
of work schedules and time sheets, 132–133
Study tips
  counting syllables, 187
  making connections, 227
  spelling aloud while writing, 167, 207
  study habits, 52–53, 63
  testing yourself, 7, 67
  writing personal sentences, 127

Writing
  of abbreviations
    for days of the week, 132
    for months, 78
    for street addresses, 118
  capital letters in
    for days of the week, 143
    for months, 83
    for names, 23
    to start sentences, 36, 43
  checklists for, 43, 63, 83, 103, 123, 143, 163, 183, 203, 223, 243
  about clothes, 103
  about daily activities, 127
  of dates, 78–79
  about family members, 83
  about favorite day of week, 143
  about favorite room at home, 123
  about food, 163
  about friends, 43
  giving examples in, 198
  about health habits, 223
  about job skills, 243
  punctuation in
    apostrophes in possessive nouns, 71
    commas in lists, 103
    periods ending sentences, 43
  spelling
    aloud, while writing, 167, 207
    of names and titles, 10–11
  on sticky notes, 107
  about street and community, 203
  about study habits, 63
  using details in, 123
  using examples in, 198
  on vocabulary cards, 27, 47
  about weather, 183
  about yourself, 23

CIVICS
Life skills
  calendar and time
    calculating time, 133, 139
    capital letters for months, 83
    community weekend schedules, 200–201

278 Index

days of the week, 132, 143
saying and writing dates, 78–79, 214
communities, 185–204
   giving locations of places in, 188–189
   identifying places in, 186–187
   public libraries in, 198–199
   transportation in, 191–193
   weekend plans in, 200–201
   writing about, 203
daily activities, 125–144
   during free time, 138–139
   frequency of, 136–137, 142
   identifying types of, 126–127
   making plans for, 128–129
   relaxing, 140–141
   timing of, 130–131
   on weekends, 134–137, 200–201
   work schedules and time sheets of, 132–133
   writing about, 127
emergencies
   asking about activities during, 174–175
   hurricanes as, 178–179
   planning for, 172–173
families, 65–84
   blended, 72–73
   family trees, 67, 69, 71
   giving child's age, 80–81
   identifying members of, 66–67
   separating work and home life, 84
   speaking about, 68–69
   writing about, 83
food, 145–164
   healthy, 158–161
   identifying names of, 146–147
   labels on, 158–159
   ordering in restaurants, 154–155
   prices of, 157
   shopping for, 150, 157
   speaking about likes and dislikes in, 148–149
   writing about, 163
health and healthcare, 205–224
   doctors' instructions in, 211–212
   giving advice in, 220–221
   identifying body parts in, 206–207
   making good decisions in, 224
   medicine labels in, 213, 222
   reading about jobs in, 38–39
   reading about walking and, 218–219
   speaking about health problems, 214–215
   writing about, 223
homes, 105–124
   ads for, 108–111, 118–119
   asking about, 114–117
   identifying rooms and items in, 106–107
   smoke alarms in, 112–113
   speaking about, 108–109
   street addresses of, 118
   writing about favorite room of, 123
interpersonal communication
   asking for and giving phone numbers, 32–33
   calling to explain absence, 208–209
   giving email addresses, 33
   text messaging, 211
money and prices, 92–93
   of bus transportation, 194–195
   of clothes, 93
   of food, 157
   of rental houses, 108
   speaking about, 92–93
   tax rates, 93
school, 45–64
   calling to explain absence from, 208–209
   giving and following instructions in, 48–51
   giving child's grade in, 80–81
   identifying items in, 46–47
   identifying places at, 58–59
   rules in, 50–51
   speaking about items in, 54–55
   speaking about places at, 60–61
shopping, 85–104
   asking for sizes and colors in, 94–95
   with credit cards and debit cards, 98–99
   for food, 150, 157
   for gifts, 88–89
   identifying colors and clothes in, 86–87
   for needs and wants, 88–91
   prices in, 92–93, 157
   receipts for, 93
   returning items in, 100–101
transportation
   asking about bus routes and costs, 194–195
   reading bus signs and schedules, 193
   reading street addresses, 118
   reading street signs, 192
weather, 165–184
   in hurricanes, 178–179
   identifying types of, 166–167
   speaking about, 168–169
   understanding reports on, 180–181
   writing about, 183

GRAMMAR

Adjectives
   adverbs of degree before, 182
   possessive, 70
Adverbs
   of degree, 182
   of frequency, 136–137
Affirmative statements
   with *can*, 230–231
   imperative, 50–51
   in past, with *be,* 216–217

INDEX

in present continuous, 170–171
with *should*, 222
in simple present
  with *be*, 14–15, 20–21, 22
  with *need, want, have*, 90–91
  with *work* and *live*, 42
Articles
  a/an, 30–31
  the, 195
Contractions
  with *be*, 14–15, 20–21, 22, 216
  can't, 229–231
  don't/doesn't, 96–97, 102
  pronouncing, 13
  shouldn't, 222
  that's, 56
  there's, 110–111
Negative statements
  with *can't*, 230–231
  imperative, 50–51
  in past, with *be*, 216–217
  in present continuous, 170–171
  with *shouldn't*, 222
  in simple present
    with *be*, 15, 21
    with *don't/doesn't*, 102
Nouns
  compound, 115
  count and non-count, 150–151, 162
  possessive, 71
  singular vs. plural, 31
Prepositions
  of direction and location, 122
  of place, 190
  of time, 130–131
  using correct, 203
Pronouns
  object, 62
  subject, 62, 70
Questions
  choice, with *or*, 155, 156
  with *how, how much, where*, 196–197
  with *how many/how much*, 162
  with *how often*, 142
  with *how old*, 82
  with *is there/are there*, 116–117

with *was/were*, 242
Wh-, 29
with *when* and *what time*, 130–131
yes/no
  with *be*, 36–37
  with *can*, 236–237
  in present continuous, 176–177
  rising intonation in, 35
  in simple present, 96–97, 210
Sentences
  capital letters starting, 36, 43
  periods ending, 43
  subject of, 243
  topic, 223
  writing personal, 127
Verbs
  be
    contractions with, 14–15, 20–21, 22, 216
    for descriptions, 76–77
    with *I, he, she*, 13, 14–15
    past of, 216–217, 242
    with *we, you, they, it*, 20–21
  can/can't, 229–231
    in affirmative statements, 230–231
    in negative statements, 230–231
    stress on, 229, 235
    in *yes/no* questions, 236–237
  do/does
    in simple present questions, 96–97, 196, 210
    as unstressed word, 195
  don't/doesn't
    in simple present questions, 96–97
    in simple present statements, 102
  have/has
    for descriptions, 76–77
    for simple present affirmative, 90–91
  imperative, 50–51
  irregular, *have* as, 90
  past, of *be*, 216–217, 242
  present continuous
    for future plans, 202

statements in, 170–171
yes/no questions in, 176–177
should, 222
simple present affirmative
  with *be*, 14–15, 20–21, 22
  with *need, want, have*, 90–91
  with *work* and *live*, 42
simple present negative, 102
simple present questions
  with *do/does*, 96–97, 196, 210
  with *how, how much, where*, 196–197
  with *how often*, 142
  with *when* and *what time*, 130–131
  yes/no, 96–97, 210

LISTENING
About absences, 208–209
To advice, 220–221
To ages and grades in school, 80–81
About bus routes and costs, 194–195
To classroom instructions, 48–49
To classroom item names, 54–55
About community locations, 188–189
About current activities, 168–169, 174–175
To directions, 120–121
About family, 68–69, 74–75
About food, 148–149, 154–155, 160–161
About health problems, 214–215
About housing, 108–109, 114–115
To introductions, 8–9, 28–29
About job openings, 228–229
About jobs, 28–29, 34–35, 40–41
To make plans, 128–129
To peoples' country of origin, 12–13
About relaxing, 140–141
About school, 18–19, 60–61
About shopping, 88–89, 94–95, 100–101

As soft skill at work, 44
To weather reports, 180–181
About weekend activities, 134–135
About weekend plans, 200–201
About work experience, 240–241
About work hours, 234–235

SPEAKING

About bus routes and costs, 194–195
About child's age and grade, 80–81
About classroom instructions, 48–49
About classroom items, 54–55
About contact information, 32–33
About dates, 78–79
Describing people, 74–75
About directions, 120–121, 188–189
About emergencies, activities during, 174–175
To explain absence, 208–209
About family, 68–69
About food likes and dislikes, 148–149
About health advice, 220–221
About health problems, 214–215
About hours you can work, 234–235
Identifying people, 12–13
Intonation in
    of choice questions with *or*, 155
    falling, 29
    rising, 35
Introducing others, 28
Introducing yourself, 8–9
About jobs, 28–29, 40–41
About money and prices, 92–93
About needed and wanted things, 88–89
To order food in restaurants, 154–155
About people at school, 60–61
About people's jobs, 34–35
About places at school, 58–61

About places in community, 188–189
Pronunciation in
    of compound nouns, 115
    of consonant sounds
        a before, 30
        at end of words, pronouncing, 81
    of *-es* endings, 141
    of *he's* and *she's*,
    linking words together in, 81
    of possessive *'s*, 71
    stress in
        on *can/can't*, 229, 235
        in compound nouns, 115
        on important words, 95
        lack of, 195, 215
        sound of,
        on syllables, 61, 189
        on *was/wasn't, were/weren't*, 215
    syllables in
        counting, 187
        definition of, 61
        with *-es* endings, 141
        stress on, 61, 189
    of *th*, 55
    of vowel sounds
        an before, 30
        at start of words, pronouncing, 81
About relaxing activities, 140–141
About rental houses, 108–109, 114–117
About school, 18–19
About sizes and colors of clothes, 94–95
About transportation, 191–193
About weather and activities, 168–169
About weekend activities, 134–137, 200–201
About where people are from, 12–13
About work experience, 240–241

WORK SKILLS

Career awareness
    identifying titles of jobs, 27
    identifying types of jobs, 26–27

    speaking about jobs, 28–29, 34–35, 40–41
    types of healthcare jobs, 38–39
Employability skills
    job searches, 225–244
        body language in interviews in, 238–239
        identifying duties in, 226–227
        identifying skills in, 230–231
        reading about interviews in, 238–239
        reading job postings in, 232–233, 237
        responding to help-wanted signs in, 228–229
        speaking about experience in, 240–241
        speaking about hours in, 234–235
        writing about skills in, 243
Workplace skills
    being team player, 144
    calling to explain absence, 208–209
    exchanging contact information, 32–33
    finding information, 124
    flexibility, 64
    friendliness, 24
    learning new, 184
    listening, 44
    log of, 245–246
    making good decisions, 224
    professionalism, 104
    reading and completing time sheets, 133
    reading work schedules, 132–133
    reliability, 204
    responding well to feedback, 244
    separating work and home life, 84
    taking action, 164

CREDITS

Photos:

T = top, B = bottom, L = left, C = center, R = right

Front cover: Juanmonino/Getty Images (C); Dave & Les Jacobs/Blend Images/Getty Images (L); Hill Street Studios/Blend Images/Getty Images (R).

Frontmatter

Page vi (front cover inages): Juanmonino/E+/Getty Images; Dave & Les Jacobs/Blend Images/Getty Images; Hill Street Studios/Blend Images/Getty Images; vi (MyEnglishLab screenshot): Pearson Education, Inc.; vi (ActiveTeach screenshot): Pearson Education Inc.; vi (photo in ActiveTeach screenshot): Viacheslav Iakobchuk/Alamy Stock Photo; vi (CCRS page, top, right): Illustration Forest/Shutterstock; vi (CCRS page, bottom, left): Wavebreakmedia/Shutterstock; vii: Sirtravelalot/Shutterstock; viii (1): Suhendri/Shutterstock; viii (2): Wavebreakmedia/Shutterstock; viii (3): Wavebreakmedia/Shutterstock; viii (4): Stephen Simpson/The Image Bank/Getty Images; viii (5): Auremar/123RF; viii (6): Dmitry Kalinovsky/Shutterstock; viii (7): Xinhua/Alamy Stock Photo; viii (8): Dmitry Kalinovsky/123RF; viii (9): Kali9/iStock/Getty Images; viii (10): GogaTao/Shutterstock; viii (11): Drazen/ E+/Getty Images; viii (12): Dmitry Kalinovsky/Shutterstock; viii (13): Dmitry Kalinovsky/123RF; viii (14): PR Image Factory/Shutterstock; viii (15): Ingram Publishing/Getty Images; viii (16): Welcomia/123RF;ix (Left page: TL): David Mager/Pearson Education, Inc.; ix (Left page: BL): FotoAndalucia/Shutterstock; ix (Right page: TL): Dmitry Kalinovsky/123RF; ix (Right page: TL): PR Image Factory/Shutterstock; ix (Right page: TL): Real Deal Photo/Shutterstock; ix (Right page: CL): Wavebreakmedia/Shutterstock; ix (Right page: CL): Medioimages/Photodisc/Getty Images; ix (Right page: BL): Andersen Ross/Photodisc/Getty Images; ix (Right page: BR): Kali9/iStock/Getty Images; x (Left page: T): RedChopsticks Batch 3/Glow Asia RF/Alamy Stock Photo; x (Left page: B): Hero Images/Getty Images; xi (Left page: T): Denys Semenchenko/123RF; xi (Right page: C): Andrew Poplavsky/123RF; xii (Left page: L): Medioimages/Photodisc/Getty Images; xii (Left page: C): Blue Jean Images/Alamy Stock Photo; xii (Left page: R): Kzenon/Shutterstock; xiii (Right page: T): Sirtravelalot/Shutterstock; xxii (T): Courtesy of Sarah Lynn; xxii (C): Courtesy of Ronna Magy; xxii (B): Courtesy of Federico SalasIsnardi.

Unit 1

Page 5: Steve Debenport/E+/Getty Images; 8 (CR): David Mager/Pearson Education, Inc.; 8 (TL): Sirtravelalot/Shutterstock; 8 (TC): Jennifer Lam/Shutterstock; 8 (TR): Betsie Van der Meer/DigitalVision/Getty Images; 8 (CL): David Mager/Pearson Education, Inc.; 8 (CC): David Mager/Pearson Education, Inc.; 11 (C): David Mager/Pearson Education, Inc.; 10: Tyler Olson/Shutterstock; 11 (TC): David Mager/Pearson Education, Inc.; 11 (TC): David Mager/Pearson Education, Inc.; 11 (TR): Ghislain & Marie David de Lossy/DigitalVision/Getty Images; 11 (BL): Ryan McVay/Photodisc/Getty Images; 11 (BC): Lisa F. Young/Shutterstock; 11 (BR): Jhorrocks/E+/Getty Images; 12 (C): David Mager/Pearson Education, Inc.; 12 (BL): David Mager/Pearson Education, Inc.; 12 (BC): David Mager/Pearson Education, Inc.; 13 (T): Leungchopan/Shutterstock; 13 (C): Don Mason/Blend Images/Getty Images; 13 (B): Karen Struthers/Shutterstock; 14 (all photos): David Mager/Pearson Education, Inc.; 15 (L): David Mager/Pearson Education, Inc.; 15 (R): David Mager/Pearson Education, Inc.; 15 (T): Andersen Ros/Blend Images/Getty Images; 16 (TC): Sakala/Shutterstock; 16 (TR): Arne Pastoor/Stock4BRF/Getty Images; 18: David Mager/Pearson Education, Inc.; 20: Dragon Images/Shutterstock; 24: Vstock/UpperCut Images/Getty Images.

Unit 2

Page 25: Sirtravelalot/Shutterstock; 26 (1): Suhendri/Shutterstock; 26 (2): Wavebreakmedia/Shutterstock; 26 (3): Wavebreakmedia/Shutterstock; 26 (4): Stephen Simpson/The Image Bank/Getty Images; 26 (5): Auremar/123RF; 26 (6): Dmitry Kalinovsky/Shutterstock; 26 (7): Xinhua/Alamy Stock Photo; 26 (8): Dmitry Kalinovsky/123RF; 26 (9): Kali9/E+/Getty Images; 26 (10): GogaTao/Shutterstock; 26 (11): Drazen/E+/Getty Images; 26 (12): Dmitry Kalinovsky/123RF; 26 (13): Dmitry Kalinovsky/123RF; 26 (14): PR Image Factory/Shutterstock; 26 (15): Ingram Publishing/Getty Images; 26 (16): Welcomia/123RF; 28 (T): David Mager/Pearson Education, Inc.; 28 (BL): FotoAndalucia/Shutterstock; 28 (BR): Dmitry Kalinovsky/123RF; 29 (TL): PR Image Factory/Shutterstock; 29 (TR): Real Deal Photo/Shutterstock; 29 (CL): Wavebreakmedia/Shutterstock; 29 (CR): Medioimages/Photodisc/Getty Images; 29 (BL): Andersen Ross/Photodisc/Getty Images; 29 (BR): Kali9/iStock/Getty Images; 30 (T): RedChopsticks Batch 3/Glow Asia RF/Alamy Stock Photo; 30 (B): Andersen Ross/Photodisc/Getty Images; 32: Denys Semenchenko/123RF; 33: Erwinova/Shutterstock; 34 (TCL): Andres/E+/Getty Images; 34 (TCR): Evgeny Atamanenko/Shutterstock; 34 (TCR): Kjetil Kolbjornsrud/Shutterstock; 34 (CR): David Mager/Pearson Education, Inc.; 38 (T): Hero Images/Getty Images; 38 (C): Blue Jean Images/Alamy Stock Photo; 38 (R): Kzenon/Shutterstock; 40: PhotosIndia.com RM 11/Alamy Stock Photo; 40 (CL): Steven Frame/Alamy Stock Photo; 40 (CR): David Mager/Pearson Education, Inc.; 41 (TL): Stephen Coburn/Shutterstock; 041 (TR): Africa Studio/Shutterstock; 40 (BL): Blend Images/Andersen Ross/Brand X Pictures/Getty Images; 41 (BL): Dmitry Kalinovsky/Shutterstock; 41 (BR): Hongqi Zhang/123RF; 42 (C): Ariwasabi/123RF; 42 (C): Syda Productions/Shutterstock; 42 (B): Pressmaster/Shutterstock; 44: Sirtravelalot/Shutterstock.

Unit 3

Page 45: Goodluz/Shutterstock; 46 (1): Svetlana Happyland/Shutterstock; 46 (2): Gt29/Shutterstock; 46(3): Igor Zakharevich/123RF; 46 (4): Skoda/Shutterstock; 46 (5): Aigars Reinholds/123RF; 46 (6): Andrey_Kuzmin/Shutterstock; 46 (7): Alexander Kharchenko/123RF; 46 (8): Valentin Agapov/Shutterstock; 46 (9): Coleman Yuen/Pearson Education Asia Ltd.; 46 (10): Tobkatrina/Shutterstock; 46 (11): Ed Phillips/Shutterstock; 46 (12): Suradech Prapairat/Shutterstock; 46 (13): Yurakp/123RF; 46 (14): Natalya Erofeeva/Shutterstock; 46 (15): Shtanzman/123RF; 46 (16): J. Helgason/Shutterstock; 48: David Mager/Pearson Education, Inc.; 49 (TL): Suradech Prapairat/Shutterstock; 49 (TC): You Touch Pix of EuToch/Shutterstock; 49 (TR): Tobkatrina/Shutterstock; 49 (BL): David Mager/Pearson Education, Inc.; 49 (BC): Julia Ivantsova/Shutterstock; 49 (BR): Yurakp/123RF; 52: Viacheslav Iakobchuk/Alamy Stock Photo; 54: Anton Samsonov/123RF; 54 (TR): Adisa/Shutterstock; 54 (CR): David Mager/Pearson Education, Inc.; 55 (TL): Christophe Testi/Shutterstock; 55 (TC): Igor Zakharevich/123RF; 55 (TR): Aigars Reinholds/123RF; 55 (BL): Stillfx/Shutterstock; 55 (BC): Dan Bucko/Shutterstock; 55 (BR): Akekoksomshutter/Shutterstock; 59: Hill Street Studios/Sarah Golonka/Blend Images/Getty Images; 60 (TL): Kurhan/Shutterstock; 60 (TCL): Radius Images/Alamy Stock Photo; 60 (TCR): Andersen Ross/Blend Images/Getty Images; 60 (TR): Radius Images/Alamy Stock Photo; 60 (B): David Mager/Pearson Education, Inc.; 61 (L): ColorBlind Images/Blend Images/Getty Images; 61 (R): Cheryl Savan/Shutterstock; 64: Maroke/Shutterstock.

Unit 4

Page 65: Hill Street Studios/Blend Images/Alamy Stock Photo; 68 (TL): Priscilla Grant/Everett Collection; 68 (TR): Rehan Qureshi/Shutterstock; 68 (BR): Caiaimage/Tom Merton/OJO+/Getty Images; 69: Frederic Cirou/PhotoAlto Agency RF Collections/Getty Images; 71 (Ross): Iofoto/Shutterstock; 71 (Mary): Absolut/Shutterstock; 71 (Ryan): SteveLuker/iStock/Getty Images; 71 (Eva): Nurlan/Shutterstock; 71 (Tess): Fullvalue/E+/Getty Images; 71 (Ed): Jacob Wackerhausen/iStock/Getty Images; 71 (Pat): Alberto Zornetta/Shutterstock; 71 (Alex): Lisa F. Young/Shutterstock; 71 (Meg): Iofoto/Shutterstock; 71 (Jake): Dolgachov/123RF; 74: Deborah Suarez/Shutterstock; 76 (TL): Joseph/Shutterstock; 76 (TC): Pkchai/Shutterstock; 76 (TR): Art Vandalay/DigitalVision/Getty Images; 76 (BL): Brosa/iStock/Getty Images; 76 (BC): Ariel Skelley/DigitalVision/Getty Images; 76 (BR): Ebtikar/Shutterstock; 79: Volt Collection/Shutterstock; 80 (CR): David Mager/Pearson Education, Inc.; 80 (BR): David Mager/Pearson Education, Inc.; 81 (T): Fuse/Corbis/Getty Images; 81 (C): Design Pics/Con Tanasiuk/Getty Images; 81 (B): Alexkatkov/Shutterstock; 82 (1): RPM Pictures/The Image Bank/Getty Images; 82 (2): Sylva Villerot/Photononstop/Alamy Stock Photo; 82 (3): ESB Basic/Shutterstock; 82 (4): Bill Bachmann/Alamy Stock Photo; 82 (5): Fuse/Corbis/Getty Images; 82 (BL): Euan Cherry/Retna/Photoshot/Everett Collection; 82 (BCL): Photoshot/Everett Collection; 82 (BCR): ZUMA Press, Inc./Alamy Stock Photo; 82 (BR): Kristin Callahan/Everett Collection; 84: Andy Chadwick/Alamy Stock Photo.

Unit 5

Page 85: Monkey Business Images/Shutterstock; 86 (1): Tarzhanova/Shutterstock; 86 (2): Elnur/Shutterstock; 86 (3): Magdalena Wielobob/Shutterstock; 86 (4): Sagir/Shutterstock; 86 (5): Karkas/Shutterstock; 86 (6): Sripfoto/Shutterstock; 86 (7): Elenovsky/Shutterstock; 86 (8): Dmitry Zimin/Shutterstock; 86 (9): MstudioG/Shutterstock; 86 (10): Rj Ierich/Shutterstock; 86 (11): Suradech Prapairat/Shutterstock; 86 (12): DR Travel Photo and Video/Shutterstock; 88 (TL): Pathdoc/Shutterstock; 88 (TR): Mila Supinskaya Glashchenko/Shutterstock; 88 (BL): Lepas/Shutterstock; 88 (BC): J. Helgason/Shutterstock; 88 (BR): Elnur/Shutterstock; 89 (TL): Comstock/Shutterstock; 89 (TC): Theerasaki/Shutterstock; 89 (TR): Monkey Business Images/Shutterstock; 89 (BL): Bogdan Florea/Shutterstock; 89 (BC): Karkas/Shutterstock; 89 (BR): Olga Popova/Shutterstock; 90 (T): Nivek Neslo/Stone/Getty Images; 90 (T [inset]): Elnur/Shutterstock; 90 (B): Leungchopan/Shutterstock; 90 (B [inset]): Maxstockphoto/Shutterstock; 92 ($1): Nimon/Shutterstock; 92 ($5): Robynrg/Shutterstock; 92 ($10): Reiulf Grønnevik/Shutterstock; 92 ($20): Robynrg/Shutterstock; 92 (penny): Vladimir Wrangel/Shutterstock; 92 (nickel): Bennyartist/Shutterstock; 92 (dime): Pearson Education, Inc.; 92 (quarter): Jackhollingsworth.com/Shutterstock; 92 (quarter, dime, nickel): Jackhollingsworth.com/Shutterstock, Pearson Education, Inc., Bennyartist/Shutterstock; 92 (dime, nickel, penny quarter,): Pearson Education, Inc., Bennyartist/Shutterstock, Vladimir Wrangel/Shutterstock, Jackhollingsworth.com/Shutterstock; 92 ($10, $1, nickel, penny): Reiulf Grønnevik/Shutterstock, Nimon/Shutterstock, Bennyartist/Shutterstock, Vladimir Wrangel/Shutterstock; 92($5, dime, penny): Robynrg/Shutterstock, Pearson Education, Inc., Vladimir Wrangel/Shutterstock; 94 (BR): David Mager/Pearson Education, Inc.; 94 (green sweater): Elnur/Shutterstock; 94 (red sweater): Elnur/Shutterstock; 94 (blue sweater): Elnur/Shutterstock; 95 (BL): Sagir/Shutterstock; 95 (BC): Karkas/Shutterstock; 95 (BR): Maxstockphoto/Shutterstock; 96: Goncharov Artem/Shutterstock; 98 (TL): Africa Studio/Shutterstock; 98 (TC): Jeramey Lende/Alamy Stock Photo; 98 (TR): Seeme/Shutterstock; 100 (TL): Himchenko.E/Shutterstock; 100 (TCL): Image Source/Getty Images; 100 (TCR [jeans]): Elenovsky/Shutterstock; 100 (TCR [shirt]): Bonetta/iStock/Getty Images; 100 (TR): Stanley45/iStock/Getty Images; 101 (T): Alexandr Makarov/Shutterstock; 101 (C): Nina Buday/Shutterstock; 101 (B): Aleksandar Mijatovic/Shutterstock; 104: Odua Images/Shutterstock.

Unit 6

Page 105: Monkey Business Images/Shutterstock; 106 (TL): Whitestar1955/Shutterstock; 106 (TR): Breadmaker/Shutterstock; 106 (CL): Interior Design/Shutterstock; 106 (CC): Gaf_Lila/Shutterstock; 106 (BL): Diane Uhley/Shutterstock; 108 (TL): LuckyPhoto/Shutterstock; 108 (TC): Artazum/Shutterstock; 108 (TCR): Robert Kneschke/Shutterstock; 108 (BL): Abd/Shutterstock; 108 (BCL): AnnaTamila/Shutterstock; 108 (BCL): Pavel L Photo and Video/Shutterstock; 108 (BR): Wavebreakmedia/Shutterstock; 112 (TL): TerryM/Shutterstock; 112 (TC): Thanatos Media/Shutterstock; 112 (TR): Goodluz/Shutterstock; 114: David Mager/Pearson Education, Inc.; 115: Iofoto/Shutterstock; 116 (TR): Gaf_Lila/Shutterstock; 116 (BR): Interior Design/Shutterstock; 119 (CL): Vadim Ovchinnikov/Shutterstock; 119 (CR): Artazum and Iriana Shiyan/Shutterstock; 120 (TL): Scanrail/123RF; 120 (TC): Andrew Michael/Alamy Stock Photo; 120 (CR): T.W. Van Urk/123RF; 121: Gareth Boden/Pearson Education Ltd; 124: Praet/Shutterstock.

Unit 7

Page 125: Tyler Olson/Shutterstock; 126 (1): PeopleImages/DigitalVision/Getty Images; 126 (2): ESB Professional/Shutterstock; 126 (3): BJI/Blue Jean Images/Getty Images; 126 (4): Rido/Shutterstock; 126 (5): PaylessImages/123RF; 126 (6): Monkey Business Images/Shutterstock; 126 (7): Antoniodiaz/Shutterstock; 126 (8): Périg Morisse/123RF; 126 (9): Iakov Filimonov/Shutterstock; 126 (10): Maskot/Getty Images; 126 (11): Elnur/Shutterstock; 126 (12): Africa Studio/Shutterstock; 126 (13): Rommel Canlas/Shutterstock; 128 (TL): Syda Productions/Shutterstock; 128 (TCL): Monkey Business Images/Shutterstock; 128 (TCR): Wavebreak Media Ltd/123RF; 128 (TR): Goran Bogicevic/Shutterstock; 128 (CR): William Perugini/Shutterstock; 128 (BL): Syda Productions/Shutterstock; 128 (BR): Andriy Popov/123RF; 129 (T): Nick White/Getty Images; 129 (C): Gpointstudio/Shutterstock; 129 (B): Elyse Lewin/The Image Bank/Getty Images; 130: David Mager/Pearson Education, Inc.; 134 (TL): BE&W agencja fotograficzna Sp. z o.o./Alamy Stock Photo; 134 (TC): Tom Stewart/Corbis/Getty Images; 134 (TR): William Stall/Shutterstock; 134 (BR): David Mager/Pearson Education, Inc.; 135 (cook): David Tothill/Photofusion Picture Library/Alamy Stock Photo; 135 (bike): CandyBox Images/Shutterstock; 135 (stay home): Peathegee Inc/Blend Images/Getty Images; 135 (basketball): David Buffington/Blend Images/Alamy Stock Photo; 135 (read): Mira/Alamy Stock Photo; 135 (dancing): Pressmaster/Shutterstock; 135 (laundry): Adam Crowley/Photodisc/Getty Images; 135 (beach): Robert Warren/The Image Bank/Getty Images; 135 (wash car): Katarzyna Bialasiewicz/123RF; 135 (play cards): JGI/Blend Images/Alamy Stock Photo; 135 (video games): Phillip Jarrell Photographer/The Image Bank/Getty Images; 135 (swimming): Wavebreak Media Ltd/123RF; 138 (T): Dolgachov/123RF; 138 (C): Dinis Tolipov/123RF; 138 (BC): Todd Arena/123RF; 138 (B): Image Source/Getty Images; 140 (TL): Blend Images/Shutterstock; 140 (TC): Asia Images Group/Shutterstock; 140 (TR): Tyler Olson/Shutterstock; 140 (BL): Mel Yates/Getty Images; 140 (BC): Fuse/Corbis/Getty Images; 140 (BR): EdBockStock/Shutterstock; 141: Wavebreak Media Ltd/123RF; 144: Lightpoet/Shutterstock.

Unit 8

Page 145: Andresr/E+/Getty Images; 146 (1): Peter Jochems/Shutterstock; 146 (2): Ingvald Kaldhussater/Shutterstock; 146 (3): Baloncici/Shutterstock; 146 (4): Norman Chan/Shutterstock; 146 (5): Frances L Fruit/Shutterstock; 146 (6): Chernyanskiy Vladimir Alexandrovich/Shutterstock; 146 (7): Lisa F. Young/Shutterstock; 146 (8): Robert Milek/Shutterstock; 146 (9): Marlee/Shutterstock; 146 (10): Mikeledray/Shutterstock; 146 (11): MaraZe/Shutterstock; 146 (12): Nataliya Peregudova/Shutterstock; 146 (13): Cokemomo/123RF; 146 (14): Feng Yu/Shutterstock; 146 (15): Elena Elisseeva/Shutterstock; 146 (16): Pixelrobot/123RF; 146 (17): Kamenetskiy Konstantin/Shutterstock; 146 (18): Africa Studio/Shutterstock; 146 (19): You Touch Pix of EuToch/Shutterstock; 146 (20): Trinacria Photo/Shutterstock; 146 (21): Feverpitched/123RF; 148 (TCL): Hurst Photo/Shutterstock; 148 (TCR): Sergey Peterman/Shutterstock; 148 (TR): Yeko Photo Studio/Shutterstock; 148 (BR): David Mager/Pearson Education, Inc.; 149 (TL): Viktor1/Shutterstock; 149 (TR): Michael C. Gray/Shutterstock; 149 (CL): Siamionau pavel/Shutterstock; 149 (CR): Foodiepics/Shutterstock; 149 (BL): Emil Vasiliev Iliev/Shutterstock; 149 (BR): Khz/Shutterstock; 151 (B): Mikeledray/Shutterstock; 152 (TL): Didecs/Shutterstock; 152 (TCL): ASuruwataRi/Shutterstock; 152 (TCR): ND700/Shutterstock; 152 (TR): Didecs/Shutterstock; 152 (BL): Corbis/VCG/Getty Images; 152 (BCL): PlanetSD LLC/Shutterstock; 154 (tomato soup): MichaelJohn Wolfe/Shutterstock; 154 (coffee): Stocksnapper/Shutterstock; 154 (turkey sandwich): SoleilC/Shutterstock; 154 (fries): Gabriela Trojanowska/Shutterstock; 154 (soda): Africa Studio/Shutterstock; 154 (potato): Joe Gough/Shutterstock; 154 (hamburger): Sergey Peterman/Shutterstock; 154 (iced tea): Rob Byron/Shutterstock; 154 (salad): Bochkarev Photography/Shutterstock; 154 (fruit): Muhammad Kamran Akhlaq/Shutterstock; 154 (apple pie): Marjanneke de Jong/Shutterstock; 154 (ice cream): M. Unal Ozmen/Shutterstock; 154 (BR): Dmac/Alamy Stock Photo; 156: Wavebreakmedia/Shutterstock; 158 (top row, left): Thomas M Perkins/Shutterstock; 158 (top row, center left): Danny Smythe/Shutterstock; 158 (top row, center): Sergei Gorin/123RF;158 (top row, center right): Matka_Wariatka/Shutterstock; 158 (top row, right): Sukharevskyy Dmytro (nevodka)/Shutterstock; 158 (center row, left): Emil Vasiliev Iliev/Shutterstock; 158 (center row, center left): Michael C. Gray/Shutterstock; 158 (center row, center right): Olga Lyubkin/Shutterstock; 158 (center row, right): Cameramannz/Shutterstock; 158 (bottom row, left): Pogonici/Shutterstock; 158 (bottom row, center left): Gabriela Trojanowska/Shutterstock; 158 (bottom row, center right): Evgeny Karandaev/Shutterstock; 158 (bottom row, center right): Lisa F. Young/Shutterstock; 160 (salad): Bochkarev Photography/Shutterstock; 160 (potato): Joe Gough/Shutterstock; 160 (fried chicken): Unpict/Shutterstock; 160 (grilled chicken): Andrey Starostin/Shutterstock; 160 (apples): Frances L Fruit/Shutterstock; 160 (milk): Lana Langlois/Shutterstock; 160 (rice): Mikeledray/Shutterstock; 160 (cake): Helen bird/Shutterstock; 160 (fruit): April Turner/Shutterstock; 160 (hamburger): Sergey Peterman/Shutterstock;160 (green beans): Cameramannz/Shutterstock; 161 (shrimp): Magdanatka/Shutterstock; 161 (tomatoes): Monika Olszewska/Shutterstock; 161 (turkey): Paul Cowan/Shutterstock; 161 (peppers): Fredredhat/Shutterstock; 161 (salmon): Brian Senic/Shutterstock; 161 (cucumbers): Viktar Malyshchyts/Shutterstock; 161 (roast beef): Margouillat photo/Shutterstock; 161 (avocados): Workmans Photos/Shutterstock; 161 (mango): Svetlana Kuznetsova/Shutterstock; 161 (nuts): Oksana2010/Shutterstock; 161 (spinach): Reika/Shutterstock; 161 (carrots): Goncharuk; 161 (scallions): Binh Thanh Bui/Shutterstock; 161 (watermelon): Tatiana Popova/123RF; 164: Wavebreakmedia/Shutterstock.

Unit 9

Page 165: David Grossman/Alamy Stock Photo; 166 (TL): Evgenii Emelianov/Shutterstock; 166 (TR): Suzanne Tucker/Shutterstock; 166 (TL): Steve Dunwell/Photolibrary/Getty Images; 166 (BR): Srnicholl/123RF; 168 (T): Vgstockstudio/Shutterstock; 168 (B): Sam74100/123RF; 169 (L): Robert Kneschke/Shutterstock; 169 (C): Pavels/Shutterstock; 169 (R): Robert Hoetink/Shutterstock; 172 (1): Trekandshoot/Shutterstock; 172 (2): Playalife2006/123RF; 172 (3): Minerva Studio/Shutterstock; 172 (4): JellevdWolf/Shutterstock; 172 (5): Mishoo/123RF;172 (6): Adrian Sherratt/Alamy Stock Photo; 172 (7): Dainis Derics/Shutterstock; 172 (8): Fotostory/Shutterstock; 173: Elizabeth Leyden/Alamy Stock Photo; 174: David Mager/Pearson Education, Inc.; 175 (L): Tyler Olson/Shutterstock; 175 (C): Montgomery Martin/Alamy Stock Photo; 175 (R): Gareth Byrne/Alamy Stock Photo; 177: EpicStockMedia/Shutterstock; 180 (1 [shirt]): Africa Studio/Shutterstock; 180 (1 [trousers]): Gogoiso/Shutterstock; 180 (2): Tudor Photography/Pearson Education Ltd; 180 (3): Dainis/Shutterstock; 180 (4): Ixer/Shutterstock; 180 (5): Gvictoria/Shutterstock; 180 (6): John Nairne/Shutterstock; 180 (7): Bjphotographs/Shutterstock; 180 (8): Mega Pixel/Shutterstock; 180 (9): Ingvald Kaldhussater/Shutterstock; 180 (10): Yuyangc/Shutterstock; 180 (11): Sasha Davas/Shutterstock; 180 (12): Coprid/Shutterstock; 181 (CR): Avid_creative/iStock/Getty Images; 184: Sergei Denisov/Shutterstock.

Unit 10

Page 185: Tzido Sun/Shutterstock; 186 (1): Kinn Deacon/Alamy Stock Photo; 186 (2): RaksyBH/Shutterstock; 186 (3): James R. Martin/Shutterstock; 186 (4): David R. Frazier Photolibrary, Inc./Alamy Stock Photo; 186 (5): 06photo/Shutterstock; 186 (6): Mangostock/Shutterstock; 186 (7): Whitestar1955/Shutterstock; 186 (8): Maifly/123RF; 186 (9): Auremar/123RF; 186 (10): Annkozar/Shutterstock; 186 (11): Inga Spence/Alamy Stock Photo; 186 (12): Tyler Olson/123RF; 186 (13): Skydive Erick/Shutterstock; 186 (14): Fiphoto/Shutterstock; 186 (15): Wavebreakmedia/Shutterstock; 186 (16): Lakov Filimonov/123RF; 188 (CL): Olyniteow/Shutterstock; 186 (19): Nick Ut/AP Images; 189 (BL): Wavebreakmedia/Shutterstock; 189 (BR): RichLegg/E+/Getty Images; 191 (T): Isaak/Shutterstock; 191 (TC): Kickstand/E+/Getty Images; 191 (BC): Andrus Ciprian/Shutterstock; 191 (BC): Anthony Hall/Shutterstock; 191 (BR): Laura Ashley/Alamy Stock Photo; 192 (1): Dcwcreations/Shutterstock; 192 (2): Zoart Studio/Shutterstock; 192 (3): Robert J. Beyers II/Shutterstock; 192 (4): Idea.s/Shutterstock; 192 (5): Vitezslav Valka/Shutterstock; 192 (6): Mr. Alien/Shutterstock; 192 (7): Paul Brennan/Shutterstock; 192 (8): Thitipong Chotwicha/Shutterstock; 192 (9): Shah Rohani/Shutterstock; 194: David Mager/Pearson Education, Inc.; 195 (park): Destinyweddingstudio/Shutterstock; 195 (bus 15): Milkovasa/Shutterstock; 195 (Green's store): Fiphoto/Shutterstock; 195 (bus 16): Milkovasa/Shutterstock; 195 (post office): Underawesternsky/Shutterstock; 195 (bus 8): Milkovasa/Shutterstock; 195 (bus 9): Martindm/E+/Getty Images; 197 (chocolate): Lemonpink Images/Shutterstock; 197 (tissues): Graham Stewart/Shutterstock; 197 (milk): Hurst Photo/Shutterstock; 197 (pens): Nattika/Shutterstock; 198 (TL): Todd Strand/Independent Picture Service/Alamy Stock Photo; 198 (TC): Ronnie McMillan/Alamy Stock Photo; 198 (TR): Robnroll/Shutterstock; 198 (BR): Wavebreakmediamicro/123RF; 202: David Mager/Pearson Education, Inc.; 204: Antonio Diaz/123RF.

Unit 11

Page 205: AVAVA/Shutterstock; 206 (L): Michal and Yossi Rotem/Shutterstock; 206 (inset): Michal and Yossi Rotem/Shutterstock; 206 (R): Dolgachov/123RF; 208 (T): David Mager/Pearson Education, Inc.; 208 (1): Narikan/Shutterstock; 208 (2): Philippe Renaud/123RF; 208 (3): Lucidio Studio Inc/Corbis/Getty Images; 208 (4): Ben Gingell/123RF; 214 (CR): David Mager/Pearson Education, Inc.; 218: PaylessImages/123RF; 221 (woman): Katarzyna Bialasiewicz/123RF; 221 (man): Imtmphoto/123RF; 221 (inset, tea): Anmbph/123RF; 221 (inset, honey): Dustin Dennis/Shutterstock; 224: Shutterpix/Shutterstock.

Unit 12

Page 225: Monkey Business Images/Shutterstock; 226 (1): Elnur/Shutterstock; 226 (2): Fuse/Corbis/Getty Images; 226 (3): Andriy Popov/123RF; 226 (4): Wavebreakmedia/Shutterstock; 226 (5): Top Photo Corporation/Top Photo Group/Getty Images; 226 (6): Solomiya Malovana/Shutterstock; 226 (7): Barros & Barros/Photographer's Choice RF/Getty Images; 226 (8): Monty Rakusen/Cultura/Getty Images; 226 (9): Herjua/123RF; 226 (10): Kadmy/123RF; 226 (11): Andrew Woodley/Alamy Stock Photo; 226 (12): Andrew Woodley/Alamy Stock Photo; 226 (13): Akurtz/E+/Getty Images; 226 (14): Ernest R. Prim/Shutterstock; 228 (CR): David Mager/Pearson Education, Inc.; 228 (1a): Suhendri/Shutterstock; 228 (1b): Gstockstudio/Shutterstock; 228 (1c): Wavebreakmedia/Shutterstock; 228 (2a): Chris Bence/Shutterstock; 228 (2b): Sergey Peterman/Shutterstock; 228 (2c): Dustin Dennis/Shutterstock; 233: Andriy Popov/123RF; 234 (BR): David Mager/Pearson Education, Inc.; 237 (L): Leung Cho Pan/123RF; 237 (R [inset]): Chatuporn Sornlampoo/123RF; 238 (B): Tanya Constantine/Blend Images/Getty Images; 240: Dragon Images/Shutterstock; 241 (TR): Fuse/Corbis/Getty Images; 241 (salon): TheDesignTrade/Shutterstock; 241 (stylist): Antoniodiaz/Shutterstock; 241 (grocery store): Montgomery Martin/Alamy Stock Photo; 241 (cashier): Ariel Skelley/Blend Images/Alamy Stock Photo; 241 (clothing store): Fiphoto/Shutterstock; 241 (sales assistant): Sirtravelalot/Shutterstock; 244: Buddit Nidsornkul/Shutterstock.

Backmatter

Page 248: Fuse/Corbis/Getty Images; 249: Daniel M Ernst/Shutterstock; 251: Digital Vision/Photodisc/Getty Images; 254 (T): Wavebreak Media Ltd/123RF; 256 (B): Designs by Jack/Shutterstock.

Illustrations: Steve Attoe, pp. 97, 101; Kenneth Batelman, pp. 111, 253; Luis Briseno, pp. 18, 52, 91, 93, 109, 150, 160, 193; Laurie Conley, pp. 12, 31, 51, 55, 74, 194, 196, 212–213 (top), 218, 250; Deborah Crowle, pp. 6, 168, 181; Len Ebert represented by Ann Remen-Willis, pp. 2 (top); ElectraGraphics, pp. 24, 37, 44, 48, 50, 58, 64, 72, 78, 79, 84, 104, 114, 119, 124, 132, 142, 146–147, 144, 146, 172, 173, 176, 178, 184, 186, 204, 213 (bottom), 214 (top), 217 (top), 224, 234, 244, 275–277; Brian Hughes, pp. 94, 112, 117, 120, 122, 157, 162, 188–190, 228, 259; Steve MacEachern, pp. 13, 80; André Labrie, pp. 182, 210, 217 (bottom), 231, 236, 238; Luis Montiel, pp. 67, 72 (bottom); Alan Moon, pp. 69, 71, 72, 214; Michel Rabagliati, pp. 9, 36, 62, 216; Roberto Sadi, pp. 77; John Schreiner/Wolfe LTD, pp. 159; Steve Schulman, pp. 3, 76, 137, 174; David Silva, pp. 18–19, 209, 229; Neil Stewart/NSV Productions, pp. 42; Anna Veltfort, pp. 2 (bottom six), 20, 21, 56–57, 80, 102, 170–171, 200–201, 206, 220, 247, 256; Rose Zgodzinski, pp. 166, 222.

282 Credits